Golfing
the CAROLINA
GRAND STRAND

Golfing the CAROLINA GRAND STRAND

TOMMY WOODRUM

PELICAN PUBLISHING COMPANY

Gretna 1999

First edition, February 1993
Second edition, January 1999

The word "Pelican" and the depiction of a pelican are
trademarks of Pelican Publishing Company, Inc., and are
registered in the U.S. Patent and Trademark Office.

Library of Congress Cataloging-in-Publication Data

Woodrum, Tommy.
    Golfing the Carolina Grand Strand / Tommy Woodrum.—2nd ed.
       p.   cm.
    ISBN 1-56554-338-6 (hardcover : alk. paper)
    1. Golf courses—South Carolina—Guidebooks. 2. South Carolina—
Guidebooks. I. Title.
    GV982.S6W66 1998
    796.352'06'8757—dc21
                                            98-25992
                                                CIP

Area maps by Michael Forsythe

Course maps by Lawrence H. Woodrum, AIA

Printed in Hong Kong

Published by Pelican Publishing Company, Inc.
1000 Burmaster Street, Gretna, Louisiana 70053-3110

CONTENTS

INTRODUCTION

Since the first edition of *Golfing the Carolina Grand Strand* was published, golf has continued to grow at a phenomenal rate in this self-styled, aptly named "Golf Capitol of the World." This second edition introduces twenty-nine new golf courses that were not described in the original edition, and several others (at least seven) are either on the verge of completion or are under construction at various locations on the Grand Strand.

The courses continue to get better and better. Some of them cost in the neighborhood of $5 million to build as developers and designers strive for top ratings—which, indeed, they are garnering. Major Senior PGA and LPGA tour events are played in the area, and top players are quick to put their expertise to work as architects. Jack Nicklaus, Arnold Palmer, Gary Player, and Larry Nelson creations were here before this second edition, and in this update you will find additional golf-course gems designed or planned in cooperation with household golfing names such as Raymond Floyd, Hale Irwin, Fred Couples, and John Daly. Greg Norman also is building a championship course here that is scheduled to open in 1999.

Newcomers to golf design have made quite an impression here on the Grand Strand. Mike Strantz, and Tim Cate have designed award winners and are placing their names alongside architects such as Tom Fazio, Pete Dye and P. B. Dye, Rees Jones, Willard Byrd, Clyde Johnston, Dan

Maples, Tom Jackson, Russell Breedon, Gene Hamm, Ken Tomlinson, and Larry Young, who all have built outstanding golf facilities and continue to be active in the Myrtle Beach area. Then, too, there are some great courses that have withstood the test of time because of the foresight and design talents of legendary golf architects such as Robert Trent Jones, Arthur Hills, Donald Ross, and George Cobb.

It isn't difficult to find an outstanding, well-designed golf course on the Grand Strand. The biggest problem is finding the time to play them all—or, worse, having to pick and choose the right ones for you in a limited stretch of time!

One of the most noticeable changes in this area since the original edition of *Golfing the Carolina Grand Strand* first appeared on the bookstore shelves is the profusion of total golf facilities. More and more people, enchanted with their visit to the sandy shores of the Grand Strand, have determined that this is the area they want to call home, and golf courses have responded with a massive but carefully considered building program, offering condominiums, home sites, and homes built around the fairways.

The aggressive marketing program at Wild Wing puts that four-course facility at the forefront of golf-course living, but it's hard to beat the facilities at the three-course Legends, the three-course Ocean Ridge, and the three-course St. James Plantation. The two splendid courses at "downtown" Myrtlewood and the three beauties at Myrtle Beach National are attracting their share of new homeowners, and Deer Track's two courses have always been a clarion call for those who want to live where they play. Tidewater and Wachesaw Plantation are upscale communities with highly rated playing facilities. Brunswick is making a major splash, and Burning Ridge markets its properties to various income and age groups!

Most golf-course developers are buying excess land, planning to establish the course and then add housing—for example, Arrowhead and Meadowlands.

There are many others, and all of them are well planned. Homes, constructed by a private builder, are going up even at the traditional Surf Club alongside its tenth fairway, and some of the opportunities on the south end of the Beach are spectacularly beautiful.

In no way is this intended to be a complete summary of golf-course real-estate possibilities, and the reader, if he or she is inclined to make the Grand Strand home, should look at all possible options, many of which are not listed here.

Getting away from individual options, the clubhouses are so big and so good they really deserve a book of their own. Whether you prefer the massive Legends clubhouse—a great interpretation of the one at St. Andrews, Scotland—or antebellum treasures such as the ones at DeBordieu, Pawleys Plantation, Heritage Club, and Wedgefield, you are going to be impressed with the size and beauty of these Myrtle Beach-area clubhouses. The magnificent, relatively new $2 million facility at the Surf and the remodeled beauty of The Dunes present a gracious form of service and comfort second to none.

Of a different architectural bent, Wild Wing is modern, opulent, and memorable.

No, we have not forgotten the graciousness of Pines Lakes International, the granddaddy, nor the historic quaintness of Litchfield.

A large new beauty is coming out of the ground at Myrtle Beach National and will be exceptional. The Tradition is handsome, Caledonia wins awards, and many of the newer facilities such as Wachesaw have separate clubhouses for each golf course at the facility. The Wizard and Man O' War, located on the same piece of real estate in Carolina Forest, also have individual and very distinctive clubhouses.

Getting there is part of the delight of the total experience. It is a thrill to drive into Myrtlewood, surrounded by trees and lush golf holes. The Ocean Ridge courses, again with separate clubhouses for Lion's Paw, Panther's Run, and Tiger's Eye, offer a similar sensation. The drive through dense forest to Ocean Harbor and scenic lowlands of The Legends, past centuries-old magnolias to Wedgefield, Pawleys, DeBordieu, The Heritage, and Caledonia can make the Old South come alive and the senses tingle. Then, too, it is a pretty spectacular ride into Tidewater, Heather Glen, Glen Dornoch, Blackmoor, and the Litchfield properties.

Sea Trail is a great example of a well-planned residential and rental facility. Then there are some unusual methods of reaching some great golf courses. How about a skyway tram to Waterway Hills or a five-mile ferryboat ride to Bald Head Island?

It's not difficult to see that golf is more than a way of life in the Myrtle Beach area.

Golf is big business. Myrtle Beach Golf Holiday, the spearhead of marketing Grand Strand golf around the world, is a nonprofit group comprised of golf-course and hospitality-lodging owners. Golf Holiday, now a partner with the new TPC venture in staging the Senior PGA Championship's year-end tournament, receives more than a million telephone calls every year requesting reservations and information about golf at Myrtle Beach. It is estimated that more than 3.5 million rounds of golf are played yearly on the Grand Strand, but golf—while No. 1—is not the only game in town.

Visitors now come to the Grand Strand for its wide, recently renourished beaches and for excellent entertainment bulwarked by theaters owned and operated by the Gatlin Brothers, Alabama, and country-music impresario Calvin Gilmore (with his very popular Carolina Opry). The House of Blues has come to town; the Palace Theatre offers the Rockettes from Radio City Music Hall at Christmas and Broadway plays and top-name performers at other times. A Hard Rock Cafe, a Ripley's Believe It or Not, a splendid aquarium, the nation's first NASCAR Cafe, Planet Hollywood, and an All-Star Sports Cafe restaurant (which fittingly has a Tiger Woods' Locker Room), an Eddie Miles Theatre for this Elvis Presley look-alike, and an IMAX Theatre have all set up shop in the area.

Golf is still the king, evidenced by its con-tinuing growth. The game has indeed blossomed around the country and around the world, but nowhere so much as in the Myrtle Beach area. As my book goes to press, this golfing mecca boasts well over 100 golf courses, most of them pictured and described in this second edition of *Golfing the Carolina Grand Strand*.

I hope you will enjoy playing these courses and reading this book as much as I have enjoyed visiting these marvelous facilities, playing most of them with the host professionals, and then sitting down to compose this book.

Any endeavor of this size requires a lot of time and a lot of help.

I am indebted to the golfing professionals and golf-course owners of the Grand Strand; to photographers such as Michael Slear, Bill Woodward, and others; to advertising agencies such as Brandon and Himmelsbach; to good friend George Wilson, who had a major hand in typing and looking for discrepancies; and, of course, to Pelican Publishing and to the man assigned to edit this book, Patrick Davis.

Thanks again—all of you.

THE CAROLINA GRAND STRAND

SUNSET BEACH

SOUTHPORT

Yaupon Beach

Long Beach

Hwy. 17 North
To WILMINGTON, N.C.
50 miles

Hwy. 211

Hwy. 133

SUPPLY

Hwy. 211

Hwy. 130

SHALLOTTE

Holden Beach

Hwy. 17 North

Hwy. 179

Hwy. 130

GRISSETTOWN

Hwy. 904

Hwy. 904

LONGWOOD

Hwy. 904

Hwy. 179

Ocean Isle Beach

Hwy. 57

Hwy. 17 North

Hwy. 179

Hwy. 179

Calabash Creek

Sunset Beach

LITTLE RIVER

LITTLE RIVER

Little River River

BROOKSVILLE

Hwy. 905

HWY. 9 WEST

Hwy. 9

Hwy. 9

Hwy. 57

Hwy. 90

Kings Hwy. U.S. 17 North

North Myrtle Beach

LONGS

Waccamaw River

WAMPEE

To I-95

Hwy. 905

Hwy. 90

NORTH CENTRAL SECTION

Hwy. 17 Bypass

Waccamaw

Intracoastal

MYRTLE BEACH

FROM CONWAY ON HWY. 501

Hwy. 501

Hwy. 501

Hwy. 501

CONWAY

Waterway

AYNOR

To I-95, I-20, I-26, I-75, I-77

Hwy. 544

Hwy. 17 Bypass

Kings Hwy. U.S. 17 South

SOUTH END

Hwy. 701

Waccamaw River

Murrells Inlet

Black River

Pawleys Island

Georgetown

Hwy. Alternate 17

Winyah Bay

To I-95

ATLANTIC OCEAN

Golfing
the CAROLINA
GRAND STRAND

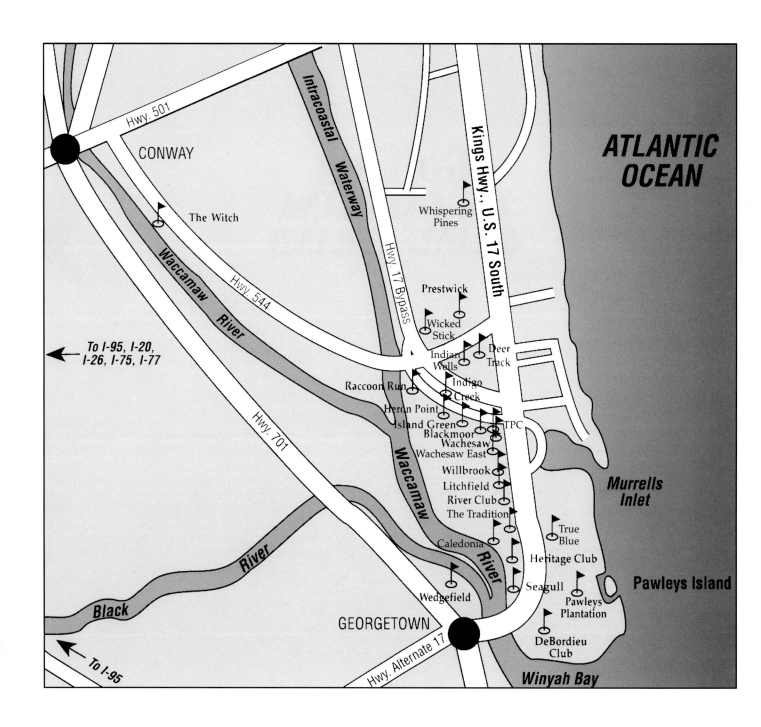

ATLANTIC OCEAN

Hwy. 501

CONWAY

Intracoastal Waterway

Kings Hwy., U.S. 17 South

Whispering Pines

The Witch

Waccamaw River

Hwy. 544

Hwy. 17 Bypass

Prestwick

To I-95, I-20, I-26, I-75, I-77

Wicked Stick

Indian Wells

Deer Track

Raccoon Run

Indigo Creek

Heron Point

Hwy. 701

Island Green

Blackmoor

TPC

Wachesaw

Waccamaw River

Wachesaw East

Willbrook

Litchfield

Murrells Inlet

River Club

The Tradition

True Blue

Caledonia

Black River

Heritage Club

Pawleys Island

Seagull

Wedgefield

Pawleys Plantation

GEORGETOWN

DeBordieu Club

To I-95

Hwy. Alternate 17

Winyah Bay

The South End of Myrtle Beach

A stand of oaks guards #1 green at Wedgefield. (Courtesy Himmelsbach Communications/Bill Woodward)

Wedgefield

HOLE NUMBER	1	2	3	4	5	6	7	8	9	OUT	10	11	12	13	14	15	16	17	18	IN	TOT	HCP	NET
CHAMP.	523	382	217	536	436	202	436	434	416	3582	482	425	445	203	433	398	213	482	372	3453	7035		
MEDAL	516	376	193	504	427	196	412	406	386	3416	461	410	436	183	405	382	207	443	362	3289	6705		
MIDDLE	485	357	150	467	401	186	382	391	367	3186	448	388	393	160	393	371	200	435	351	3139	6325		
HANDICAP	9	11	17	15	1	7	5	3	13		12	8	4	18	2	6	14	10	16				
PAR	5	4	3	5	4	3	4	4	4	36	5	4	4	3	4	4	3	5	4	36	72		
FORWARD	450	335	112	375	383	152	314	328	287	2736	393	298	316	104	274	321	147	373	287	2513	5249		
HANDICAP	9	3	17	15	1	7	11	5	13		12	10	8	18	2	4	16	6	14				
PAR	5	4	3	5	5	3	4	4	4	37	5	4	4	3	4	4	3	5	4	36	73		

WEDGEFIELD PLANTATION

Highway 701 North   100 Manor Dr.   Georgetown, SC 29440
(843) 546-8587

Architect: Porter Gibson   Year opened: 1972

Course rating/Slope rating:
Black - 73.4/123   White - 69.3/116
Blue - 71.7/120   Red - 69.6/119

Many good things have been said about Wedgefield Plantation Country Club and, as far as we are concerned, they are all true. If there is any one thing that limits the popularity of this truly wonderful Porter Gibson design, it is the geographical location of the course.

Even "The Links Guide," published by the golf course, seems to recognize this when it captions one page in the pamphlet "Is It Worth the Trip?" Quoting from *Golf Traveler* magazine: "Set like a coveted jewel at the end of a string of pearls, Wedgefield Plantation Country Club is located at the southernmost tip of Myrtle Beach's renowned Grand Strand, secluded within historic and picturesque Georgetown, South Carolina."

Secluded is the key word, and that is both a liability and an asset. Golfers who find Wedgefield will feel that they have stepped back into another time, and some confess that they keep looking for Rhett Butler and Scarlett O'Hara to appear at any moment. The site, once a flourishing rice plantation, sits astride the Black River and provides a succession of breathtaking vistas. Even the circular entrance to the Manor House is spectacular, framed with moss-draped live oaks that have been there for centuries. While Wedgefield has gone through a series of owners and has seen better times, it remains a picture book, with oaks, dogwoods, magnolias, and a wide variety of flowering plants that abound alongside a menagerie of wildlife. Again, we agree with the publicists who say, "In short, this is a setting so beautiful and serene it can easily distract your attention from the game."

However, if you want to post a good score it would be better to concentrate, because this is a fair but difficult golf course. This course is mature in every sense of the word, and has thrilled and challenged golfers since it opened more than twenty years ago. There are no tricks or gimmicks at Wedgefield—what you see is what you get, a course that rewards well-placed shots, chastises mediocre ones, and punishes bad shots. It is a long course, even from the white tees where most of the four pars play to a length of approximately 400 yards, but the five pars are relatively short and provide excellent birdie opportunities.

While there are many good golf holes at Wedgefield, #14 is the signature, a four par, 433 yards from the championship tees. It is not a trick hole, but it requires accuracy, nerve, and concentration. The hole plays as a dogleg left, providing a landing area some 200 yards from the tee or challenging the long hitter to hit the ball left, carrying water and trees. This ploy is not recommended!

If the golfer plays to the shorter landing area, the hole probably will require three shots to reach the green. But a five on this one isn't all that bad. . . .

Numbers 11-12-13-14 form the "Amen

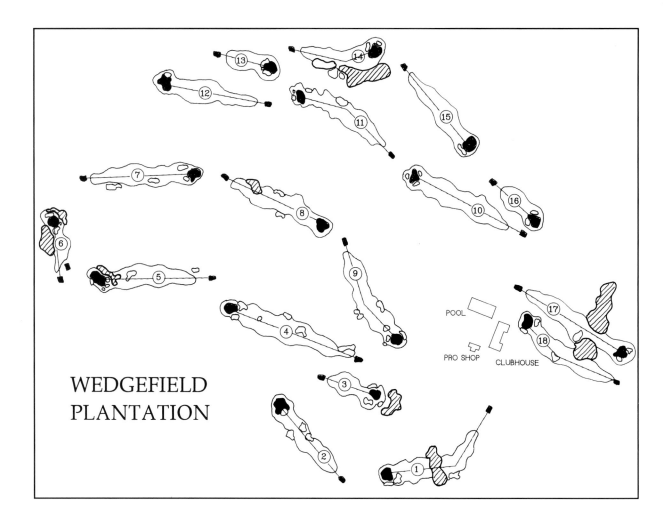

WEDGEFIELD PLANTATION

Corner" for Wedgefield, and they are as pretty as they are difficult. Mounds of love grass, magnolia trees, abundant water, elevated tees, and even the resident alligator who hangs out between #11 and #14 make this a setting you'll long remember.

Number 1 is a very fair, very good starting hole, and #9, with water before the green, is a fine finishing hole, but golfers are more apt to remember 4 and 5. They are similar in appearance as they parallel the road into Wedgefield. Four is a five par featuring a medium-width fairway bordered by pine trees on the right and the road to the left. Both are out of bounds, placing a premium not only on the drive, but on every shot until

the golfer reaches the green, which is protected on the right by a large pond.

Number 5 has been labeled as "undeniably amongst the best holes on any golf course is South Carolina—a par four from the back tees and a par five from the forward tees for Ladies and Seniors." The hole demands not only an accurate drive down the right center, but a long one as well. Even a long, well-placed drive from the back tees will leave the golfer a long iron shot to a green well protected by four spectacular sand bunkers and completely fronted by water. In other words, the approach shot must carry all the way to the putting surface.

18

INDIGO CREEK

Highway 17 Bypass   Garden City, SC
P.O. Box 15437   Surfside Beach, SC 29587
(843) 650-0381

Architect: Willard Byrd   Year opened: 1990

Course rating/Slope rating:
Back - 72.4/134   Regular - 69.7/126   Ladies - 69.2/120

A fine course on the Grand Strand, Indigo Creek, a Willard Byrd design, is easy to find. Not far from the center of Myrtle Beach, Indigo Creek is directly across Bypass 17 from Indian Wells.

This is a relatively short course that places a premium on accuracy.

Opened in the summer of 1990, Indigo Creek is now pleasingly mature, with plenty of grass in the fairways and no weeds hidden in the very good Bermuda greens. The course certainly is long enough for the average player, but the long hitter must "think" his way around the course, avoiding the driver on most holes, hitting long irons or a 4 or 5 fairway wood for position. Although it is not necessary to hit long, you do need to hit straight. Many holes seem to have small or nonexistent landing areas, but at your tee you will find they are fairly open. Better players will enjoy this course.

The golfer is more apt to come away from

Indigo Creek. (Courtesy Brandon Advertising/Michael Slear)

Indigo Creek remembering the back nine. It is more scenic than the front, and there are some excellent holes. Number 11 is a par three over water. With a large waste bunker to the left and pot bunkers on the right, the green slopes toward the water. It is a very appealing hole, long at 200 yards, but one that surprisingly has given up more than its share of holes-in-one.

Number 12 probably will become one of the most talked-about holes on the Beach.

Quite unique, it plays as a severe dogleg with the green 90 degrees to the left. Actually, standing on the tee, you can see the green directly ahead of you, but you had better not try to reach this one with your driver. Instead, hit with a long iron or fairway wood to the left side of the dogleg turn, leaving a shorter shot to the green.

Numbers 16 and 17, both par fours featuring bumps, mounds, and grass bunkers, are also memorable.

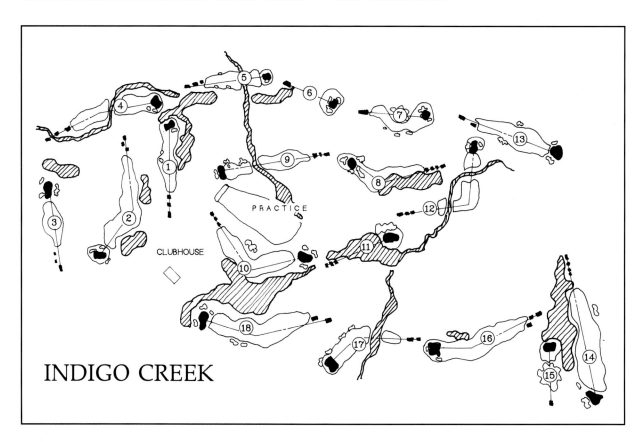

INDIGO CREEK

Indigo Creek

HOLE NUMBER	1	2	3	4	5	6	7	8	9	OUT	10	11	12	13	14	15	16	17	18	IN	TOT	HCP	NET
BLUE	390	375	190	520	420	200	390	365	535	3385	390	195	395	405	510	180	380	375	530	3360	6745		
WHITE	360	360	165	485	380	155	365	340	515	3125	355	170	355	375	435	145	355	325	505	3020	6145		
YELLOW	330	320	150	450	340	135	325	325	480	2855	315	130	335	355	415	110	330	295	455	2740	5595		
RED	305	290	120	395	300	115	295	265	425	2510	285	100	290	310	385	95	295	260	390	2410	4920		
MEN'S HCP	9	17	5	11	1	13	3	15	7		6	12	2	4	8	16	14	18	10				
PAR	4	4	3	5	4	3	4	4	5	36	4	3	4	4	5	3	4	4	5	36	72		
LADIES' HCP	1	11	15	7	3	17	5	13	9		6	16	2	4	10	18	12	14	8				

LITCHFIELD/WILLBROOK PLANTATION/RIVER CLUB

Purchased in 1990 by Myrtle Beach National, three great golf courses on the south end of the Grand Strand—Litchfield, Willbrook Plantation, and River Club—continue to function in the same location.

The three courses are an integral part of a total resort complex, Litchfield By The Sea, which stretches from the Atlantic Ocean to the Intracoastal Waterway, embracing 4,500 lush, semitropical acres. In addition to golf on the three challenging eighteen-hole championship courses, the resort offers two dozen all-weather tennis courts, indoor and outdoor swimming pools, a fitness center, two theaters, and seven and a half miles of wide, white beaches.

It doesn't matter which of these three courses you play—you're going to be happy with your choice!

Litchfield was here first, opened to the public in 1968, and this course is every bit as good today as it was then, if not better. With its irrigation system, the course now stays very green. Before the irrigation system was installed, some very low scores were posted at Litchfield, including a 61 by Randy Glover, which is believed to be the course record.

No one puts those kinds of numbers on the board today at this 6,874-yard par-72 championship course designed by Willard Byrd, nor at the other courses. Joe Inman holds the record at River Club—66—and that same score is the best mark at Willbrook.

LITCHFIELD

Highway 17   P.O. Box 379   Pawleys Island, SC 29585
(843) 448-3331   (800) 845-1897

Architect: Willard Byrd   Year opened: 1968

Course rating/Slope rating:
Gold - 72.4/120   White - 68.8/116
Blue - 70.6/119   Ladies - 70.8/119

This mature, very good golf course winds through a pleasant residential section, and has featured many local and Carolina professional and amateur championship tournaments.

Highly respected by men and women who know the game, Litchfield doesn't have one bad hole. It is a long and fair course.

The first hole is a dogleg to the left, measuring 417 yards from the championship tees to the center of a well-trapped green, and hole #2, a 528-yard par five, has water all the way from tee to green on the left side. Actually, it is a sharp dogleg right and the man or woman who hits a long ball will have to choose carefully the proper club for the shot from the tee. Two traps are set on the left, 225 yards from the championship tee, and, if the drive carries beyond the traps, the golfer is going to find that he is

Number 3 does not get a whole lot easier. As a matter of fact, it is the number-one handicap hole on the golf course, 435 yards in length, with water on the right threatening the golfer's second shot.

So you're weary from playing those first three and would welcome a three par? You've got it, but the hole is 215 yards from the championship tees, 190 yards from the men's tees, and is set at an angle which demands an accurate tee shot!

Number 11, a sharp dogleg left, remains to most people the hardest hole on which to post a good score. More than 430 yards in length, it is virtually impossible to "cut the dogleg" because the fairway seems to be carved from a forest of very large oaks and pines.

Number 18 is a very good finishing hole. It measures 403 yards and requires a drive of approximately 250 yards to reach the elbow into the dogleg.

This course deserves its lofty rating.

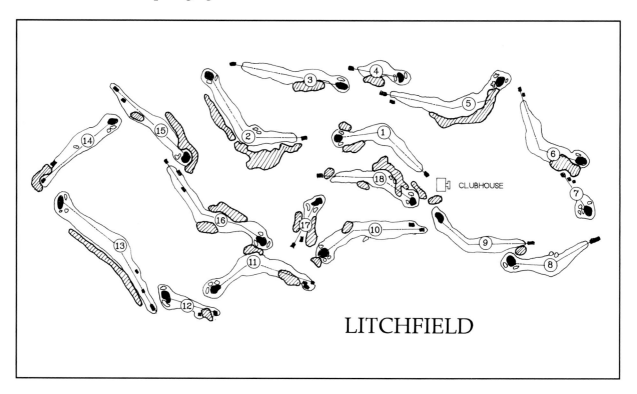

LITCHFIELD

Litchfield

HOLE NUMBER	1	2	3	4	5	6	7	8	9	OUT	10	11	12	13	14	15	16	17	18	IN	TOT	HCP	NET
GOLD	405	519	425	202	499	393	186	385	258	3352	389	424	219	520	366	354	538	184	406	3400	6752		
BLUE	385	501	401	185	479	363	170	347	339	3170	375	387	189	498	340	330	502	165	386	3172	6342		
WHITE	356	469	393	164	445	346	151	304	319	2947	361	358	170	463	313	321	474	151	359	2970	5917		
MEN'S HCP	5	7	1	9	13	3	17	15	11		12	2	8	10	14	16	4	18	6				
PAR	4	5	4	3	5	4	3	4	4	36	4	4	3	5	4	4	5	3	4	36	72		
LADIES'	317	433	362	133	392	331	130	292	292	2672	326	350	161	397	286	282	376	111	303	2592	5264		
LADIES' HCP	5	7	1	15	9	3	17	13	11		10	2	14	8	18	12	4	16	6				
LADIES' PAR	4	5	4	3	5	4	3	4	4	36	4	4	3	5	4	4	5	3	4	36	72		

Litchfield, first of three great courses within the Litchfield Complex. (Courtesy Brandon Advertising/Michael Slear)

Willbrook Plantation, another of the fine courses within Litchfield. (Courtesy Brandon Advertising/Michael Slear)

WILLBROOK PLANTATION

Highway 17   Litchfield Beach, SC   P.O. Box 379
Pawleys Island, SC 28585   (843) 237-4900
Architect: Dan Maples   Year opened: 1988
Course rating/Slope rating:
Blue - 72.5/131
White - 69.6/120
Red - 67.7/118

One of the best kept secrets of the Grand Strand golfing scene is Willbrook Plantation, a fine eighteen-hole course designed by Dan Maples and a fitting companion to sister courses Litchfield and River Club.

The course, which takes its name from an eighteenth-century rice plantation, has few members and, until recently, the only way you could get on its manicured fairways was to stay at the Waccamaw House or tour the eighteen holes with a member of the Litchfield course.

If you get a chance to play Willbrook, do not miss it.

The course is good and it's fun. The scenery is delightful, and Maples has come up with a design that is pleasing, playable, and difficult enough to test the ability of every golfer, whether the player is a high handicapper or scratch.

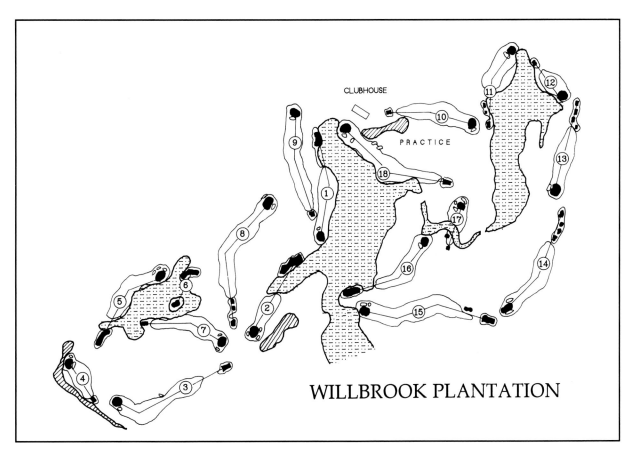

WILLBROOK PLANTATION

It has everything—water, marsh, sand, trees, bunkers, waste bunkers, boards, mounds, and good greens. If a critic has a complaint it would be that the first hole is too hard, 440 yards with hazards between tee and green. But once the golfer has conquered (or yielded to) the first hole, he or she will have a delightful round, and maybe a good score—until reaching #14. From that moment on, the five closing holes compare favorably to any closing stretch on the Strand and a couple of five pars—#15 and #18—will be remembered for years to come.

Can you hit your drive far enough to get your second shot over the water? If you don't, you can't reach #15 in three. And #18 is the type of five par that low handicappers love. It can be reached in two, if you can hit an accurate 225- to 250-yard second shot through a narrow opening and keep the pellet from bouncing off a boarded fairway!

Number 16, too, is an awesome four par, requiring distance and accuracy to an elevated green.

Good golf course!

Willbrook

HOLE NUMBER	1	2	3	4	5	6	7	8	9	OUT	10	11	12	13	14	15	16	17	18	IN	TOT	HCP	NET
BLUE	428	394	553	180	383	127	355	519	355	3294	379	336	199	363	419	572	404	173	535	3380	6674		
WHITE	404	360	503	155	369	107	324	485	322	3029	334	292	180	325	380	538	381	147	471	3048	6077		
HANDICAP	7	5	11	13	3	15	9	1	17		14	8	16	10	12	2	4	18	6				
PAR	4	4	5	3	4	3	4	5	4	36	4	4	3	4	4	5	4	3	5	36	72		
RED	281	264	452	106	332	87	280	410	220	2432	294	251	156	275	334	438	234	129	421	2532	4964		
HANDICAP	9	7	3	15	1	13	11	5	17		12	18	8	16	6	2	10	14	4				
PAR	4	4	5	3	4	3	4	5	4	36	4	4	3	4	4	5	4	3	5	36	72		

RIVER CLUB

Pine Drive   P.O. Box 379   Pawleys Island, SC 29585
(843) 237-8755

Architect: Tom Jackson   Year opened: 1986

Course rating/Slope rating:
Black - 72.4/128
White - 70.4/121
Red - 67.7/120

We played River Club on a warm February afternoon with two professional golfers, one from Virginia, who was seeing this course for the first time. It was a fine day, and though the sun was playing peekaboo with the clouds, the temperature was in the high 60s and the wind was no factor.

"I really like this course," said Billy Woolard. "There aren't any bad holes!"

"When you play the River, you're probably going to lose your religion," laughed Mayor Mason Barber of Ocean Isle Beach. "I don't think I ever saw so much water and so much sand."

The good mayor was right about the preponderance of sand and water, but to us the River was a very fair, challenging, and fun golf course. There was a lot of water—coming into play on fifteen of the eighteen holes—and the greens were well guarded with a bevy of sand traps on every hole. The Bermuda greens were converting to bent, and the course was well kept, a fitting companion to its sister courses, Litchfield and Willbrook. All three are good, truly championship golf layouts, and River Club may be the most challenging of the trio.

There are several memorable holes, particularly #18, which bears a remarkable resemblance to the famed monster 18th at Doral in Florida.

From the back tees you have to carry the ball 240 to 245 yards over the water, but if you do you're in position to get home in two and have an excellent chance to make birdie, even eagle. If you clear the pond you're going to be able to get home with a second shot of 180 to 190 yards. However, be warned. The approach shot to the green is also over water guarding the front of the green.

Most golfers will not be able to hit the ball far enough to clear the water and will elect to play a safe shot to the right, then hit a second shot up close to the water and use a short iron to negotiate the final water hazard.

This is a good hole, but not the most difficult.

That distinction probably belongs to #9, although there can be a lot of argument among River Club devotees. Many will opt for #15 when naming the hardest hole on the course. Others will talk about #11 and there are some who will tell you that it is the combined toughness of the three-par holes that makes River Club such a challenge.

One hole certain to catch your attention is the par-five 6th. This would be among our "eighteen best" except that the narrow green slopes to the left, allowing surface water to run off. And, since the green is exposed to sun and wind, it can become very hard. With these factors it is hard to "hold" anything but a lofty iron on the approach to the green. Because it is a five-par hole the hard surface makes it difficult to post subpar numbers.

The shot to the green not only must carry over a large pond, but the green is narrow and a tremendous trap running the entire length of the green is directly behind the putting surface. If you come up short you're in the water, but if you hit the green with a wood or a long iron, chances are you're going to be in that back trap.

Still, it is a spectacular hole, fun to play, and a real challenge.

Those aspects—spectacular, fun, and challenging—summarize the entire golf course, which was designed by Tom Jackson. Add to this the fact that it is placed in a beautiful setting and adorned with a modern, circular clubhouse offering wide vistas of the playing area as the golfer relaxes in overstuffed furniture or enjoys a sandwich and beverage at the lounge, and it is easy to see why River Club is destined to be a favorite.

Aerial view of River Club, one of three eighteen-hole courses at Litchfield. (Courtesy Brandon Advertising/Michael Slear)

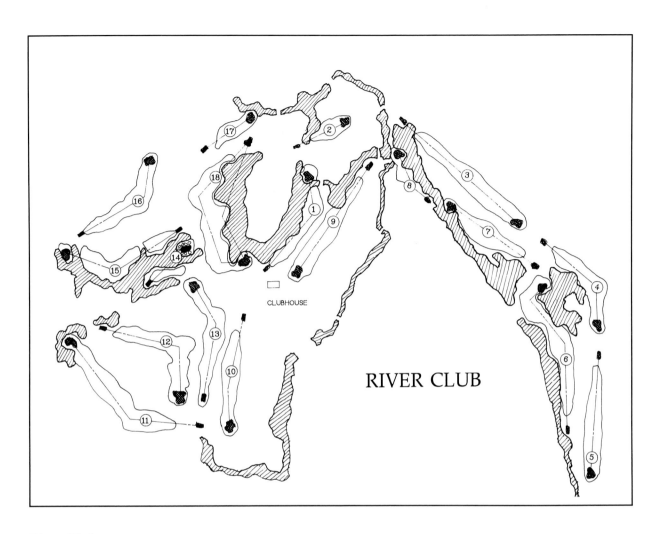

River Club

HOLE NUMBER	1	2	3	4	5	6	7	8	9	OUT	10	11	12	13	14	15	16	17	18	IN	TOT	HCP	NET
BLACK	390	198	545	349	399	481	372	181	414	3329	383	546	386	363	185	412	368	191	506	3340	6669		
WHITE	372	176	514	330	376	462	338	168	395	3131	368	523	364	350	160	386	352	168	481	3152	6283		
HANDICAP	9	17	1	15	5	3	11	13	7		8	4	12	10	16	2	14	18	6				
MEN'S PAR	4	3	5	4	4	5	4	3	4	36	4	5	4	4	3	4	4	3	5	36	72		
RED	293	116	450	271	295	382	241	100	294	2442	300	453	298	262	118	275	271	116	363	2456	4898		
HANDICAP	9	17	1	15	7	3	11	13	5		8	2	12	10	16	6	14	18	4				
LADIES' PAR	4	3	5	4	4	5	4	3	4	36	4	5	4	4	3	4	4	3	5	36	72		

Hole #7 at Wachesaw Plantation is long, narrow, and difficult. (Courtesy Wachesaw Plantation/Brian Morgan)

WACHESAW PLANTATION

P.O. Box 1578   Murrells Inlet, SC 29576
(843) 357-1500   (800) 922-5834
Architect: Tom Fazio   Year opened: 1985
Course rating/Slope rating:
Gold - 73.5/132
Blue - 70.8/125
White - 68.8/119

You have to see the Wachesaw Plantation golf course to discover how good it really is. Granted, Tom Fazio had a beautiful tract of ground on which to design a championship layout, and most agree he made the most of it.

A sales brochure for Wachesaw has a particularly apt description:

It is a place away, a time apart. The natural charms of Wachesaw Plantation are just as they were two hundred years ago, when this historic natural expanse boasted a gracious rice plantation.

A few things have changed at Wachesaw Plantation since the 1700s. Now, instead of rice crops, a championship signature golf course meanders through the property and along the river.

Rated number one on South Carolina's Grand Strand by *Golf Digest* magazine, the course is carved artfully out of the forest and wanders beside the river's breathtaking bluffs ... rolling fairways, grass bunkers, elevated tees, love grass hazards. These are some of the features which set the Wachesaw Golf Course apart.

Yes, the Wachesaw golf course is handsome—but it is also difficult!

Wachesaw, from the back tees, is just shy of 7,000 yards, and while it appears to be open and inviting, that appearance can be most deceptive. J. P. Waldron has the course record of 65, set in 1987 and unchallenged since.

In the words of NCNB bank executive Jim Watson, a good amateur player who often tours Wachesaw, "this is a good course, fun to play, but it can be challenging. Wachesaw is a course that rewards a good shot but can severely punish you if you hit the ball off line.

"Take #4 as an example. This is a par five which good players can reach in two, but they must be extremely accurate. Hit it straight and the opportunity for birdie is excellent, but get off line and you're going to be bunkered or, worse than that, in the love grass."

In Watson's opinion, the three pars are excellent and that is an opinion shared by many.

Number 7 is the signature hole, and perhaps the prettiest hole on the entire course. There is water on the left, jutting into the fairway, guarding most of the green to create an island-type green. Banks of love grass are on the right, and with five different tee boxes this hole can change radically depending on which tee you are playing.

Number 15 is a good hole that behooves the golfer to forget temporarily the history lesson he or she has learned by walking from the 14th green to this tee, because the hole demands undivided attention.

There are plantation ruins located on the hill between green and tee, and a historical marker commemorating Richmond Hill Plantation:

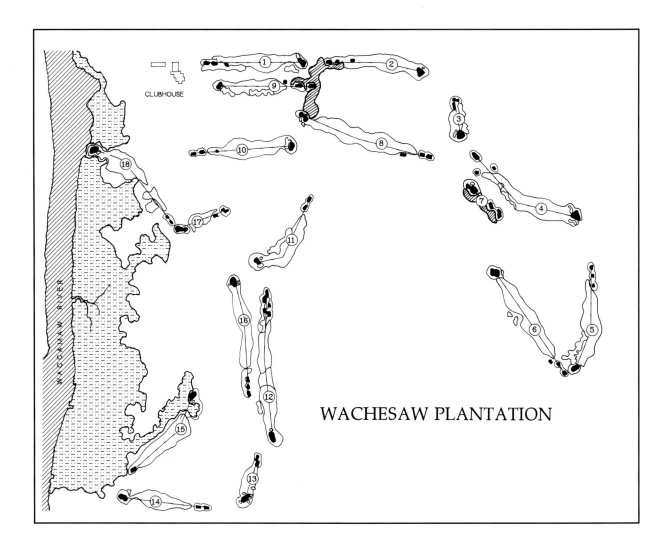

WACHESAW PLANTATION

The brick piers are built on the original foundation footing laid down by members of the Austin family in 1810. Doctor John Magill, physician and rice planter, acquired the plantation in 1825 and married Mary Eliza Vereen. Here, in this small residence, the Magills managed the plantation consisting of 1,000 acres and 200 slaves.

Back to golf! The 15th is a par-four, dog-leg-left, 378-yard hole that features steep slopes. The fairway sets up about eye level with a lateral hazard, and falls off sharply to the left. Trees line the right side and the fairway is open, but your tee ball is going to roll to the left, making the second shot difficult as you hit uphill to a plateaued green guarded in front by a ravine.

While on the subject of steep slopes, let's consider the three-par 17th hole. If the golfer misses the green short or to the right, there is a strong possibility that this errant tee shot will roll all the way down the hill into the water hazard. And, if the ball isn't wet, the second shot is quite demanding, with the impression that you must hit the ball straight up to get it onto the green.

Having successfully maneuvered his way through 17 holes, the player now finds himself at #18, and this is the one most golfers go home talking about (or talking to themselves!). Par five and 573 yards from the professional tees, this hole goes toward the

Intracoastal Waterway, which runs behind the green.

There are many different ways to play the hole, but probably the best way is a long iron or a fairway wood off the tees, clearing a deep chasm filled with water, hoping to hit a very tight landing area. The second shot is even more difficult because everything, fairway and rough, slopes sharply to the left, with water paralleling the entire length of the fairway. The prudent, better player will hit a long iron, leaving an approach of 130 to 150 yards.

The temptation is to hit this second shot to the right, but let it slide too much and you are out of bounds or looking at a shot out of the rough from a side hill lie.

The green is hard to read, like every green on this Fazio layout. They feature very subtle breaks and when the bent grass is cut close, they are fast as lightning. An expert putter definitely has an advantage at Wachesaw.

Wachesaw is a private club. To get on the course you must play with a member or rent an on-premise guest cottage. However, if there is any way to play Wachesaw, it is strongly recommended as one of the most interesting courses on the Strand.

See page 71 for Wachesaw East.

Wachesaw Plantation

HOLE NUMBER	1	2	3	4	5	6	7	8	9	OUT	10	11	12	13	14	15	16	17	18	IN	TOT	HCP	NET
GOLD	407	426	165	475	415	455	177	537	386	3443	412	355	569	179	330	378	443	207	573	3446	6889		
BLUE	368	376	125	470	384	427	159	506	345	3160	378	325	535	155	302	369	412	171	535	3182	6342		
HANDICAP	7	9	17	13	5	3	11	1	15		10	14	2	18	16	6	8	12	4				
PAR	4	4	3	5	4	4	3	5	4	36	4	4	5	3	4	4	4	3	5	36	72		
WHITE	285	293	97	377	324	371	87	414	296	2544	312	245	430	122	227	281	307	111	410	2445	4989		
HANDICAP	11	9	17	7	3	5	15	1	13		6	16	2	18	14	10	8	12	4				

Clubhouse at Heritage Club, a Larry Young development. (Courtesy Himmelsbach Communications/Bill Woodward)

Heritage Club

HOLE NUMBER	1	2	3	4	5	6	7	8	9	OUT	10	11	12	13	14	15	16	17	18	IN	TOT	HCP	NET
GOLD	410	570	440	440	410	205	430	165	370	3440	610	170	365	235	440	460	410	440	530	3660	7100		
BLUE	380	540	410	415	395	185	400	155	350	3230	520	140	340	200	400	440	380	415	510	3345	6575		
WHITE	360	510	380	345	370	165	370	145	330	2975	500	125	315	175	350	420	365	385	490	3125	6100		
HANDICAP	7	11	3	1	15	13	5	17	9		10	18	16	8	4	2	14	6	12				
PAR	4	5	4	4	4	3	4	3	4	35	5	3	4	3	4	4	4	4	5	36	71		

HERITAGE CLUB

River Road   P.O. Box 2038   Myrtle Beach, SC 29585
(843) 237-3424   (800) 552-2660

Architect: Dan Maples   Year opened: 1986

Course Rating/Slope Rating:
Gold - 74.1/142
Blue - 72.0/132
White - 69.6/129

"Tee to green, as far as aesthetics are concerned, this is my best golf course ever," says Larry Young, developer. Many people will agree with him even after playing his other masterpieces—including Oyster Bay, Marsh Harbour, and the three splendid courses at The Legends (Heathland, Moorland, and Parkland).

"You just can't beat Larry Young golf courses," says George Hendrix, golf professional. "They are very, very tough, and very, very good."

Almost everyone will agree that Heritage Club belongs in the top ten of Grand Strand golf courses, and there can be legitimate argument that it is the very best of all. The Heritage is scenic, difficult, well planned, and immaculately conditioned.

A par 71, the Heritage features vast areas of putting surface, and is adorned with live oaks, some of them 300 years old, and giant magnolias. Built on the former site of two eighteenth-century rice plantations—True Blue and Midway—the Heritage is a fantasy re-creation of the Old South, complete with spiral staircase in the colonial-style clubhouse and the avenue of live oaks leading to that gracious facility.

Not only are the greens huge, but they also undulate!

With an abundance of marsh, water, sand, strategically placed trees, and those big, undulating greens, this is a course that doesn't "give you anything," and although the golf course has been a favorite since it opened in February of 1986, no one has bettered the 69 (2 under par) that PGA Tour professional Leonard Thompson fired from the back tees.

In addition to referring constantly to the huge greens, Heritage visitors will tell you about the hole that has two parallel fairways; the 235-yard, par-three island-green hole; pot bunkers; tight doglegs; and the long iron shot over an old slave cemetery.

As though par-five holes aren't tough enough for most golfers, #2 at the Heritage has water curving into the middle of the fairway, making accurate placement shots most important.

Number 4 is a long par four and has a line of live oaks on the right side. One oak tree stands as a silent sentinel in the middle of the fairway. Even the best of golfers can hit a great tee shot and still need a three iron to get home with the second shot.

Number 9 is described as a fine finishing hole, requiring an accurate drive. It is not a particularly long hole, and big hitters will be using a short iron to reach the green. However, that's where the rub comes in to play. This green is so undulated that it can cause nightmares.

The 13th hole is spectacular, 235 yards from the championship tee to an island green. The green itself is a masterpiece for golf architect Dan Maples, who routed this course for Young, featuring pot bunkers to the right and a yawning sand trap to the left.

Fourteen is testy. The tee shot is over water, and, if you are on the left side of the fairway, you must go over the water again to reach the green.

Hole #17 plays as a dogleg right and measures 440 yards, and the architects have left trees in critical spots, just to get in your way.

Number 18 is characterized by professionals as a good finishing hole, one of those five pars you can reach in two if you're a gambler. This is a hole that rewards the spectacular shot, but can become very pun-

ishing. Yes, you can reach the beautiful hourglass-shaped green with your second shot, but it is a shot that must carry all the way over water. Most players will play it short and use a wedge to get the ball close.

The Heritage is rated in the top fifty courses in the United States by *Golf Digest*. Golfers coming to the Strand for the first time will not have made a bad choice if they choose to play all the Larry Young courses. However, if you are going to challenge any of the courses from the very back tees, bring plenty of golf balls!

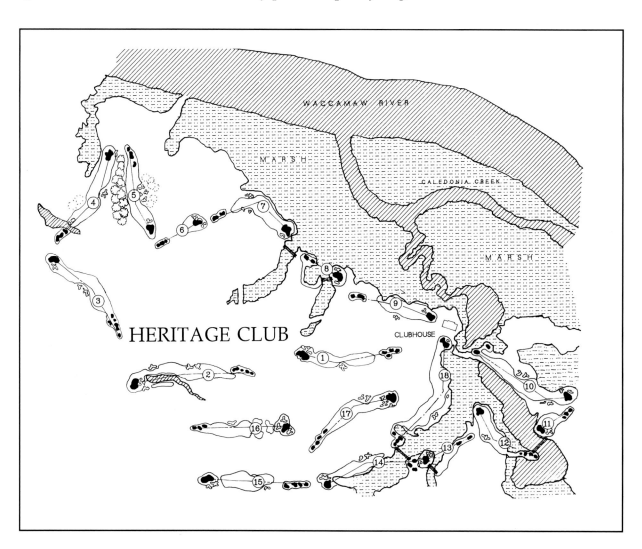

HERITAGE CLUB

PAWLEYS PLANTATION

Highway 17   70 Tanglewood Drive   P.O. Box 2070   Pawleys Island, SC 29585
(843) 237-1736   (800) 545-5973

Architect: Jack Nicklaus   Year opened: 1988

Course rating/Slope rating:

Gold - 74.8/140   Blue - 71.9/133
White - 70.5/125   Red - 73.0/130

Among the ninety-six golf courses of the Grand Strand that are featured in this book, two were designed by Jack Nicklaus. The head professional of Pawleys Plantation, located on the south end of the Strand, not only has the opportunity of playing an occasional round of golf with Nicklaus, but has the pleasure of hanging his hat here every day.

Most of the people who get the chance to play here are convinced that Pawleys is an exceptional golf course. It is very demand-ing, with wonderful subtleties built into it by Nicklaus. A scratch player can be very proud of shooting 75 on this course.

Pawleys is a picturesque course, with much of the back nine fronting marshland. First-time visitors will be particularly impressed as they leave the four-par 12th hole and drive their golf cart right out through the marsh across a dike.

The dike was part of the old rice plantation on this site, and the Coastal Council allowed the golf club to use it as an access.

The clubhouse at Pawleys Plantation. (Courtesy Pawleys Plantation)

Number 12 at Pawleys Plantation. (Courtesy Pawleys Plantation)

Instead of just getting a nice view of the marsh, golfers at Pawleys join the scene with the wildlife.

Number 13 actually is a double green, and the golfer plays this green again when he plays #16. This is the signature hole at Pawleys, and the green is so large that few golfers realize they are playing a double green. But the landing area for #13 green is very small and difficult to hit.

The approach to #16 is much less demanding, but it is a very memorable and challenging four-par hole. This entire section of the golf course—#12 through #17—is played in, around, and over marshland, and is as hard as it is picturesque.

Golfers with a sense of history will look forward to playing #14 if for no other reason than that Nicklaus owns a home on this fairway.

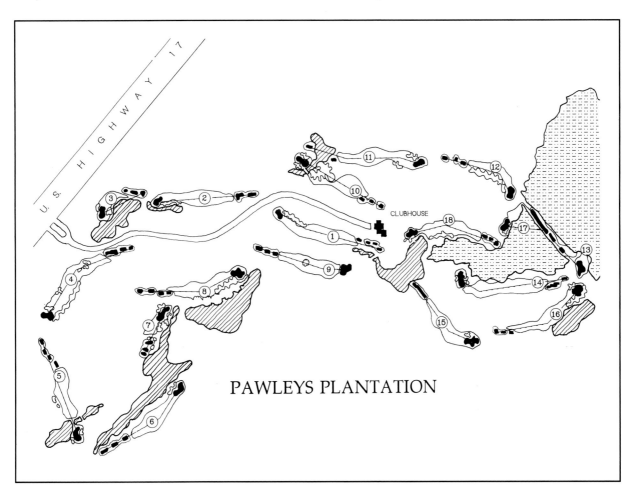

PAWLEYS PLANTATION

Pawleys Plantation

HOLE NUMBER	1	2	3	4	5	6	7	8	9	OUT	10	11	12	13	14	15	16	17	18	IN	TOT	HCP	NET
GOLD	511	461	194	543	390	432	172	452	416	3571	361	563	382	145	525	391	444	201	443	3455	7026		
BLUE	495	441	170	498	371	391	151	419	387	3323	330	548	345	115	495	374	423	167	402	3199	6522		
WHITE	484	408	162	468	353	382	131	387	358	3133	301	542	331	69	471	364	405	139	372	2994	6127		
MEN'S HCP	17	1	11	13	5	7	15	3	9		12	16	18	6	8	14	2	10	4				
PAR	5	4	3	5	4	4	3	4	4	36	4	5	4	3	5	4	4	3	4	36	72		
RED	426	354	127	450	322	367	124	361	351	2882	278	442	309	40	446	351	360	122	342	2690	5572		
LADIES' HCP	17	5	13	1	3	11	15	7	9		10	16	18	6	4	14	2	12	8				

The front and back nines of this splendid golf course are radically different. The back side is the one customers will remember because of the scenery and pinpoint precision needed to play "target" golf. While the front side has more of a traditional look, it is long, beautifully manicured, well bunkered, and stacks up against the best around.

Pawleys is more than a good golf course. It is a golfing experience, taking visitors back in time as they drive through the "guard" gate up a winding lane to a beautiful clubhouse that is even more delightful inside.

The dining rooms are spacious and well appointed. The private member rooms are beautifully paneled, and the service and hospitality are legendary.

The famous double green of #13 is set in the marshlands. (Courtesy Pawleys Plantation)

SEAGULL

Highway 17   P.O. Box 196   Pawleys Island, SC 29585   (843) 237-4285
Architect: Gene Hamm   Year opened: 1967
Course rating/Slope rating:
Blue - 74.0/134
White - 70.9/129
Red - 74.4/120

The senior member in a group of golf courses operated by Ken Fowlkes and known as "The Links Group," Seagull is one of the southernmost courses on the Grand Strand. Other courses in this group, all of them well conditioned and a good test of golf, include Quail Creek, Colonial Charters, The Tradition, Indigo Creek, Indian Wells, Cypress Bay, Island Green, and the two courses at Burning Ridge.

When you play Seagull for the first time, two things probably will impress you: the tremendous size of the golf course and the vast difference between the front nine and the back.

The front nine is long and relatively flat, while the back has much more roll and movement than most Beach courses, with two large lakes cutting across fairways on the back side. There are impressive mounds, doglegs, and several man-made hazards on the back, created by "boarding" the sides of bunkers.

Gene Hamm did a fine design job, and even though this Seagull course was opened in 1967, it holds up very well against the competition of the 1990s.

The signature hole is #12, but several other holes, such as #6, #7, #9, and #18, warrant special attention.

Number 12 is memorable in that it has two greens! One green, for the ladies, sits on the tee-box side of a large lake and plays as a par four. The other green lies beyond the lake and is the finishing point of a difficult 525-yard par-five hole (the ladies' four par is 330 yards in length). Few male golfers can reach this one in two; they must play a calculated second shot short of the pond and still face an iron shot of 140 yards or more to a well-bunkered green.

Number 9 is another five par which golfers will remember because it is the hole visible from Highway 17, with the green tucked almost under the motel rooms. It is a double dogleg and you must hit the ball right, then left, and finally straight ahead to a well-bunkered green. If "well-bunkered green" sounds redundant, just take a look at the scorecard. None of the holes can be played without the specter of a sand trap to be negotiated!

Seagull

HOLE NUMBER	1	2	3	4	5	6	7	8	9	OUT	10	11	12	13	14	15	16	17	18	IN	TOT	HCP	NET
BLUE	440	395	185	535	185	415	420	420	545	3540	510	210	525	380	420	365	165	425	370	3370	6910		
WHITE	400	375	160	510	160	385	380	375	510	3255	480	180	485	330	385	315	150	390	345	3060	6315		
MEN'S HCP	9	11	15	5	17	3	13	1	7		8	16	6	12	4	14	18	2	10				
PAR	4	4	3	5	3	4	4	4	5	36	5	3	5	4	4	4	3	4	4	36	72		
RED	330	285	110	480	130	320	300	345	455	2755	425	135	330	290	300	255	135	340	285	2495	5250		
HANDICAP	7	9	17	1	11	5	13	15	3		2	16	8	12	6	14	18	4	10				
PAR	4	4	3	5	3	4	4	5	5	37	5	3	4	4	4	4	3	4	4	35	72		

Walled bunker at Seagull. (Courtesy Brandon Advertising/Michael Slear)

Number 6 features water on the left side into the fairway. The right side heads for the woods, making it a very difficult tee shot. A good player would still use a driver and a medium iron if he can keep the ball in the fairway!

The 7th hole is a good tee-shot hole. There is water on the left and, even from the whites, the golfer must carry the ball 180 yards to hit the fairway. If the golfer cannot clear the water, he has to keep it to the right and it is a sharp dogleg left to get home.

From the championship tees, #7 is 420 yards long, but that is the rule, not the exception. There are five four pars on the front, and all five are 400 yards or more!

Number 18 was redesigned several years ago by putting large mounds behind the green to block out the parking lot. In many tournaments played here, even though it is a short par four, the average score has been over double bogey. This is not the number-one handicap hole, yet it is one of the most difficult holes on the course, and one of the best finishing holes on the entire Grand Strand.

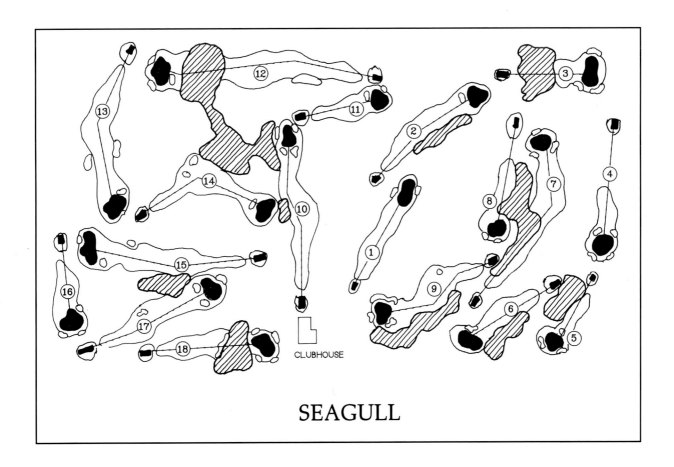

SEAGULL

DeBordieu Club's #9, beautiful and dangerous. (Courtesy DeBordieu Club)

DeBordieu Club

HOLE NUMBER	1	2	3	4	5	6	7	8	9	OUT	10	11	12	13	14	15	16	17	18	IN	TOT	HCP	NET
PROFESSIONAL	381	377	468	170	430	568	465	212	513	3584	420	497	364	427	194	427	213	449	566	3557	7141		
CHAMPIONSHIP	375	370	437	165	413	543	413	189	500	3405	410	490	335	405	185	400	200	423	555	3403	6808		
BACK	370	365	415	151	370	515	380	175	455	3196	392	467	302	395	152	385	185	376	550	3204	6400		
MIDDLE	300	340	365	143	365	500	375	140	451	2979	361	457	276	392	145	350	149	376	515	3021	6000		
MEN'S HCP	17	11	3	13	5	1	7	9	15		4	16	18	10	14	12	8	2	6				
PAR	4	4	4	3	4	5	4	3	5	36	4	5	4	4	3	4	3	4	5	36	72		
FORWARD	237	298	332	106	319	432	301	117	405	2547	354	397	240	298	107	305	120	289	456	2566	5113		
WOMEN'S HCP	17	9	7	15	3	1	11	13	5		16	6	10	12	18	8	14	4	2				

DeBORDIEU CLUB

Highway 17   P.O. Box 1996   Georgetown, SC 29442
(843) 546-1525
Architect: Pete Dye   Year opened: 1986
Course rating/Slope rating:
Professional - 75.4/144   Middle - 68.5/120
Championship - 73.7/137   Forward - 70.6/128
Back - 71.4/130

Golfers—professionals who should know—tell us that it doesn't get any better than this Pete Dye design, which is just as beautiful as it is tough. With a slope of 145 and a rating of 75 against the par of 72, DeBordieu Club, on paper, is the most difficult golf course on the Grand Strand.

It is a big golf course in every way—long, big greens, wide fairways, all spread over vast acreage. This is a private club and development with 325 golfing members, most of them from out of the area. In October 1991, only sixty families lived at beautiful DeBordieu the year round.

A new colonial-style clubhouse was added in 1990, and it is magnificent—30,000 square feet of paneling, chandeliers, carpeting, and hardwood floors.

The golf course, naturally, is the prime attraction of DeBordieu and draws rave reviews. Bob Drum, who does a golf show called "Drummers' Beat" for CBS, summed up his reaction by calling DeBordieu a "Pete Dye course without the whips and chains . . . Of all the Pete Dye courses I have seen, this one is the most mellow."

But this does not mean that DeBordieu is easy, at least not from the professional and championship tees. With five sets of tees, this course can become friendly, but there is water on sixteen holes, and the last two are very difficult.

We have been told that variety is the spice of life, which makes this golf course fun

every time you play it, because it seems to be a different course each time. It is always a challenge because of wind and tee placements, with good bent-grass greens and an assortment of carefully cultivated grasses throughout the course. The fairways are Bermuda, the roughs are centipede, and there is a ring of zoysia around the greens.

DeBordieu is a course so carefully designed that there are no bad holes. A major reason for this is that Dye was given unlimited acreage on which to build the course and the results are super.

While all the holes are good, everyone has a favorite.

Number 5 should be on everybody's list of best holes on the Strand. The hole is played from an elevated tee built onto the face of a hill. From this elevation, the good golfer hits a driver into the flat part of the fairway and still needs a long iron to get home on this 420-yard par four. The second shot must carry over water that cuts in front of the green and guards the entire putting surface on the right. A four here beats the world!

Another excellent hole on the front side is #4, a short three par over water. With the tee box on the right, the shot to the green is completely over a formidable lake, and requires a carry of 165 yards from the championship tees. This does not sound terribly difficult, but Dye has built a huge mound at the back of the green, causing the wind to swirl and making proper club selection an adventure in itself. In diabolical fashion, he also ringed the green with a myriad of sand traps, and this is a very difficult par three.

Be careful on #9. Relatively short at 500 yards, the hole affords the big hitter a chance to make this five par a two-shot hole, but there is plenty of trouble on this sharp dogleg to the left. If the golfer tries to cut the dogleg, there is a strong likelihood of driving the tee shot into the large lake on the left of the fairway. Water again comes into play on the second shot as it runs down the right side from the corner of the dogleg all the way to and behind the green. This is a hole that rewards great shot making, but assigns the maximum penalty to wayward souls.

Numbers 17 and 18 are exceptional, with water all the way on the right of both holes. They are beautiful but frightening—a vast expanse of fairway, marsh, water, and sand—but wide open and a wonderful example of good links design.

Number 17 is a dogleg to the right, a 449-yard par four with water from tee to green guarding the right side of the hole—very intimidating.

Number 18 is one of those big, big par fives—566 yards with water and a waste bunker on the left and a huge body of water running the length of the hole on the right. The golfer crosses a footbridge to reach the tee and quickly gets the feeling of being isolated. Actually, there is a lot of landing area for the tee shot, but the second shot is exceedingly tough as you hit toward the water. Slice it or push it and you're dead. Hit the ball left and you contend with some typical Pete Dye mounds and traps. This is not an easy hole and birdies are rare.

To dyed-in-the-wool residents, DeBordieu has an almost legendary aura. Very private and very difficult, it is a tough ticket—the kind of course golfers would sell their souls to play. It is beautiful. If you ever get a chance to play this one, don't miss it.

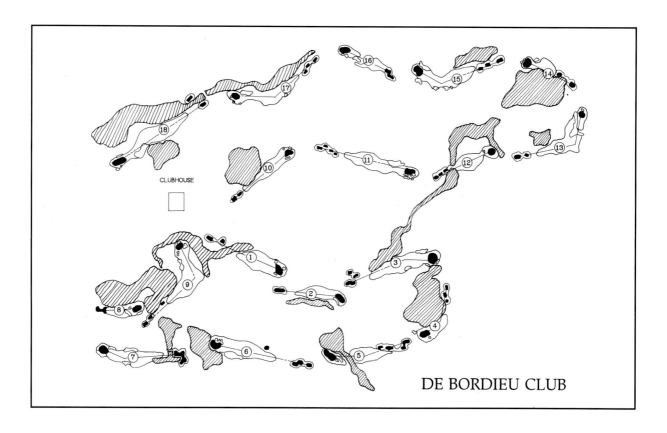

DE BORDIEU CLUB

THE WITCH

1900 Highway 544   Conway, SC 29526   (843) 448-1300
Architect: Dan Maples   Year opened: 1989
Course rating/Slope rating:

Black - 71.2/133
Orange - 69.0/109
White - 68.3/121

Without exception, golfers of our acquaintance enjoy playing The Witch. It is, as described in the golf course's brochure, an incredible course, eighteen holes of wilderness winding its way through 500 acres with no houses in sight.

Located between Conway and South Myrtle Beach on SC Highway 544, The Witch was created as a world of its own, carefully removed from the distractions of homes, hotels, and developments. Along with the Wizard and Man O' War, it is one of the three fine layouts owned and operated by Claude Pardue and Richard Lee.

Like other Dan Maples courses, The Witch features a natural layout, with no unnatural obstacles to impede maintenance. The average player can enjoy himself here while the better player can still be challenged.

"There is probably not another course like this Dan Maples jewel anyplace in the world," writes *Golf Magazine*.

The Witch was not an easy course to build, and more than 4,000 feet of bridges connect the holes, winding through cypress-tree swamps, across lakes, and over wetland areas filled with numerous species of flowers and plants.

Alligators, deer, black bear, and ducks can be spotted on the attractive course. You can really get away from it all here. And since there is no residential development, The Witch will be able to retain this pleasing wildness in the future.

The Witch "theme" is fun.

Tee markers, in traditional Halloween colors, are white, orange, and black, and the pins have orange, black, or striped poles letting the golfer know whether the pin is set front, back, or middle of the green. At the driving range, a first-time visitor might be startled to see three cardboard witches apparently flying across the range. Actually, they hold signs indicating distances. Tourists can take home The Witch logo on tee shirts, sweatshirts, caps, visors, and balls.

The Witch, whose name suggests a treacherous golf course, has two distinctly different looks on the front and back.

The front nine is relatively flat, built in and around the wetland areas, while the back nine is "hilly" by Beach standards, with drops in elevation of thirty feet or more. Maples chose Bermuda greens, using Bermuda 419 as tee and fairway ground cover. Because The Witch is carved from forest and swamp, Bermuda is well-suited to its damp and shady areas.

The Witch has a lot of good golf holes.

Some favorites that bring golfers back again and again are #9, #15, #17, and #18. The 9th is a relatively short par four, dogleg left which requires great accuracy, since golfers must place the tee shot in a tight landing area and then hit uphill to a well-bunkered green. Measuring 373 yards from the black (back) tees, this hole is only 217 yards in length for the ladies when they tee up from the orange markers.

Number 15 is a demanding four par, 425 yards from the black tee box. The golfer

Natural terrain dictates the layout of The Witch's #15. (Courtesy The Witch)

must hit a big drive to be in position to carry the wetlands, which come into play on the second shot, extending nearly to the green itself. Number 17 is interesting because of the drop in elevation, leaving a downhill shot to the green on this pretty three par. The second shot on the finishing hole is downhill and quite picturesque, with the clubhouse in the background.

The Witch is not a long course, measuring 6,700 yards when played all the way back and 4,812 yards from the ladies' tees. How-ever, there can be many a slip twixt the first tee shot and the final putt.

At first glance, it does not seem awesome and water is directly in the line of flight on only three holes—at #2, #4, and #6. Even then water only partially invades the fair-way except on #6, a short four par which is played directly over a large body of water. But with all the wetland areas to the side of most holes, accuracy is still called for.

The course record is an 8-under-par 64, fired by professional Ronnie Parker.

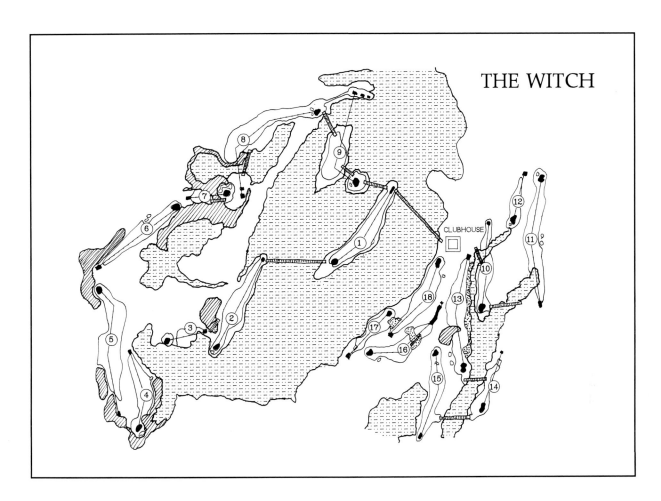

The Witch

HOLE NUMBER	1	2	3	4	5	6	7	8	9	OUT	10	11	12	13	14	15	16	17	18	IN	TOT	HCP	NET
BLACK	420	416	169	386	570	447	185	592	373	3558	375	542	193	520	142	425	382	177	388	3144	6702		
ORANGE	384	389	118	319	529	403	147	559	344	3192	338	511	163	478	119	379	337	143	351	2819	6011		
WHITE	317	320	70	282	470	344	102	477	217	2599	277	387	113	409	86	301	276	112	252	2213	4812		
HANDICAP	1	3	5	17	11	9	13	7	15		2	4	6	14	18	8	16	12	10				
PAR	4	4	3	4	5	4	3	5	4	36	4	5	3	5	3	4	4	3	4	35	71		

Heron Point's difficult #18. (Courtesy Himmelsbach Communications/Bill Woodward)

HERON POINT

Highway 707   6980 Blue Heron Blvd.   Myrtle Beach, SC 29575
(843) 650-6664

Architect: Willard Byrd   Year opened: 1988

Course rating/Slope rating:
Blue - 70.9/129
White - 69.2/121
Red - 69.2/121

With strategically placed sand and water hazards, Heron Point is characteristic of a Willard Byrd design as it winds its way through a pine forest and a comparatively dense housing development.

There are some excellent holes on this challenging, tight course, and the final four are most memorable. Some words of advice: bring plenty of golf balls and resolve to leave your driver in the bag much of the time.

Numbers 7 and 9 are five-par holes on the front side that offer birdie opportunities, as both are straightaway and reasonably short. Number 9, however—like much of this course—demands unerring accuracy, with large bodies of water on both sides of the fairway halfway from the second shot to the green.

The final four holes can leave a lasting impression on visiting golfers. The 18th is particularly exciting, running 511 yards from tee to green from the back tees, with a large lake down the left side and sand traps on the right.

As though that isn't enough, Byrd designed this hole to be even more demanding by hiding a couple of traps in the fairway and leaving two tall pine trees in that same fairway. To get to the 18th hole, the golfer has just played a demanding par three, 190 yards in length, with a large bunker running in front of most of the green.

Nor is #16 a "piece of cake," 521 yards in length, with two ponds strategically located on the left. At least #16 is straight. The hole preceding it is a severe dogleg right, and the green is hidden from the tee box by tall pines on the right. If the golfer attempts to avoid the pines and get an open shot to the green, there is danger of hooking the tee shot into a pond on the left at the elbow of the dogleg.

Heron Point is a golf course that surprises a lot of people. They get the impression that it is fairly easy, but there are some real horror stories told by some pretty fair golfers who play Heron Point for the first time.

Plan to lose some golf balls, and it wouldn't be a bad idea to leave the driver at home. It

Heron Point

HOLE NUMBER	1	2	3	4	5	6	7	8	9	OUT	10	11	12	13	14	15	16	17	18	IN	TOT	HCP	NET
BLUE	340	394	386	165	367	175	508	394	546	3275	426	179	380	355	378	381	521	193	511	3324	6599		
WHITE	320	374	359	148	346	156	475	368	515	3061	385	158	362	323	357	363	484	176	482	3090	6151		
MEN'S HCP	8	6	4	17	15	10	11	13	2		3	16	9	18	14	12	5	7	1				
PAR	4	4	4	3	4	3	5	4	5	36	4	3	4	4	4	4	5	3	5	36	72		
RED	272	335	325	112	327	113	431	334	432	2681	337	123	337	300	306	308	426	154	418	2709	5390		
LADIES' HCP	12	6	10	18	8	17	2	14	4		5	16	7	15	9	13	1	11	3				

is a very tight course, and it is fairly short, 6,100 yards from the white tees, 6,500 from the blues, 5,200 yards from the women's markers. While Heron Point is the type of course that can cause trouble for the low-handicap player, it remains a course that the average player can enjoy and post a good score. Mid- to high handicappers will love Heron Point.

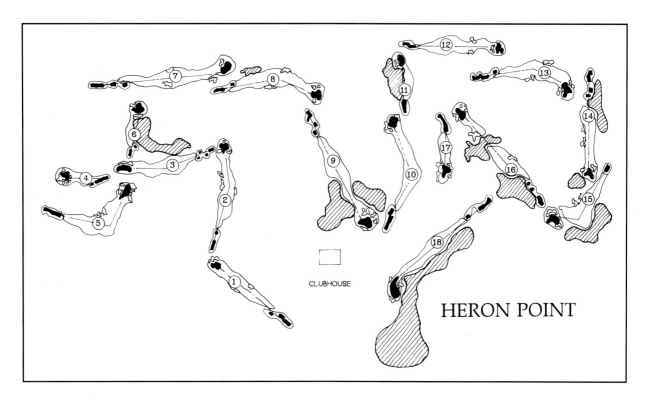

CLUBHOUSE

HERON POINT

RACCOON RUN

8950 Highway 707 [between Socastee and Murrells Inlet]
Myrtle Beach, SC 29575   (843) 650-2644

Architect: Gene Hamm   Year opened: 1977

Course rating/Slope rating:
Blue - 74.0/120   Red - 69.5/109
White - 72.6/116   Gold - 69.2/113

Raccoon Run is not mentioned in the same sentence as premier courses such as Tidewater, The Dunes, Heather Glen, Wild Wing Plantation, Heritage Club, The Legends, Caledonia, The Surf Club, Myrtle Beach National, Belle Terre, Glen Dornoch, and others, *but* this course has several distinctions. It is arguably the most affordable golf course on the Grand Strand, and, without argument, it *is* the longest.

When many courses were charging $60 to $115 for green fees and carts in the spring of 1998, Raccoon Run opened its doors to thousands of golfers who liked the $25 total price tag—and, if you wanted to walk, $20 would do the trick.

The golfers would find a very challenging Gene Hamm designed golf course measuring 7,400 yards from the championship tees and 6,800 yards from the men's regular markers. They would go home shaking their heads but praising the Run's own version of "Amen Corner"—holes 15 through 18.

Beginning with a 248-yard par three

Water guards the 18th at Raccoon Run. (Courtesy Resort Media Consultants)

which has water on both sides of the fairway, this Amen Corner concludes with a monster 450-yard four par dogleg right. It is necessary to hit the tee shot some 240 yards to get an open shot to the green and, to complicate further the efforts of a golfer, there is a pond on the left front of the green.

Number 16 is another long par four with water running the length of the fairway on the left and woods guarding the right. This one is 458 from the blues, 420 from the whites. Number 17 is a little shorter, but not much easier. With woods on both sides of the fairway, it measures 387 and is described as a tough little hole.

While these four tough finishing holes are extremely difficult, Raccoon Run for the most part is wide open. However, the awesome length of the course (#10 is 610 yards from tee to green and #4 measures 585) makes it hard for anyone to put a low score on the board.

The course was opened in February 1977, and the best score is believed to be 69, posted by a North Carolina amateur playing the white tees. Knowing that the course is devilishly long, especially for the vast number of senior players who patronize Raccoon Run, the course has built a new set of tees (gold) for seniors. Even then, the course measures almost 6,300 yards. Nor do the ladies get a lot of aid. Raccoon Run is 5,535 yards from the red tees.

The greens and tees are elevated, some more than others, with a good Bermuda putting surface for the 300 members and frequent tourist players. The ladies' group at Raccoon Run is very active, and the women members play a lot of golf.

There are quite a few bunkers: "We have three or four sand traps on every hole."

RACCOON RUN

Raccoon Run

HOLE NUMBER	1	2	3	4	5	6	7	8	9	OUT	10	11	12	13	14	15	16	17	18	IN	TOT	HCP	NET
BLUE	536	388	450	585	450	190	413	484	209	3705	610	252	398	466	375	248	458	387	450	3644	7349		
WHITE	510	353	415	550	420	160	382	460	175	3425	575	210	367	455	363	215	420	354	415	3374	6799		
HANDICAP	3	17	9	1	5	15	7	11	13		2	6	16	18	14	12	4	10	8				
MEN'S PAR	5	4	4	5	4	3	4	5	3	37	5	3	4	5	4	3	4	4	4	36	73		
RED	422	301	331	460	330	114	294	400	155	2807	498	148	318	349	237	172	348	298	360	2728	5535		
LADIES' PAR	5	4	4	5	4	3	4	5	3	37	5	3	4	4	4	3	4	4	4	35	72		

ISLAND GREEN

Highway 707   455 Sunnehanna Drive   Myrtle Beach, SC 29575   (843) 650-2186

Architect: Willard Byrd   Year opened: 1988

Course rating/Slope rating:
Blue - H34.6, D34.4/118
White - H33.4, D32.8/111
Red - H33.0, D32.0/113

The premium is on accuracy at the twenty-seven-hole Island Green course situated just off SC Highway 707. This course forms one leg of a triangle of three "fun" courses (the others are Heron Point and Raccoon Run).

Island Green is relatively short and very narrow and features crowned greens that can lead to some difficult pin placements. Because the course is short, measuring only 6,100 yards from the championship tees regardless of which choice of three nines is utilized, the unwary golfer might be lulled into a sense of false security, feeling this is an easy golf course. That golfer would be wrong!

Island Green stretches in a narrow strip between rows of condominiums, rental units, and bands of pine over rolling terrain. Because many of the holes are short, the long hitter will find that it is better to play Island Green from the tee with long irons or a three wood. Even on five-par holes the fairways are so narrow that discretion might well be the better part of valor, making the driver an obsolete club for the scratch or low-handicap player.

Island Green is an excellent golf course for seniors and ladies. It is not the easiest course in the area, but after all those tough courses on the Grand Strand, playing Island Green can be a treat. With less pressure here, golfers can relax.

The greens are crowned for a good reason. They drain so well that the course never has to close.

Until 1992, when tournaments were played at Island Green, "Tall Oaks" and "Holly" were the two nines used to form the eighteen-hole layout. However, "Dogwood" is the prettiest of the three, and plans are to use that nine in tournaments in the future.

Number 7 on Dogwood is a good hole, but the signature hole at Island Green is #9 on Holly. It is a par four with an island green. You tee off with a three or two iron and then use anything from a wedge to a seven iron to the island green. You can look down at the green for your approach shot, since it is a straightaway hole and the fairway rolls uphill. Many people go in the water or give up.

Dogwood's 7th hole is a par five, about 475 yards. A long hitter might make it in two shots, but because it is a very narrow area into the green, many people opt to lay up.

Most think of #9 on Tall Oaks as the prettiest hole at Island Green. It also is one of the most difficult. It is a par-four, straightaway hole with water paralleling the fairway all the way up the left side. A three wood is recommended off the tee and a short iron into the 360-yard hole, which is distinguished by a green that is very difficult to play because of a tremendous crown in the center and a green that slants left to the lake. So even if you nail the green, your ball can roll into the lake!

Because of the crowned greens, it is difficult to "throw a shot at the pin," but there is a compensating factor. There are no bunkers in front, so you can roll a shot up most of them.

With many winter members, Island Green gets a lot of play, and many of these winter members choose to walk. This is hard on the Bermuda greens, but they remain good and very quick.

Island Green, twenty-seven holes set amidst lakes and sand. (Courtesy Himmelsbach Communications/Bill Woodward)

Dogwood Course

HOLE NUMBER	1	2	3	4	5	6	7	8	9	TOT
BLUE	390	157	289	140	410	350	475	330	535	3076
WHITE	337	143	265	120	380	336	455	308	500	2844
HANDICAP	4	8	6	9	2	5	3	7	1	
PAR	4	3	4	3	4	4	5	4	5	36
RED	246	87	208	86	330	279	360	254	401	2251
HANDICAP	4	8	6	9	2	5	3	7	1	

Holly Course

HOLE NUMBER	1	2	3	4	5	6	7	8	9	TOT
BLUE	371	460	198	473	371	323	149	383	332	3060
WHITE	361	423	162	441	337	300	138	361	312	2835
HANDICAP	4	2	8	1	5	7	9	3	6	
PAR	4	5	3	5	4	4	3	4	4	36
RED	248	357	101	405	300	258	104	308	230	2311
HANDICAP	6	4	9	1	5	7	8	2	3	

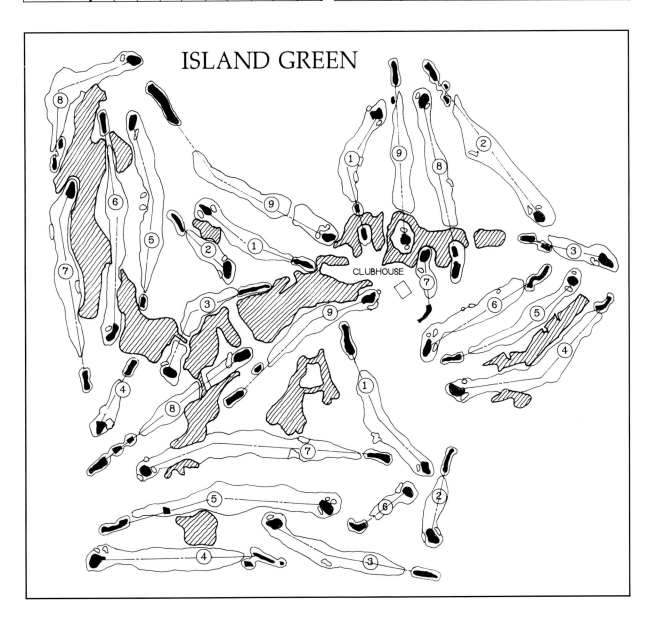

ISLAND GREEN

Number 15 at Blackmoor, a three par, one of designer Gary Player's favorites. (Courtesy Brandon Advertising/Michael Slear)

BLACKMOOR

Off Highway 707   Murrells Inlet   [P.O. Box 2010]   Myrtle Beach, SC
(843) 650-5555
Architect: Gary Player   Year opened: 1991
Course rating/Slope rating:
Black - 71.1/126
White - 69.3/118
Red - 68.0/110

Golf professional turned architect Gary Player has built a golf course near Murrells Inlet which seems destined to become one of the most talked about courses on the Grand Strand. It also will be ranked among the best, as Player has utilized rolling land, great stands of cypress, oak, and pine, natural wetlands, marsh, river, and rice fields to create a 6,600-yard championship course which can be a test from any of the tees.

Elevated tees afford the golfer good views of the scenic beauty of this course, and he will appreciate another Gary Player design characteristic—he doesn't believe in placing hazards in front of a green. Instead you will find sand traps to the sides of the greens, causing trouble on a shot to the green only if you hit it off line.

However, the Blackmoor course certainly is not easy.

Number 1 demands a long carry over water with your initial drive and the length (421 yards from the championship markers) negates dreams of early birdies. The 2nd hole is a very pretty three par, framed by traps carved into the mounds on either side

of the green. The five-par 3rd is a birdie opportunity, but beware of the large wetlands area which bisects the fairway. Four is another three par, and while it's relatively short, there is very little between the tee and green but water. Don't look up or top it. Better have plenty of club, too.

These are good holes, but the best is yet to come.

Number 6 features a two-tier fairway which is separated by a rough, and is devilishly long at 412 yards. Player stipulated the narrow rough running in the middle of the fairway from tee to green to give more definition to two separate fairways. However, it can penalize a good straight drive, making it extremely difficult to reach the green, which is guarded left front with a grass bunker.

Seven is mean, too, and the golfer must be aware of a large waste bunker which can be reached with a long drive. Eight will have most golfers scratching their heads. Depending on your point of view, this can be the most ingenious hole ever designed—or the worst hole in history. There are two ways to reach the hole: hit a long drive into

Blackmoor

HOLE NUMBER	1	2	3	4	5	6	7	8	9	OUT	10	11	12	13	14	15	16	17	18	IN	TOT	HCP	NET
BLACK	421	182	514	162	376	412	544	371 290	372	3354 3273	411	332	366	499	390	166	413	174	509	3260	6614 6533		
WHITE	393	170	490	140	343	400	520	347 270	358	3161 3084	365	318	342	478	362	150	390	158	493	3056	6217 6140		
HANDICAP	12	18	4	16	6	8	2	14	10		9	11	13	1	3	15	5	17	7				
PAR	4	3	5	3	4	4	5	4	4	36	4	4	4	5	4	3	4	3	5	36	72		
RED	299	142	415	106	161	356	443	278	273	2473	271	250	260	400	315	114	286	124	399	2419	4892		

the dogleg on the left side of the large stand of trees, or go for broke over a grassy area dotted with bunkers and mounds on the right. There isn't much fairway if you attempt the latter route, but it is much shorter —290 yards from the championship tees, 270 from the whites. If you choose to stay on the short grass, hit it left, and play the dogleg right, the hole is 371 yards long.

The builders moved more dirt on the backside, and it is truly beautiful. Player's favorite hole is the three par 15th, and rice fields abound on the back. Golfers find themselves playing a championship course set in the midst of an antebellum rice plantation, recalling one of the most opulent eras of Southern culture.

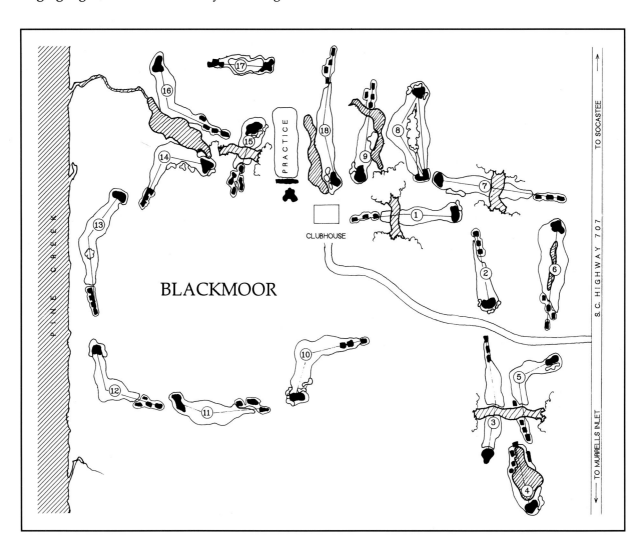

BLACKMOOR

PRESTWICK

1001 Links Rd.   Myrtle Beach, SC 29575   (843) 293-4100
Architects: Pete and P. B. Dye   Year opened: 1989
Course rating/Slope rating:
Medal - 74.3/137   Middle - 68.5/115
Champ - 72.6/132   Forward - 70.0/123
Back - 70.7/124

Prestwick, designed by Pete and P. B. Dye with a strong Scottish flavor, is a beautiful and sometimes difficult private golf course. From all the way back this course measures an awesome 7,156 yards, but the architects, complying with requests from the owners of this superb development property, made concessions to the average and high-handicap player.

"One thing I would like to stress," says the Prestwick golf director, "is that this course can be fun for anyone. Many people think that Pete Dye seems to build courses that only the pros can play. Maybe that has some validity, but not here. One of the things he had in mind with this concept was that this was to be a 'member's' golf course."

Prestwick officials wanted a playable golf course, and that is why there are five sets of tees on every hole. Actually, there are placements on twelve holes for a sixth set of tees, which will be for juniors and beginning women. This allows for tailoring the game to individuals.

"Another thing—we have only four holes which have a 'forced' carry," said a professional who had served at Prestwick. "You know what I mean. We didn't want to have very many holes where the beginner stands on the tee box and continually hits the ball short of the fairway, ending up in the love grass or the water."

In keeping with the Scottish concept, flags on the green are much shorter than the average American pin, and the tees are not designated as men's or women's. "Mrs. Dye had a lot of input in designing these courses, and she has a theory that there should be no discrimination between men and women's golfing. Nor does she believe in color differences, so we simply call our five tees medal, championship, back, middle, and forward."

The holes are so good that any one hole has the potential of becoming someone's favorite. Number 2, a demanding 467-yard four par, will remain in the memory of many, but one pro says that his favorite is #14.

"It just has a lot of things going for it that are beyond description. You just have to play it to appreciate the nuances of this one. It doesn't go out to the ocean. There are no trees. But still . . . this hole is really something."

This is one of the four holes that does require a "forced" carry. From the championship tees the golfer must hit a drive of at least 220 yards to carry a large pond and rough area which block the entrance to the fairway landing area. Once the drive is properly positioned, the golfer faces a very long second shot to a narrow entrance of a well-bunkered green which is elevated with railroad ties.

The 14th at Prestwick has similarities to another Dye masterpiece—Oak Tree—and, when the course was being routed and the trees tagged, Pete left one to the left of the green for the express purpose of capturing the feeling of Oak Tree.

Every green is undulated, and Dye carefully built the greens to be cosmetically correct. For example, if the hole requires playing a left-to-right shot, Dye designed the green from right to left so that it would hold the shot.

The bunkers and mounds border on the spectacular. There are pathways for the golfer to descend into and then walk out of the deep bunkers, and sometimes they are so steep that a ladder is built into the side of the hazard!

Invariably the championship golf courses of Scotland feature at least one hole where a driver is required to reach the green, and that, too, can be found at Prestwick. Number 8 is 246 yards from the back tees and, because a driver is needed by most players, the green is oversize, 52 yards across and 28 yards deep.

First-time players will be struck by the different atmosphere found on the two 9 holes. Specifically, after the 10th hole, there are very few trees, giving the impression of wide-open, windswept Scottish links.

A variety of grasses, heavy mounding, deep bunkers—a typical hole at Prestwick.
(Courtesy Lesnick, Himmelsbach, Wilson, Hearl & Dietz)

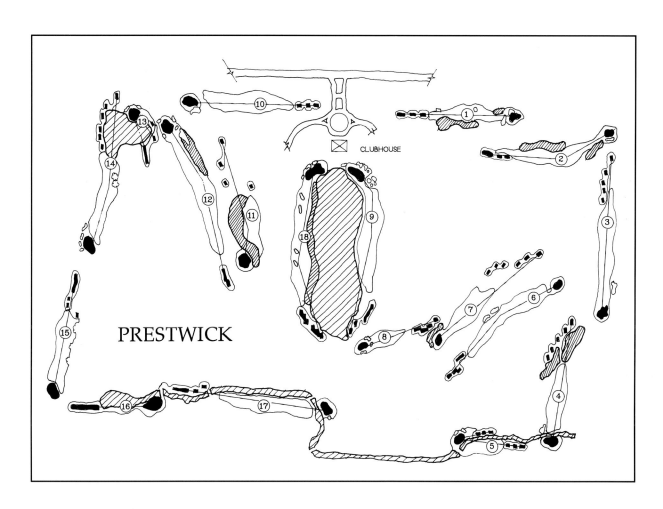

Prestwick

HOLE NUMBER	1	2	3	4	5	6	7	8	9	OUT	10	11	12	13	14	15	16	17	18	IN	TOT	HCP	NET
MEDAL	367	448	470	340	195	522	446	246	537	3571	398	412	529	152	451	374	199	531	441	3487	7058		
CHAMP.	362	427	458	319	183	491	416	211	507	3374	388	400	520	144	431	365	188	515	419	3370	6744		
BACK	341	387	444	305	164	459	384	193	486	3163	373	344	504	135	409	350	174	499	396	3184	6347		
HANDICAP	9	5	1	15	17	11	7	13	3		12	10	8	18	2	16	14	4	6				
PAR	4	4	4	4	3	5	4	3	5	36	4	4	5	3	4	4	3	5	4	36	72		
MIDDLE	318	358	403	290	135	435	333	163	454	2889	349	318	478	118	381	332	153	472	373	2974	5863		
FORWARD	302	307	357	234	108	415	296	136	423	2578	319	269	450	83	343	312	115	405	336	2632	5210		
HANDICAP	9	5	1	13	17	7	11	15	3		12	10	8	18	4	16	14	2	6				

Deer Track. (Courtesy Brandon Advertising/Michael Slear)

Deer Track North

HOLE NUMBER	1	2	3	4	5	6	7	8	9	OUT	10	11	12	13	14	15	16	17	18	IN	TOT	HCP	NET
BLUE	549	401	246	411	391	384	229	462	526	3600	538	427	172	415	393	414	387	219	524	3489	7089		
WHITE	529	362	187	391	368	345	189	423	487	3281	510	385	145	375	355	375	355	162	485	3147	6428		
HANDICAP	5	15	17	3	11	9	13	1	7		2	8	18	4	14	10	12	16	6				
PAR	5	4	3	4	4	4	3	4	5	36	5	4	3	4	4	4	4	3	5	36	72		
RED	448	283	109	312	335	308	99	338	421	2653	458	312	128	318	289	311	292	122	451	2681	5334		
HANDICAP	7	13	15	5	9	11	17	3	1		2	6	18	8	14	12	10	16	4				

Deer Track South

HOLE NUMBER	1	2	3	4	5	6	7	8	9	OUT	10	11	12	13	14	15	16	17	18	IN	TOT	HCP	NET
BLUE	543	391	415	200	528	399	189	400	426	3491	474	432	364	179	401	362	521	156	411	3300	6791		
WHITE	491	341	379	157	501	347	145	378	399	3138	401	389	325	138	380	314	456	117	368	2988	6126		
HANDICAP	7	9	13	15	1	11	17	3	5		8	6	14	16	10	12	4	18	2				
PAR	5	4	4	3	5	4	3	4	4	36	5	4	4	3	4	4	5	3	4	36	72		
RED	409	329	313	121	438	291	98	315	315	2635	316	305	302	123	339	274	431	99	303	2492	5127		
HANDICAP	1	5	11	15	3	13	17	9	7		12	4	8	16	14	6	10	18	2				

DEER TRACK

Highway 17   P.O. Box 14430   Surfside, SC 29587   (843) 650-2146

Architect: Porter Gibson   Year opened: 1974

Course rating/Slope rating:

NORTH	SOUTH
Blue - 74.7/129	Blue - 72.9/119
White - 71.2/127	White - 69.3/119
Red - 70.4/117	Red - 69.6/117

The one impression that comes to mind when people mention Deer Track is "big." The North course especially is big in every way. It is long. The greens are huge, and it is possible to put some big numbers on the board. A lot of good golfers have given it their best shot, and the course record is 63, posted by Deer Track instructor Chuck Wike.

The two courses of Deer Track were designed by golf architect Porter Gibson and consultant Bob Toski. The North course, totally different from the South course, has a lot of length and is fairly open. It is a real challenge for the better player. The South course is shorter, but it has much more water. It is an exacting course requiring great accuracy.

Actually, both courses are long, with the North measuring almost 7,100 yards from the championship tees and the South stretching for 6,800 yards.

The North is still a lot of golf course from the white tees, too, as it stretches 6,500 yards. That's when the distance is measured from the center of the green. When the tees are back and the pins are on the back of these huge greens, you can add another 200 yards!

Since the first edition of *Golfing the Carolina Grand Strand* was published, both of the Deer Track courses have undergone an intensive face-lift and are better than ever. Some of the traps have been reshaped, and the greens have been switched to Bermuda grass.

Golfers will have another impression of Deer Track. With condominiums and homes bordering many of the fairways, the course, on occasion, has a canyonlike appearance. At the opposite extreme, several holes seem to stretch for miles, wide open, a vast expanse of green grass and blue skies. The course does, indeed, offer a lot of variety.

The layout is distinctive, with holes that will impress themselves on the memory of the golfer who played there. The three pars are particularly good and most memorable. Three of the four three-par holes on the North course exceed 200 yards in length, and one, #3, is 246 yards from the championship tee. When the wind is blowing, as it frequently does, this is a very difficult par.

The South, too, has good three pars, and #4 is a jewel, with water fronting the green on both sides of the fairway, leaving a thin strip of fairway for the golfer who cannot carry the green. Number 11 is another favorite of golfers who play the South. Water runs across the fairway and then parallels it, forming a formidable lake that extends almost to the green.

Nor will golfers forget the par-four 8th hole on the North course, a 462-yard monster made even more difficult by a pond fronting the green on the left.

None of the five-par holes on the North are "gimme" birdie holes so typical of many courses. Number 1 indicates from the get-go what the golfer will face as he plays a 549-yard hole. No relief is in sight when he turns to the back side, either. Number 10 not only has a large lake on the right all the way to the green, but it throws in eight sand traps, all strategically located to catch his best effort.

The hole many golfers will remember most of all is #18 on the North. It is tight, with condominiums bordering both sides of the fairway, three ponds very much in play, and two traps fronting the green with another directly behind. Oh, yes, it is 524 yards from tee to green. . . .

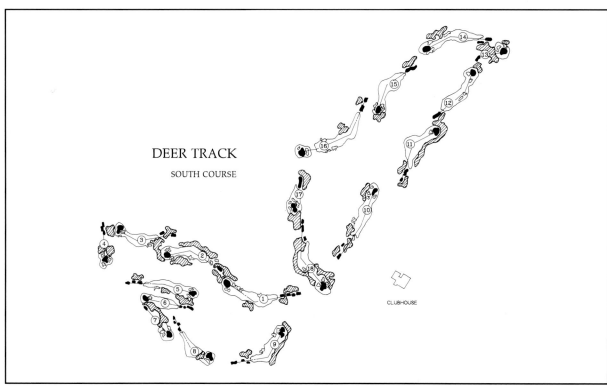

66

INDIAN WELLS

Highway 17 Bypass   Garden City, SC   P.O. Box 15418
Surfside Beach, SC 29587   (843) 626-8228   (800) 833-6337
Architect: Gene Hamm   Year opened: 1984
Course rating/Slope rating:
Blue - 71.5/121   Gold - 67.7/111
White - 69.7/116   Red - 67.0/118

Directly across Bypass 17 from Indigo Creek, Indian Wells is a challenging golf course, designed by Gene Hamm and opened in October of 1984. Water is very evident on this course, a lurking danger on fifteen of the eighteen holes!

The course is deceptively long. Listed as 6,624 yards from the blue tees, this number takes on added significance when it becomes apparent that long hitters can gamble on reaching at least three of the five pars in two.

"The holes allow you to hit over large blue lakes and reach home in two shots, if you wish to gamble," says the Indian Wells brochure. "In our opinion this challenge exemplifies the essence of golf and what makes it such a great game."

But if the par fives are a little shorter at Indian Wells, you can bet that the par threes and par fours are a little bit longer and tougher, since the course is more than 6,600 yards.

The five pars are great holes, but the design of the course with tough finishing holes on both nines also keep the crowds coming back. And there's not a single five par among the final three on either side!

Some golfers refer to Indian Wells as a "shotmaker's" course, implying that it is tight and invites the golfer to search for landing areas. However, the player who approaches Indian Wells aggressively with a driver in hand is more apt to challenge the course record of 66, which is held by area golf professional Randy Broughton. Most people play better when they go ahead and swing at the ball, instead of cautiously trying to guide it. You must still play smart, but you don't have to let up at Indian Wells.

Number 10 is a particularly difficult starting hole as a large lake guards the left side of the fairway and comes into the fairway, an obstacle which must be cleared on the second shot. However, #9 is the most talked about hole on this course, and has been a consistent member of the Dream 18 annually selected by the Myrtle Beach *Sun News*. Again, there is an abundance of water in the path of the golfer, this time flowing from right to left across the front of the green. At #9, you must go down the left side and hit it pretty long to get around a pine tree which juts into the fairway. Otherwise you are forced to navigate a diagonal lake. It is critical to have a big drive here.

The greens also pose a problem. Designed as oversize putting surfaces, some of the greens have been reduced in size but are irregularly shaped; there is a lot of square footage in these greens. Some are narrow and very deep, while others are wide but angled to such an extent that the landing area seems quite small. Hurricane Hugo of

1989 caused some damage, and both #14 and #17 were rebuilt and enlarged with improved drainage.

The putting surface is Bermuda and the greens are good. The course itself is built in lowlands and, on occasion, can be quite wet. However, the superintendent does an excellent job and tourist golfers usually are well pleased with their round at Indian Wells.

Number 2 at Indian Wells in the foreground, #6 on right. (Courtesy Brandon Advertising/Michael Slear)

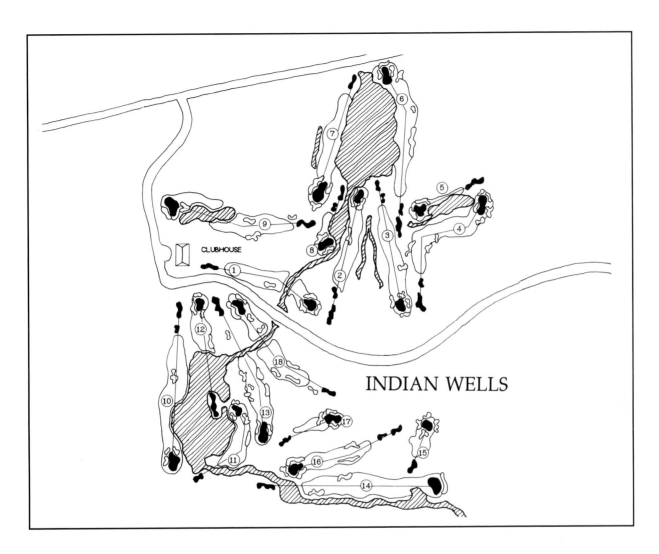

Indian Wells

HOLE NUMBER	1	2	3	4	5	6	7	8	9	OUT	10	11	12	13	14	15	16	17	18	IN	TOT	HCP	NET
BLUE	348	401	382	481	167	484	396	210	410	3279	491	388	355	430	526	167	375	193	420	3345	6624		
WHITE	333	383	337	465	154	458	369	186	383	3068	471	371	323	401	504	154	355	181	397	3157	6225		
GOLD	315	363	302	445	127	433	350	158	362	2855	447	342	297	366	494	134	338	164	374	2956	.5811		
RED	293	289	255	390	119	356	316	110	304	2432	371	312	271	298	353	118	282	155	320	2480	4912		
HANDICAP	17	7	15	5	13	3	11	9	1		8	10	14	2	4	18	16	12	6				
PAR	4	4	4	5	3	5	4	3	4	36	5	4	4	4	5	3	4	3	4	36			
LADIES' HCP	11	9	13	5	15	1	7	17	3		4	10	12	8	2	18	16	14	6				
LADIES' PAR	4	4	4	5	3	5	4	3	4	36	5	4	4	4	5	3	4	3	4	36			

Wachesaw East, a Clyde Johnston masterpiece, is the site of an annual LPGA tournament. All the natural elements combine for a terrific and highly regarded golf course. (Courtesy Brandon Advertising/Michael Slear)

WACHESAW EAST

911 River Wood Road   Murrells Inlet, SC 29576
Wachesaw Plantation, Highway 17 South   (800) 797-8425   (843) 357-2090
Architect: Clyde Johnston   Year opened: 1996
Course rating/Slope rating:
Green - 73.6/135   Blue - 72.0/133
White - 70.3/130   Gold - 67.9/117
Red - 68.8/117

A newcomer to the Myrtle Beach golf scene, Wachesaw East already is recognized as one of the best and one of the best-known courses in America. The course has gained notoriety as the site of a nationally televised LPGA tournament that not only affords the best women golfers in the world an opportunity to display their skills but also brings the natural beauty of Wachesaw in the spring into millions of homes across the country.

Wachesaw East is best described as a traditional golf course with a Scottish flavor, and—while the length of this tough beauty makes it anything but a "target" course—shooting a good score here requires much thought and skillful management of your game. You also must be aware of the wind. Golfers most often find themselves playing into a wind blowing in a northwesterly direction, but when it is blowing to the northeast, the already demanding course becomes two or three shots more difficult.

For example, holes #5 through #9 usually play downwind, as do #15 through #18, but if you are forced to play those holes into the wind, they can become monsters.

Understated—but very accurate—is a hole-by-hole synopsis of the entire golf course, supplied to the author by veteran professional David Schueck, who was lured away from his home of twenty-one years at the respected, impressive duPont Country Club in Wilmington, Delaware, to come to this more southerly clime. Schueck was on board before construction began and worked closely with architect Clyde Johnston as this course came to fruition.

Head golf professional Hank Gabriel says his favorite holes are #17 and #18.

We are particularly fond of #18. Every hole has a name, and this one is simply called "Johnston" in honor of the architect. The very large bunker to the left of the green is shaped as a convoluted C—that's for Clyde, of course!

"Johnston" is the finale of a four-hole stretch that has been called all sorts of things: "beautiful," "demanding," "too hard," "exciting," "the toughest finish in golf." Without question these final four holes give you as much challenge as you would want. Just watch those LPGA Tour players challenge them on TV!

Let's not leave you with the impression that Wachesaw East is too tough to be enjoyable—it's quite the opposite. Five sets of tees make it possible for golfers at every skill level to play out on every hole. We do, however, recommend that you use the suggested tees that correspond to your handicap. You'll have much more fun that way.

Let's look at the first few holes and some other beauties on this fine course:

#1, Magnolia (par four). Some starting holes tend to be tame in nature, but the 1st at Wachesaw East challenges you with a tee shot over wetlands to this dogleg-left hole.

71

The fairway bunkers form the right side of the fairway and provide an aiming point from the tee. A middle-to-short iron is required for the approach to the green.

#2, Classic Carolina (par four). A de-

manding tee shot to a sculpted fairway is required off the tee. The left center of the fairway provides the best angle for the approach to the green, which is highlighted by the Scottish mounds and a lake on the

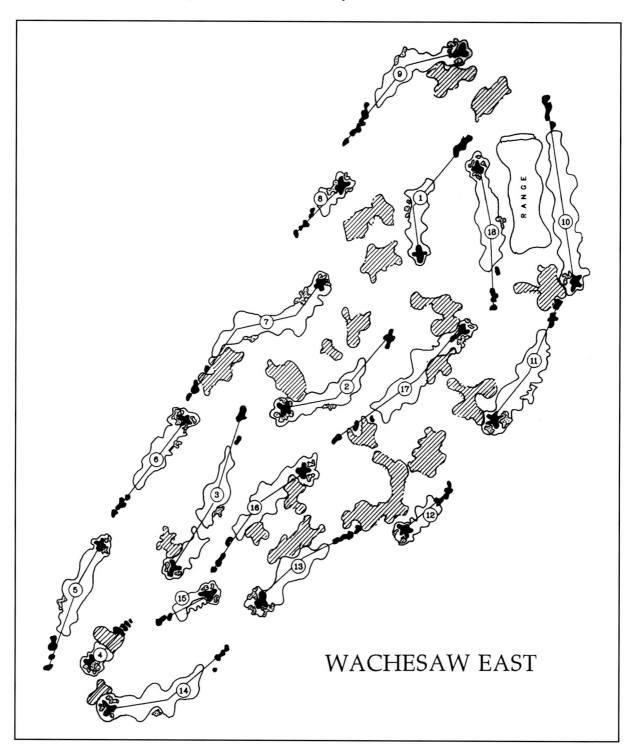

WACHESAW EAST

right. A well-struck tee shot leaves you shooting with a middle iron to the green.

#3, Riverwood (par four). Strategy is the name of the game on this par four. Keep the tee shot to the left center because the slope moves the ball to the right. The same applies to the second shot if you elect to lay up short of the wetland area. If you play your second shot over the wetland, you are left with a short pitch to a green that is guarded on the right by a bunker and a lake. This is a great risk-reward hole.

#4, Deceive (par three). Although this is a relatively short par three, being nestled in the trees makes make club selection difficult. The prevailing wind generally is in your face but is difficult to feel. Look at the top of the trees to get a good read on the wind velocity. Take one more club than you think is necessary.

#13, Plantation (par four). This beguiling par four requires a tee shot to the right center of the fairway. A middle-to-short iron is needed for the approach to the green. If the wind is blowing hard, this green allows you to play a low run-up shot into it.

#18, Johnston (par four). You want to survive this hole rather than attack it, because problems are waiting for you at every turn. If you use the right center of the fairway as your target off the tee, you are left with a middle-to-long iron into the final green. A large bunker and lake are set to the left of the green. Once you do reach the green, its large size and many undulations continue to challenge you. Be careful when the pin is back right. If you play the approach shot into the right center of the green, the ball feeds itself toward the pin. Make a par here and you will have made your day.

See also Wachesaw Plantation, p. 31.

Wachesaw East

HOLE NUMBER	1	2	3	4	5	6	7	8	9	OUT	10	11	12	13	14	15	16	17	18	IN	TOT	HCP	NET
GREEN	390	410	530	165	403	380	580	180	420	3458	545	410	185	395	405	195	410	500	430	3475	6933		
BLUE	376	385	510	155	393	365	550	173	400	3307	515	386	172	378	381	185	395	485	414	3311	6618		
WHITE	351	375	495	145	373	342	530	162	390	3163	484	356	166	358	360	170	370	470	400	3134	6297		
GOLD	328	353	445	135	328	319	490	151	363	2912	449	332	133	332	335	160	340	456	378	2915	5827		
RED	260	235	425	121	310	287	450	136	273	2497	425	290	116	262	270	140	275	415	305	2498	4995		
HANDICAP	11	7	3	17	9	13	1	15	5		2	10	18	14	12	16	8	6	4				
PAR	4	4	5	3	4	4	5	3	4	36	5	4	3	4	4	3	4	5	4	36	72		
LADIES' HCP	11	13	3	15	5	7	1	17	9		2	8	18	14	12	16	10	4	6				

Caledonia's magnificent 18th hole is shown here. Most observers agree that Caledonia is one of the "five best on the Beach." You'll see the green tucked beneath the beautiful clubhouse after you have negotiated a second shot over a large lake. (Courtesy Brandon Advertising/Michael Slear)

CALEDONIA

P.O. Box 1320   369 Caledonia Drive   Pawleys Island, SC 29585
(800) 483-6800   (843) 237-3675
Architect: Mike Strantz   Year opened: 1994
Course rating/Slope rating
Pintail - 70.9/132   Mallard - 68.8/122
Wood Duck - 66.7/114   Redhead - 68.2/113

Famous for its natural beauty and challenging layout, Caledonia, opened in January 1994, has become known as one of the very best courses in an area already known for its great golf courses. In June 1998 it was rated among the top five new courses.

With two holes on this magnificent course selected to the "Dream Eighteen" (as established by a panel formed by the Myrtle Beach *Sun News*) and four other holes considered among the best one hundred on the Strand, Caledonia can easily defend the fact that it is a surcharge golf course. Extremely popular, Caledonia is high on everyone's list of must-play courses, and tee times are not easy to come by.

Caledonia is the first course designed by golf architect Mike Strantz, who learned his skills at the hands of Pete Dye. He followed this success by creating Stone House, named the best new golf course of 1996 by *Golf Digest*.

"Mike is a marvel and great to work with," enthused Todd Weldon, Caledonia's head professional. "Unlike most of the architects, he is on site, on the job every day, a real hands-on guy."

(Strantz has again worked his magic on the south end of Myrtle Beach with his 1998 creation True Blue, an eighteen-hole championship course next to Caledonia and Heritage that also is reviewed in this book. Forest Fezler, a PGA Tour player of some renown who is learning the business of golf-course architecture, assisted Strantz on the project.)

At Caledonia, Strantz has built a visual masterpiece, carving the route of the course from impressive century-old live oaks and creating huge greens punctuated with vast expanses of sand and environmentally protected wastelands. Copious plantings of indigenous flowers and plants, along with meandering streams and imposing lakes fringed with Spanish-moss-draped oaks, make Caledonia a colorful and visually stunning golf course. A skillful golfer who has studied the course and knows how to manage his game will not have a problem with the water. "They are more of a visual attraction than a penalty," Weldon said of the water on the course.

Markers on the tee boxes are duck decoys, each painted as one of four species: Pintail, Mallard, Wood Duck and Red Head. The Southern atmosphere is further enhanced by bridges of Olde English brick and a complimentary cup of fish chowder as the golfer approaches the 10th hole.

Caledonia is a challenge to low-handicap players but is nonetheless an enjoyable course—and not just because of its natural beauty. Its four sets of carefully designed tees afford you the opportunity to score well if you can hit the ball straight. And if the course is a challenge for players, think what it must have been to architect Mike Strantz when he was called upon to build a truly first-class facility on 125 acres of ground!

Despite the space limitations there's not a bad hole on the course, and even those that have not been ranked among the one hundred best on the Strand have their fair share of devotees. Some golfers consider #9 to be the exception because it is a very short three par. It may be the only controversial hole on an exceptional layout, but even some of the loudest complainers produce double bogeys on this hole. Club selection here is critical: The green appears to be an oasis, an island in the middle of a sea of

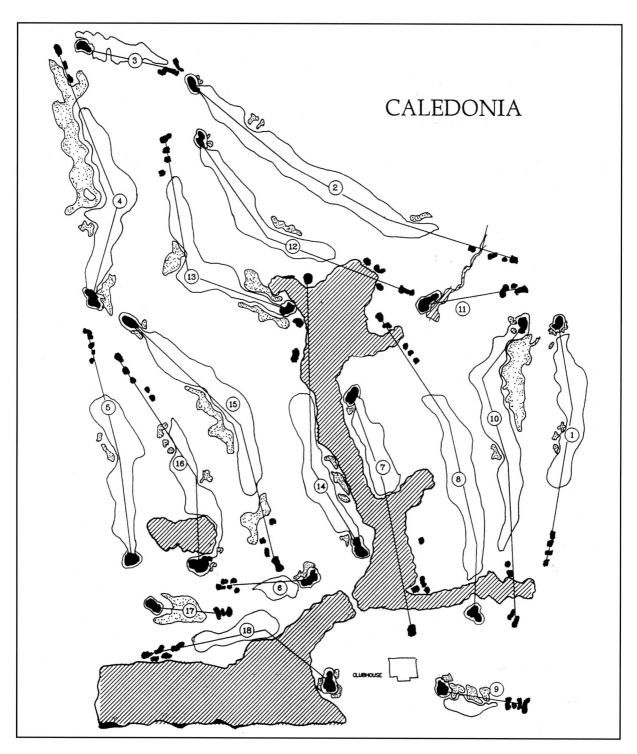

CALEDONIA

sand. There's not much fairway on this one!

The front nine basically runs around the perimeter of the course, turning to the interior at #7, which is beautiful. From the Pintail tees, the golfer must hit between overhanging oak branches—and that's just the beginning of the adventure. Oak trees come into play on the shot to the green on this 399-yard four par, and the right side is a no-no. Keep your tee shot well to left center on this one, and you might want to hit your approach shot to the center of the green regardless of your pin placement.

Water in front of the green on the par-five 8th makes this a three-shot hole for all but the most daring of long hitters, and the two-tiered green itself can pose a problem.

Believe it or not, the back nine is more difficult than the front. The tour begins with a long five par, with the approach shot going into a sunken green that is effectively guarded by a series of bunkers on the left and an awesome wasteland on the right. Again, the second shot should be hit to the left to leave a better approach.

Cited as a member of the "Dream Eighteen," #11 features a huge green and a meandering stream that begins on the right of the fairway, cuts across the fairway at a drunken diagonal, and expires at a big lake that guards at least half the green. This hole is a demanding three par, whether played from 135 or 167 yards, and pin placement here makes a huge difference.

Number 12 is difficult, too, and many professional players consider it one of the best on the course. The 13th is memorable—or maybe you would rather forget it, with its 90-degree dogleg left and a green almost entirely surrounded by sand. Although Strantz did leave a narrow alley to the green, be forewarned that if your tee shot does not hug that big oak on the left, you're not going to reach this one in two.

The 14th hole is very demanding from the back (Pintail) tees, and again my advice is to keep your tee shot left of center to avoid the long, long sand bunker. Believe me, it's even worse on the right.

Some of us think 450-yard par-four holes are just too much, and #15 falls into that category, measuring 462 from the back and more than 405 for everybody from any tee!

The 16th hole is beautiful, but pay attention. A lake guards the entire front, but you at least hit down to the green (which helps). Then again, you might want to be safe and lay up for a little pitch with your third shot.

The 18th hole is one people go home talking about. A long, narrow green sits in the lee of the clubhouse, and spectators can watch as you try to navigate the approach to a green that slopes toward the water. Hit it good off the tee (240 yards) and you still have an approach of 144 yards over unforgiving water. The approach shot, which generally ranges from 120 to 180 yards, makes this a hole that short knockers and some ladies would just as soon avoid.

Number 18 is a good golf hole on a good golf course.

Caledonia

HOLE NUMBER	1	2	3	4	5	6	7	8	9	OUT	10	11	12	13	14	15	16	17	18	IN	TOT	HCP	NET
PINTAIL	376	571	187	396	419	157	399	528	118	3151	553	167	424	398	415	462	417	156	383	3375	6526		
MALLARD	350	553	175	357	376	135	346	512	110	2914	531	153	414	380	363	441	400	148	377	3207	6121		
WOOD DUCK	319	516	153	322	347	120	323	477	92	2669	518	150	384	354	343	423	375	132	362	3041	5710		
REDHEAD	254	479	126	259	328	107	283	429	80	2345	442	135	321	291	290	404	307	121	301	2612	4957		
HANDICAP	12	8	14	6	2	16	4	10	18		15	13	9	5	7	3	1	17	11				
PAR	4	5	3	4	4	3	4	5	3	35	5	3	4	4	4	4	4	3	4	35	70		
LADIES' HCP	12	8	14	6	4	16	10	2	18		11	13	17	3	9	7	5	15	1				

This par-three #14 has it all: elevated greens, yawning sand traps, and multiple tee boxes. True Blue is a championship golf course on the south end of the Grand Strand. (Courtesy Brandon Advertising/Michael Slear)

TRUE BLUE

900 Blue Stem Drive   P.O. Box 3170   Pawleys Island, SC 29585
(888) 483-6801   (843) 235-0900

Architect: Mike Strantz   Year opened: 1998

Course rating/Slope rating:
Black - 74.3/145   Blue - 72.8/141
White - 70.1/127   Gold - 66.9/115
Red - 71.4/123

One of the newest golf courses on the Grand Strand seems destined to be one of the best. Mike Strantz, the "hot" new architect on the national scene, is very excited about this championship eighteen-hole layout that is located directly across from Caledonia, the only other course he has designed in South Carolina.

Although this course is only the fourth Strantz has created, the reputation he has almost immediately built has many people saying that his name is going to be right up there with the very best. His credentials, while growing, certainly support such claims: Caledonia is consistently rated as among the top five courses on the Strand, and the Stone House course he built near Williamburg, Virginia, was named by *Golf Digest* as the best new course of 1996. Not resting on his laurels, Strantz then designed a second course for Larry Young, again near Williamsburg, and this one, Royal New Kent, promptly was chosen as the best of 1997!

Strantz thinks True Blue fits into the same category of outstanding golf layouts. "It's entirely different. After all, the ground you are working dictates the type of course you're going to build, and the elevations on the South Carolina coast are not one bit like those you find in the Williamsburg area. True Blue has more of a Pine Valley, Pinehurst feeling. It's open, a lot of scrubby, sandy areas. Really a pretty golf course."

Just because True Blue is pretty doesn't mean that it is easy. Some of the holes here are very memorable, and all complemented by large (8,000 square feet on the average) bent-grass greens of the G2 variety.

The green on #8 sits on a high plateau completely encircled by sand and slopes off into that huge hazard. This short par four doglegs to the right, and to reach the green the golfer must get through or over a natural berm. The middle of the berm has a narrow opening, but low handicappers will hit their tee shot short of this area and then have a flip wedge to the green.

True Blue starts "long," intentionally long, so there are no two-shot par fives. Both #1 and #10 are immensely wide, with much air space. You shouldn't find much trouble on these holes, but you have to really "bust" the ball.

Then the course shortens up—for a short while. Number 2 is a short par four, and many players will choose an iron off the tee. The 3rd hole is only 140 yards long, but the green sits in the middle of a lake. Still, with the green big and the target going back, this one should not claim as many water balls as most island greens.

Then we come to #4, a hole that will be etched into the memories of those who play it. In some respects, golfers will be reminded of #13, the famed Waterloo Hole at the Dunes Club, but while it might play in similar fashion, the 4th hole at True Blue doesn't look all that much like Waterloo. For one thing, this hole plays right to left, the reverse of the Dunes Club hole. On the other hand, the green is virtually diagonal to the tee box, creating a double-dogleg effect.

This 4th hole at True Blue is called "The Cove," and this par five is a risk-reward hole whose green can be reached in two shots. The tee shot sets up the hole, but a long drive to the left of the fairway and short of the lake allows the golfer a 220-yard carry to the green.

Number 15 is spectacular, too, with sand being the key element here. A wide expanse of sand borders the hole all the way from tee to green on the left and also stretches from the tee box to the landing area on the right side. The third shot on this difficult par five is the premium play. The green—skinny, long, and narrow—is elevated, perching high above the fairway and falling off hard to the fairway on the back of the green. Increasing the degree of difficulty is that the front side slopes from the middle, and therefore a ball hit short can trickle back off the green!

While sand is the key on #15, another natural element—water—is very visible on the closing holes. On the 17th hole is an eight-acre lake that starts to the right of the fairway and extends into the fairway, effectively guarding the green from a direct approach. However, a large mound about 50 yards to the left of the green is contoured so that a shot hit into this area will funnel back into the green.

That same lake is on your left on #18, which is placed perpendicular to the 17th hole. Again the lake cuts into the fairway, and again Strantz has designed mounding, this time on the right, that lets your shot flow back into the green. Numbers 17 and 18 are two very interesting holes.

Under construction when we visited the architect, True Blue is one of the few courses we have not played. We're looking forward to that experience and expect it to be a highly ranked course.

The par-four #8 at True Blue. (Courtesy Brandon Advertising/Michael Slear)

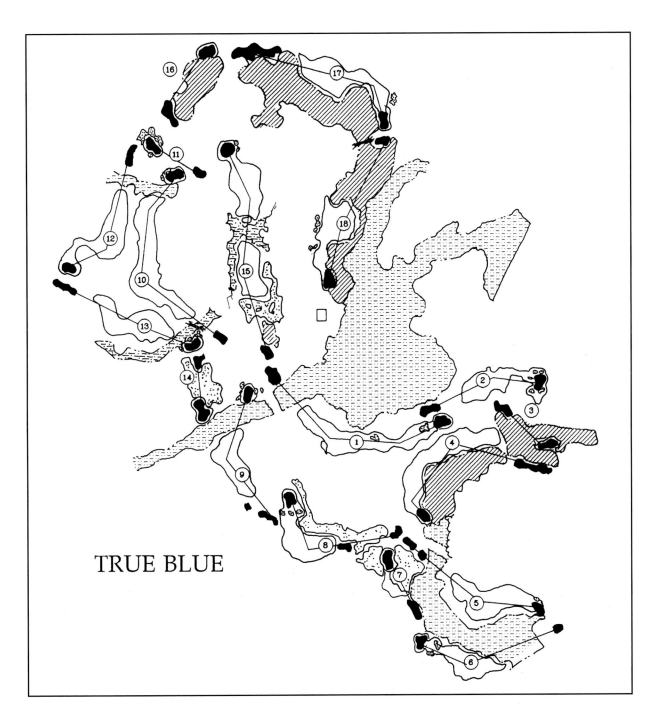

True Blue

HOLE NUMBER	1	2	3	4	5	6	7	8	9	OUT	10	11	12	13	14	15	16	17	18	IN	TOT	HCP	NET
BLACK	624	342	172	548	433	413	177	363	548	3620	599	167	407	410	161	602	208	449	437	3440	7060		
BLUE	598	333	169	533	430	406	170	350	532	3521	580	163	390	400	157	585	200	424	420	3319	6840		
WHITE	498	325	162	520	420	395	165	335	510	3330	568	158	380	390	150	575	185	392	360	3158	6488		
GOLD	440	268	134	435	358	220	118	310	458	2741	470	122	300	365	108	519	160	365	315	2724	5465		
RED	400	250	125	415	320	198	105	250	380	2443	418	115	238	325	97	496	140	348	300	2477	4920		
HANDICAP	1	13	17	3	7	9	15	11	5		4	16	12	10	18	2	14	6	8				
PAR	5	4	3	5	4	4	3	4	5	37	5	3	4	4	3	5	3	4	4	35	72		

One of the magnificent holes at the new Tournament Players Club, slated to become the home of the PGA Senior tour (Courtesy Tournament Players Club)

TOURNAMENT PLAYERS CLUB

SC Highway 707   3.5 miles west of the Atlantic Ocean
P.O. Box 159   Murrells Inlet, SC 29576
(843) 357-3399   (888) PGA-TPC1

Architect: Tom Fazio (with Lanny Wadkins)   Year opened: 1998

Course statistics:
Tee - Yardage/Par
TPC - 7,017/72

Black - 6,759/72   Blue - 6,419/72
White - 6,022/71   Red - 5,203/72

Another prestige golf course, a magnificent layout designed, owned, and operated by the PGA Tour's Tournament Players Club, opened its fairways, hazards, and bent-grass greens just 12 miles south of the heart of Myrtle Beach in October 1998 and immediately claimed its position among the premier courses of the Grand Strand.

TPC courses are designed for the intent of staging a tournament-play facility at each of its twenty locations across the United States.

The season-ending Senior Tour Championship moves from The Dunes to this impressive new facility in 1999, but Lanny Wadkins, consultant to course designer Tom Fazio, has no qualms in predicting a future PGA event for this locale.

"The finishing stretch, #13 through #18, is awesome," said Wadkins, pointing out that the TPC courses are uniquely designed to accommodate thousands of golfing fans who enjoy enhanced viewing areas with stadium seating and easy access to other prime viewing areas.

Golfers, of course, enjoy watching the game, but they enjoy playing it even more, and the opportunity of adding this course to a golf package of the Grand Strand and playing where the professionals "tee it up" adds extra excitement and spice to those golfing tours.

This is the first TPC design by highly respected architect Tom Fazio. "Tom has

always wanted to do a TPC design," said Skip Corn, general manager of the Myrtle Beach course, "and, of course, the PGA was excited about having him to do it. He certainly has built a lot of excitement and design innovations into this one!"

If there is one single "thread" that runs through the design and concept of Tournament Players Club courses, it is that these courses are a vehicle used to support the PGA Tour and the Tour players. According to a PGA Tour brochure, at the end of 1998, nineteen of these superior golf courses, maintaining high standards that set them apart from other courses, were open or under construction. Each embodies the traits that have been trademarks since the TPC at Sawgrass first opened its world-renowned Stadium course in 1980.

"Tournament Players Clubs are an important element of our overall strategy to provide value for our players, tournaments, and corporate sponsors," PGA Tour Commissioner Tom Finchem said.

The seed for the TPC Network was former Commissioner Dean Beman's vision to provide Tour players with quality golf courses that also would cater to the fans with enhanced viewing areas. Furthermore, these golf-course facilities would become a major revenue source, thus alleviating the Tour's dependency on the television dollar. And by providing rent-free venues for tournaments, *greater charitable contributions* would be generated by the tournaments held at TPCs.

There are some great name designers for these nineteen TPCs, but Fazio's Myrtle Beach creation is as good as any.

"The three-par holes are exceptional," said Wadkins, "but my favorite hole on the course may be #12. It is very similar to #10 at Riviera in Los Angeles, although the dogleg extends to the opposite direction. It is short enough for the very long hitter to cut the dogleg and reach the putting surface with his drive. Of course, there is a lot of risk involved, and such an attempt must be a very accurate shot. The fans will love it!"

This second edition of *Golfing the Carolina Grand Strand* went to press before the final subtleties were incorporated by Fazio and Wadkins, but here's the description of the eighteen magnificent holes before the course was officially opened. All yardages are measured from the TPC tee boxes:

Hole #1, a 400-yard par four: This dogleg left has several bunkers to the right of the landing area. A waste area stretches along the left side of the fairway from the turning point to the green.

Hole #2, a 537-yard par five: Lakes and waste areas line the left side of this hole. Each landing area is protected by bunkers on the right. The green is also protected by bunkers on the right and left sides.

Hole #3, a 440-yard par four: The tee shot must carry a large wetland area to reach the landing area, which has bunkers to the right. The green is protected by bunkers on the front left.

Hole #4, a 452-yard par four: Because bunkers surround the landing area, an accurate tee shot is required. The green is protected by bunkers on the right.

Hole #5, 160-yard par three: The hole sits between a lake on the left and the gallery area on the right. The lake protects the front left of the green while bunkers guard the back.

Hole #6, a 520-yard par five: Whether playing the championship tees or the back tees, the tee shot on this hole must travel through a chute of pines to a landing area that has bunkers on either side. Bunkers also surround the second landing area and the green.

Hole #7, a 178-yard par three: The shot to this green must carry a huge waste bunker extending from tee to green. There is fairway on the right if you choose to "bail out."

Hole #8, a 415-yard par four: A large waste area sits on the right side of the landing area on this dogleg right waiting to capture your tee shot. The waste area splits the fairway on the second shot and protects the left side of the fairway. Bunkers guard the left side and the back of the green.

Hole #9, a 470-yard par four: The tee area is surrounded by a lake and a wetland area. A large waste area right of the fairway creates an impression of a narrow fairway. The fairway does, indeed, narrow beyond the landing area with bunkers on the left. Additional sand hazards protect the right side and the back of the green.

Hole #10, a 395-yard par four: A few fairway bunkers sit on the left side of this landing area. A lake extends from the landing area to the green on the right side. The right half of this green actually extends into the lake, while the left side is guarded by bunkers.

Hole #11, a 437-yard par four: A lake that should not come into play sits to the right of the teeing area on this slight dogleg left. Bunkers on the left are just short of the normal landing area, while the bunkers on the right are beyond it. A long drive must be hit with accuracy to avoid these hazards. The green is protected on both sides by bunkers.

Hole #12, a 330-yard par four: A Lanny Wadkins favorite that offers a good opportunity for birdie. This short hole is surrounded by bunkers along the entire length of both sides of the fairway. The green sits to the left with bunkers on the front, back, and right side.

Hole #13, a 200-yard par three: A large bunker has been placed right in front of the green. Fairway runs up the right and left side of the bunker to the green. Two bunkers are on the back of the green, one left, one right.

Hole #14, a 490-yard par four or five: For championship play, #14 will be a four par. The tee shot on this dogleg left must carry a wetland area just in front of the tee area to reach the large landing area that is surrounded on all sides by bunkers. The fairway narrows for the second shot, with bunkers on the right side of the second landing area and a waste bunker on the left of the green.

Hole #15, a 455-yard par four: A waste area is located between the tee boxes and a large wetland area that must be carried to reach the large landing area. A narrow fairway surrounded by bunkers just beyond the landing area makes longer drives difficult. The green is well protected by bunkers on all sides.

Hole #16, a 385-yard par four: The tee shot on this hole has to carry a lake and avoid bunkers on the left side of the fairway just short of the landing area. A creek runs along the left side of the fairway and behind the green. Bunkers protect the right side of the green.

Hole #17, a 190-yard par three: A lot of water! The tee shot must carry a creek and a large waste bunker to reach this green. The green sits next to a lake that protects the right side and extends around to the back of the green.

Hole #18, a 545-yard par five: The landing area on this excellent finishing hole is protected on the left by a waste bunker and on the right by a creek. The creek cuts across the fairway just beyond the landing area to a lake that extends up the left side of the hole to the green. The green is guarded on the right side by several bunkers.

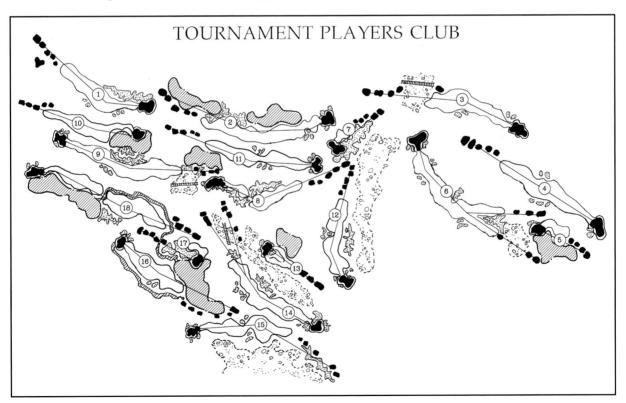

TOURNAMENT PLAYERS CLUB

A wide variety of landscapes adorns Wicked Stick, a John Daly signature course. A vast array of sand awaits the golfer at #16, shown here, plus pot bunkers, mounds, and love grass. (Courtesy Himmelsbach Communications/Bill Woodward)

WICKED STICK

1051 Coventry Road   Myrtle Beach, SC 29575
(800) 797-8425   (843) 215-2500
Architect: Clyde Johnston   Year opened: 1995
"A John Daly signature course"
Course rating/Slope rating:
Daly - 72.2/129   Blue - 70.0/122
White - 68.2/117   Red - 69.2/109

Wicked Stick, conveniently located just south of Highway 544 and facing the Highway 17 bypass, displays white fences, a pretty clubhouse, and a prominent sign on the left side of the bypass as the golfer drives south from the heart of Myrtle Beach toward Georgetown. Another splendid Clyde Johnston course, Wicked Stick has the added appeal of contributions by 1995 British Open champion John Daly, who has made this his first signature course.

To some, Wicked Stick is as controversial as the long-hitting Daly. It's one of those courses with which you fall in love or don't like it at all. Most people who play Wicked Stick belong in the first category, appreciating the nuances that Johnston and Daly have brought to this Scottish-flavored championship layout.

Wicked Stick has been widely applauded by the press, and Gary Schaal, its owner and a former PGA president, has collected some of its praises, listed below:

"One of the top 10 courses to play on the Grand Strand . . . Tee it high and let it fly." *Kansas City Golf,* October 1996.

"There are many hidden treasures in Myrtle Beach. . . . Try Wicked Stick's mini-museum, a collaboration between touring pro John Daly and past PGA President Gary Schaal." *Golfweek,* July 13, 1996.

"Wicked Stick is where to find sun, fun, and low scores. A wide open, links-style layout designed by Clyde Johnston." *USA Today,* November 8, 1996. (Wicked Stick was the only Myrtle Beach course mentioned in this *USA Today* feature.)

"The layout is a traditional, Scottish heathland style. Johnston's careful mounding transformed an uninspiring and flat piece of land into a fair test of golf." *Golf Magazine,* October 1995.

"Destination Myrtle Beach: The Best is Even Better: John Daly's long-awaited debut as an architect opened this fall. . . ." *The Washington Golf Monthly,* October 1995 (headline and sentence opener).

"Long John's first foray into course design is a huge success. Daly teamed up with veteran Clyde Johnston to create an open, Scottish-style course. Perhaps Daly's involvement with the project inspired his 1995 British Open win at the Old Course at St. Andrews. . . . You had better have your long game tuned up if you expect to conquer the 'Daly Signature tees.'" *Carolina Fairways,* Fall 1996.

There have been many other comments, but this handful gives an insight to the curiosity and delight of those who love the spare, open look of Scotland's links courses. It also explains the opposite, minority view of those who say, "It looks like you're playing in an open field." Well, that's the way many of the Scottish courses look.

In truth, Johnston's design is not entirely Scottish in nature. Almost half of the eighteen holes are more parkland in style, weaving between trees—you don't see many trees on golf courses in Scotland!

For the most part, however, Wicked Stick is an open course that features expansive dune fields, large sand wastelands with gorse-like vegetation, deep pot bunkers, and strategically placed water hazards.

One of the unique features of Wicked Stick is the absence of fairway bunkers, which makes this a truly "grip it and rip it" golf course. The golfer should find his target off the tee and let it fly. There are many opportunities for playing "bump and run" shots. Good iron play and a sharp short game will produce a low score. The golfer who can judge the wind will have a definite advantage at Wicked Stick.

Let's tour this very interesting course.

Holes #1, #2, and #3 are wide open with parallel fairways. You go away from the clubhouse on the first hole, come back in for the second, and then out again for the third hole. Number 1 is a good starting hole. You won't find any trouble here, and you don't need to "kill" your drive unless you can drive the green (it has been reached before!) Really, though, all you need is a good solid shot to the fairway and a lofted iron approach to a generous green to set up a potential birdie start.

Number 2 also is relatively short, but trouble does live here, and it's all around a green that slopes away from the golfer. If the pin is on the back, please play short. *Do not* be long on your approach.

On Number 3, just rear back and "bust it." This par five is a good birdie hole, but watch your second shot. Keep it left because out-of-bounds areas and other trouble spots abound down the right side.

Holes #4 through #6 look like they belong to a different course, much more like Carolina than Scotland. You'll encounter many trees and much water. Number 4 is consid-

ered one of the best holes at Wicked Stick. *Tip:* Aim your tee shot to the left side of the fairway because there is plenty of room there, whereas water runs the length of the fairway along the right side. The green slopes away to the right, and if the pin is back right, your second shot should favor the middle of the green.

Number 5 is a long three par and usually plays into the wind. Hit it left; the mounds will act as a backstop for the long tee shot. Number 6 is truly awesome from the Daly tees, stretching 468 yards. Out of bounds on the left and water on the right make this tee shot critical. Because of a large bunker snaking across the entire front of the green, the second shot is all carry. This hole is tough.

Now you leave the trees and come back out into the open, looking at #7, one of the signature holes and a humongous par three. The best way to play it is to miss the green short and chip to the large double green. There are grass bunkers everywhere! Par is a great score, and a bogey is not bad.

Number 9 is exceptionally tough. The major enemy on this wide-open hole is the wind, and water on the left dictates a shot to the right side of the fairway or even the rough. The wind can make a difference of three or four clubs on your second shot.

Numbers 10, 11, and 12 are wide open. *Tip:* If the wind is blowing (and it usually is), consider the punch-and-run approach instead of lofting the shot to the pin.

Eleven is the kind of hole you came to play. Truly Dalyesque, it is 611 yards from the Daly tees, 576 from the whites. This is the other half of the double green that shares its putting surface with the 7th hole.

As the golfer leaves #12, he finds the course going back into the traditional mold for this short par three, which is a difficult hole because of a very shallow green.

The 15th hole is a spectacular par four that requires a very good tee shot. Water, water everywhere, and the golfer must negotiate the tee shot into a large landing area. Better use a long iron or three wood and then hit an accurate second shot to a well-guarded green.

There's no rest for the weary on the par-three 16th hole, whose length makes it tough. Most need a long iron or fairway wood to reach the long, narrow green. Wind dictates club selection, and if pin placement is on the back, it really is a long way there. The green is 124 feet deep.

At #17, a traditional Carolina hole, I recommend that you double-check the yardage for your approach shot, because the three pot bunkers in the fairway make your sec-ond shot look much shorter than it is.

Finish the round at Wicked Stick with a relatively short par five, but don't be deceived. Water completely guards the front of the green, and three pot bunkers behind the green are there to catch a wayward shot. Be careful off the tee, because if you hit it left over the mound, you're in the water. The second shot must be laid up to the water, and caution is advised. Pay attention to the yardage. A long three wood down the middle might be too much club. Leave it short of the water, hit a great wedge, and finish with a birdie!

Love it or leave it, Wicked Stick is an interesting course that most golfers go home talking about.

Wicked Stick

HOLE NUMBER	1	2	3	4	5	6	7	8	9	OUT	10	11	12	13	14	15	16	17	18	IN	TOT	HCP	NET
DALY	336	340	565	374	193	468	265	572	403	3516	362	611	470	161	382	371	198	402	528	3485	7001		
BLUE	328	330	550	365	180	366	205	525	385	3234	350	576	438	150	367	359	172	365	496	3273	6507		
WHITE	320	326	520	346	154	339	188	485	360	3038	315	525	385	143	355	345	163	340	471	3042	6080		
RED	249	248	434	273	115	273	150	405	281	2428	261	444	344	102	280	235	134	282	401	2483	4911		
HANDICAP	15	13	1	5	17	11	7	3	9		10	2	4	18	14	8	16	12	6				
PAR	4	4	5	4	3	4	3	5	4	36	4	5	4	3	4	4	3	4	5	36	72		

This well-designed par three at Tradition is as tough as it is pretty. The green slopes back toward the water, so don't be short with your shot. Ron Garl designed this course, which is a member of the Links Group. (Photo courtesy Himmelsbach Communications/Bill Woodward)

TRADITION CLUB

at Willbrook Plantation
1027 Willbrook Boulevard   Pawleys Island, SC 29585
(800) 833-6337   (843) 237-5041

Architect: Ron Garl   Year opened: 1995

Course rating/Slope rating:
Tournament - 72.0/129   Men's - 69.6/120
Ladies - 68.4/113   Forward - 64.1/104
Senior/Low-handicap Ladies - 66.6/114

The Tradition is the jewel in the chain of ten courses in the Myrtle Beach area operated as "The Links Group" under the leadership of former Tour player and Links president Ken Fowlkes. An eleventh course, Willowpeg, is located near Savannah, Georgia, and is the first Links Group course located beyond the Myrtle Beach area.

Although a surcharge course, the Tradition offers green fees that are still far below the average of surcharge courses. "We have a quality product and want to make it available to golfers of all income means," Fowlkes said.

Ron Garl, the creator of 135 championship layouts, designed the Tradition course. The Tradition is reminiscent of golf courses in Florida, where Garl began an architectural career that is now in worldwide demand. The Tradition features wide fairways and huge, well-placed greens. The use of natural sand areas and water throughout the course creates a dimension that is unique to Myrtle Beach, and the innovative layout has found favor with golfers at every skill level.

Designed with five sets of tees, every golfer can play each hole equally regardless of handicap. The forward tees here have enjoyed great popularity, and such success is easily explained. Many people retire to Myrtle Beach, take up the game for the first time, and appreciate the opportunity of fin-

ishing a hole while playing with more experienced golfers. The expansive fairways encourage a "you can hit the ball and go find it" philosophy without having to conduct an Easter egg hunt in forbidding roughs.

Don't, however, be led into believing that this is an easy golf course—far from it. Garl's goal was to create a championship course, one both challenging and enjoyable. His task was daunting, but Garl certainly met his goal at the Tradition Club.

Before setting out on the course itself, you will want to savor the world-class practice facility and hone your game to the challenges soon to be incurred. The putting green that covers 43,000 square feet is just a part of the story. The club's conventional range lets you hit every club in your bag, and in addition you can drive your cart into one of the many coves that surround the area. These coves are hidden by trees and serve as launching pads for your multilevel chipping and pitching areas onto actual greens.

Want to work on your sand game? Bunkers and mounds also exist, and each area is completely separate and out of the way of any errant tee shots. Altogether more than eighteen acres comprise this world-class practice area, one as good as you will find anywhere.

Natural wastelands serve as boundaries on many of the holes, and seven of the first nine holes invite you to go over, around, or at least avoid the abundance of water.

The very pretty #7 is a standout that requires a second shot to an island green. The fairway here is elevated, and the second shot is to a sunken green, giving you the impression of hitting from a plateau downhill. From the back (tournament) tees, this hole measures 393 yards and requires a well-hit iron to get home. A student of golf architecture can really appreciate how this hole has been created. It is equally demanding from all five tees.

The greens at the Tradition, Bermuda topped with bluegrass, are excellent, as is the overall conditioning of this golf course.

After the front nine, the player reaches a very handsome clubhouse and also gets a second chance to pick up a snack or refresh-ment three holes later because #12 comes back to the clubhouse.

I like #12, too. It is a fairly long three par with the tee shot over a large environmentally protected area to a green that sits about 30 feet below the tee-box areas.

Garl is enthusiastic about the 14th hole. "It's the closest thing you're going to find to #15 at the Masters." The length is the same, and—sure enough—a little stream fronts the green, which sits on the bank of the creek. Both birdies and bogeys abound here, making #14 a fine example of a risk-reward hole.

Number 15 is almost too good and partially defeats Garl's effort to give players a course that plays fast. This hole has an island green that slopes back to the water with no place to go except on the green, in the traps on the left, or to a narrow landing area over the green. Hit it short and chances are good your ball will roll back into the water.

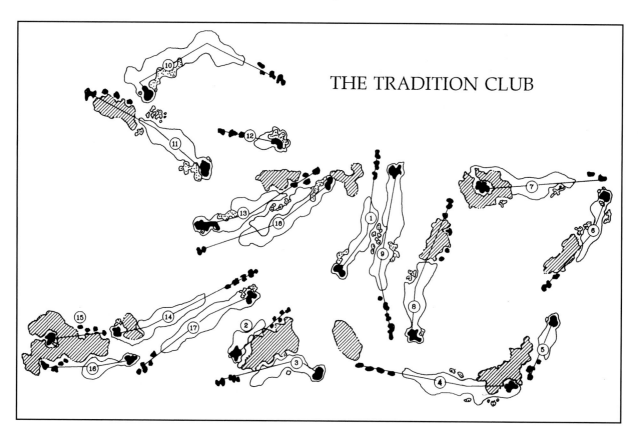

THE TRADITION CLUB

Number 18. Wow ! The green is 455 yards from the tournament tees, 430 from the regular men's tees, and a long, long 407 from the ladies' and seniors'. Sand runs the length of the fairway on the left side, and the hole is a slight dogleg to the left, finishing directly in front of that imposing clubhouse. Get home in two and you have earned the right to play with anybody, anywhere. For most of us, a bogey is not only acceptable but a good score!

Tradition Club

HOLE NUMBER	1	2	3	4	5	6	7	8	9	OUT	10	11	12	13	14	15	16	17	18	IN	TOT	HCP	NET
TOURNAMENT	373	212	350	540	203	360	393	448	507	3386	530	437	190	411	500	163	436	411	455	3533	6919		
MEN'S	356	193	329	510	179	347	377	408	490	3184	520	415	185	388	450	157	399	380	430	3324	6508		
SENIORS/LOW HCP LADIES	323	165	300	483	174	307	350	367	453	2927	453	383	147	362	433	113	377	379	407	3054	5981		
LADIES	278	125	266	442	145	254	293	330	298	2527	395	322	131	320	418	90	309	228	371	2584	5111		
FORWARD	219	124	242	352	110	250	237	270	330	2138	369	250	115	235	348	75	225	215	280	2112	4250		
HANDICAP	11	5	17	9	7	15	3	1	13		10	6	16	8	12	14	2	18	4				
PAR	4	3	4	5	3	4	4	4	5	36	5	4	3	4	5	3	4	4	4	36	72		
LADIES' HCP	17	15	11	5	13	9	1	3	7		12	2	14	6	10	16	4	18	8				

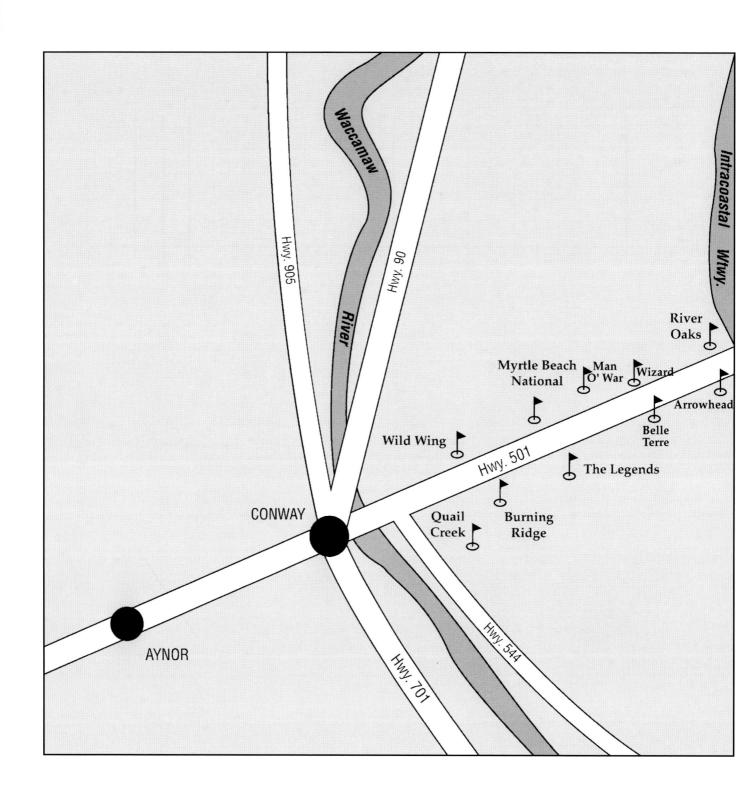

From Conway on Highway 501

One of the twenty-seven delightful holes at River Oaks. (Courtesy River Oaks Golf Links)

RIVER OAKS

Highway 501   831 River Oaks Dr.   Myrtle Beach, SC 29577
(843) 236-2222   (800) 762-8813

Architect: Gene Hamm and Tom Jackson   Year opened: 1987

Course rating/Slope rating:
Blue - 71.8/122
White - 69.7/115
Red - 68.1/118

River Oaks, operated by American Golf, which also operates Carolina Shores, has been open since 1987, commencing play with two nine-hole layouts—The Fox and The Otter—and adding a third nine—The Bear—in October of 1990.

Located behind the Waccamaw Brickyard along the Intracoastal Waterway, this is a popular course made especially tough by oversize greens which feature a lot of mounds and bumps. While these are excellent greens, the contours and undulations make them difficult to putt and three-putt greens are frequent.

Regardless of which two nines the golfer puts together to form his eighteen-hole round, there is plenty of golf course to negotiate. If the golfer chooses to play the original eighteen-hole layout, the course measures 6,791 yards. The host professional feels that the newest nine holes—The Bear—is one of the best nine holes on the Strand, and that it will be used in conjunction with The Otter for most tournaments. Then the eighteen-hole challenge becomes even longer, measuring 6,877 yards from tee to green.

The Bear, cut from a dense forest, is designed to speed up play, with only thirteen sand traps on the entire nine-hole Tom Jackson layout. Four of them, however, are placed on the finishing hole, which is both memorable and difficult. Long (547 yards), the 9th hole of The Bear resembles a half-moon, with the fairway encircling a very large lake on the right. Nor is it an easy hole to "play safe" by driving the ball down the left side. Here the trees will come into play. To complicate matters, the fairway becomes very narrow as you near the green. Almost impossible to reach in two, the golfer should consider that the farther he hits the second shot, the more the risk increases.

This is one of the host professional's favorite holes, along with two holes on The Otter (#2 and #8) and another good finishing hole, #9 on The Fox course. Both The Fox and The Otter were designed by Gene Hamm and feature many interesting designs.

Otter #2 is the most difficult hole on this twenty-seven-hole layout, in the opinion of many. It is pretty, a very scenic hole with water coming into play from the tee and then lurking as a potential danger, running all the way along the left of the fairway to and behind the green. Hamm has provided a good landing area, but hit the ball too far and you will find yourself in a trap on the right or behind a tree on either side of the fairway. Long hitters will need to go to a fairway wood, but anything longer than 240 yards probably is in trouble.

Number 8 on The Otter was named to the Myrtle Beach *Sun News'* Dream 18 and causes much comment. Water runs down the right side of the fairway, and there is a series of large mounds sculpted on the left. The hole plays as a dogleg right to an elevated green.

Fox #9 is a favorite hole. Not overly long,

a pair of grass bunkers adds interest to this hole. The second shot is demanding, as the golfer hits into a green set at an angle, and many players find they are "blocked out" for their second shot.

Other holes that immediately capture the attention of the golfer looking for something different are Fox #3 and Fox #4 (this is the nine traditionally used as the first nine).

Both are played over a big waste bunker heavily planted with large clumps of pampas grass. Number 3 is a par three, 189 yards from the blues, with traps on the left front and both sides of the green. The waste bunker seems to occupy 50 percent of the available golfing area. It's a pretty hole, as the golfer hits his tee shot into an elevated green with the Waterway running behind.

Golfers will recross that same waste bunker as they play #4, but here the big bunker is not the problem as it is located close to the tee. Instead a narrow landing area located between traps left and right provides the most formidable obstacle.

The slope rating on the original eighteen—Fox and Otter—is 68.7, but the course is much tougher than that. Since the course was rated, it has matured, and the rough has grown up, becoming much more of a factor.

Golfers like the course, and River Oaks has a plaque in the pro shop to prove it. A questionnaire was placed in the shops of thirty-one area courses, and this twenty-seven-hole layout was named number four in terms of popularity. Scoring was based on

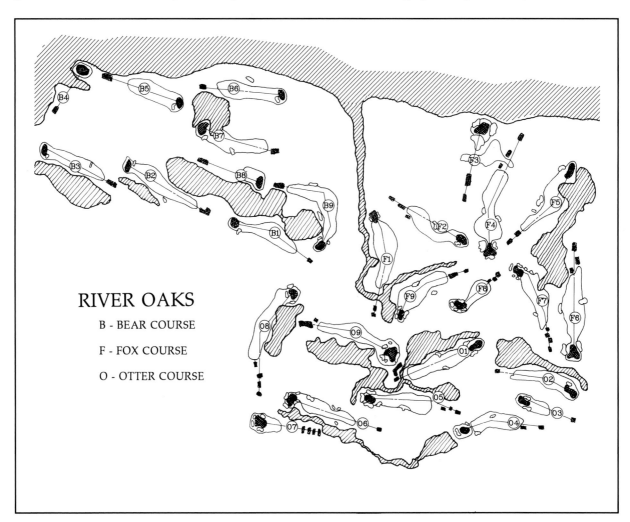

RIVER OAKS

B - BEAR COURSE

F - FOX COURSE

O - OTTER COURSE

overall value, courtesy, money value, and overall service.

Any combination of the three nines puts the premium on accuracy rather than distance. It is a "placement" course where the golfer who wears his thinking cap and clubs himself for position is going to score well. The golfer who just grabs his driver and flails away probably will get into a great deal of trouble.

The Otter

HOLE NUMBER	1	2	3	4	5	6	7	8	9	TOT
BLUE	437	405	205	367	365	524	211	410	521	3445
WHITE	415	364	186	339	340	498	198	390	498	3228
MEN'S HCP	2	3	6	9	8	4	5	1	7	
MEN'S PAR	4	4	3	4	4	5	3	4	5	36
RED	263	296	115	305	261	453	136	291	429	2549
LADIES' HCP	2	3	6	9	8	4	5	1	7	
LADIES' PAR	4	4	3	4	4	5	3	4	5	36

The Fox

HOLE NUMBER	1	2	3	4	5	6	7	8	9	TOT
BLUE	536	385	189	387	353	441	511	139	405	3346
WHITE	512	351	161	361	294	424	503	129	382	3117
MEN'S HCP	6	7	5	4	8	1	2	9	3	
MEN'S PAR	5	4	3	4	4	4	5	3	4	36
RED	404	294	120	267	251	350	420	90	298	2494
LADIES' HCP	6	7	5	4	8	1	2	9	3	
LADIES' PAR	5	4	3	4	4	4	5	3	4	36

The Bear

HOLE NUMBER	1	2	3	4	5	6	7	8	9	TOT
BLUE	460	523	377	165	409	387	341	223	547	3432
WHITE	433	497	355	153	379	358	313	193	516	3197
MEN'S HCP	2	7	5	9	4	6	8	3	1	
MEN'S PAR	4	5	4	3	4	4	4	3	5	36
RED	341	440	298	106	320	294	262	122	456	2639
LADIES' HCP	2	7	5	9	4	6	8	3	1	
LADIES' PAR	4	5	4	3	4	4	4	3	5	36

Heathland at The Legends . . . love grass, moundings, a wide-open links-style course designed by Tom Doak. (Courtesy Himmelsbach Communications/Bill Woodward)

THE LEGENDS

Highway 501, 7 miles west of Myrtle Beach   P.O. Box 2038   Myrtle Beach, SC 29578
(843) 236-9318   (800) 552-2660

Architects: Tom Doak (Heathland)   Year opened: 1990
P. B. Dye (Moorland)   Year opened: 1990
Larry Young/The Legends Group (Parkland)   Year opened: 1992

Course rating/Slope rating:
HEATHLAND
Tour Gold - 72.3/127
Green - 69.0/117   Red - 71.0/121

MOORLAND
Tour Gold - 73.1/128
Green - 69.8/121   Red - 71.0/127

PARKLAND
Tour Gold - 74.3/131   Blue - 71.9/127
White - 70.8/123   Red - 71.0/125

The Legends is one of the most spectacular golf resorts on the Grand Strand, and—like the golf courses—the amenities built into the newly opened golf villas and the various restaurant facilities are excellent.

Because of geographical location, we describe three courses—Heathland, Moorland, and Parkland—in this chapter. However, Larry Young actually operates six superb golf courses in the Myrtle Beach area and has expanded his golfing presence with two golf courses in Virginia that won back-to-back course-of-the-year honors!

The other three Larry Young golf facilities on the Grand Strand are Marsh Harbor, his first creation; Oyster Bay; and the Heritage Club. Descriptions of these great golfing layouts can be found elsewhere in this second edition of *Golfing the Carolina Grand Strand*.

In this section we will focus on the three golf courses built around the impressive 19,000-square-foot clubhouse that is fronted by three huge flags bearing the colors of the United States, Scotland, and South Carolina. Within easy access of the heart of Myrtle

Beach with a private two-mile drive extending from Highway 501, the clubhouse dominates the landscape and can be seen from everywhere on the magnificent, well-manicured courses. The Scottish influence is inescapable, so much so that anyone approaching the pro shop is assailed with the sounds of Scottish bagpipes!

Heathland, the first course to open on this plot of ground, is as close to a Scottish layout as you're going to find. "Don't like to fly? Come play the Heathland. It's a bit of Scotland in South Carolina," the Legends brochure proclaims.

And that's true. There are pot bunkers, heather, gorse, berms, and even one hole patterned after the Road Hole at St. Andrews. The big clock under the eaves of the clubhouse is another St. Andrews look-alike. Being true to the Scottish tradition of a true links course, Larry Young and his architects have removed all the trees from the playing area, allowing the wind to blow with considerably more velocity than you'll find on other Grand Strand courses.

Everything about this project is awesome in size and execution: not only the expanse of real estate (more than 1,000 acres) and the oversized, beautifully paneled clubhouse, but also the 1.3-acre putting green and the driving range that sits on 30 acres of ground in a huge circle. It is said that The Legends offers more putting surface on the putting-green facility than most courses have on all of the greens of a nine-hole layout!

Now there is more: The Legends Resorts Exclusive Golf Package, which features on-site accommodations at Turnberry Park Villa and golfing privileges at all three golf courses at this location. Visitors may also choose to go "off premises" and play one of the other three Larry Young courses.

Again borrowing from Scotland, these villas retain some of the architectural features of the hotel at Turnberry, another of the legendary Scottish golfing venues. A delightful British pub is ensconced within Turnberry Park.

The accommodations are delightful, but the primary attraction, of course, is the excellence of the Larry Young courses. In the following pages we'll take a closer look at each.

Heathland

The par-71 Heathland course, designed by Tom Doak, has been modeled in the image of the Scottish links courses, with holes reminiscent of familiar seaside layouts such as St. Andrews and lesser-known gems such as LaHinch and Cruden Bay. The challenge and difficulty of Heathland comes primarily from the unobstructed wind (which seems to blow constantly), the strategically placed bunkers, and the lush, deep rough that borders the fairways.

Shortly after Heathland opened, Hugh Gill, one of the fine golfers in the area, set a course record of 63, catching the course when the wind was only a whisper. The day after Gill set the record, the winds started blowing again, returning to their normal ferocity. "Let's call Hugh, have him come down here, and see what he shoots today," laughed Larry Young, the man most familiar with the many nuances of this fine course. Larry Young was right again. Eight years later, that 63 remains the course record!

Complicating the ability to post record numbers is the fact that the greens at Heathland are huge, presenting an interesting dilemma to players who hit their shot to the wrong portion of the green. Some of the greenside bunkers are very deep and require well-played shots to escape.

Heathland is not a "tight" course, but course knowledge is essential. Some of the bent-grass greens are 100 steps across, so you can hit the green and still be a long way from the flag. Very few of the bunkers are placed in front of the greens, so the player can bounce the ball toward the pin, knowing that the wind is a constant factor. One day you can hit a five iron to the green, but if the wind changes direction the next day, you may still need a well-hit three wood after making a good drive!

While all the holes on this course are very good (Heathland was rated as one of the top-ten new resort courses in the world when it opened in 1990), some deserve particular mention.

The first hole, a long par four, is unusual in that the fairway is 100 yards wide at one point. You need to learn how to play this hole. Hit it to one side of the fairway and the ball will roll 50 yards. Hit it to the other side and you'll be lucky if you get a roll of 15 yards after the ball hits the ground.

Number 3 is an exceptional par three and is very difficult when the wind is howling. It plays uphill through an undulating bowl of a fairway, and pin placement is the key on this oversized green, 50 yards wide. The bunker to the left is deceptive, actually 15 yards short of the putting surface. This hole was modeled after a par three at Cruden Bay, Scotland.

Number 6 is unique in that it is the only hole on this Heathland course where trees can come into play. To go over the trees, you must carry the drive at least 180 yards. You begin the hole by coming out of a "chute" and then hitting into an open green that is fronted by a bunker and a mound. At 460 yards from the back tees to the center of the green, this 6th hole is rated as the number-one handicap hole on the course.

Ironically, #7 also is 460 yards, but this one is a par five. The green and the sod-wall pot bunker guarding the green are modeled after #17 on the Old Course at St. Andrews. The green, with virtually no slope, sits atop a high plateau.

Most golfers will go home with memories of #13, which is a par five and plays downhill. Ninety percent of the time the wind is at the back of the golfer, and long hitters have an excellent chance of getting home in two even though the hole is 525 yards long. Keep left off the tee. This green slopes from right to left, and if you're going to have a chance to collect the birdie or the rare eagle, watch out for the bunker on the right.

Number 16 may be the most difficult hole on this course. A creek (berm) runs diagonally across the fairway. If the golfer can safely clear this water hazard, placing the shot on the right side of the fairway, it opens up for a clear shot past the fairway bunker to the green. Most golfers will elect to play it safe, staying away from the water by hitting the tee shot to the left side. However, such an approach leaves a long blind shot to the green. This one, too, is a very long par four, measuring 460 yards from the back tees.

In summation, Heathland is a magnificent golf course, but it certainly is not easy. The shorter holes are narrow, with love grass defining the fairways, while the longer holes are wide open and fun for the player who likes to rear back and slug it. When the wind is quiet, this course can be tame, but that doesn't happen often. When the wind is blowing, you are playing a monster.

Moorland

To some, this course is controversial, with comments ranging from "one of the very best" to "too tough," but you can expect controversy when P. B. Dye is the architect. Larry Young, developer of The Legends, asked Dye to create "the strongest challenge you can," and the renowned architect took this request to heart. Moorland is indeed very challenging, with a completely different look than other Larry Young golf courses.

A vast expanse of natural growth, sand, water, and waste areas combine with unlikely and unexpected undulations and a Dye trademark—bulkheaded areas—to present a golf course that will remind some golfers of PGA West and Pine Valley.

Moorland definitely has the aspects of a "target" course and puts a premium on accuracy. Many of the tees are elevated, and upon playing Moorland for the first time some six years ago, I was tempted to call the front nine the best nine holes of golf on the Grand Strand.

Whether you like the course or not is beside the point. This golf course is spectacular, and whenever golfers gather to discuss "the most memorable hole," "the most surprising hole," or even "the most feared hole" on the Strand, some of Dye's creations at Moorland usually enter the conversations.

You begin your round at Moorland by facing a vast waste area on #1 and lots of sand and water at #2. On this second hole—a 507-yard par five—the gambling golfer who hits a slight fade into the large depression area

Moorland at The Legends, a P. B. Dye creation. (Courtesy Himmelsbach Communications/Bill Woodward)

can play a fairway wood over the pilings onto the left of the green, but the more conservative player will lay up his second shot with a middle iron for a short pitch to the green.

If you were under the impression there is a lot of water at #2, just wait until you get to #3. Safely past this one, the golfer who plays from the back tees must hit a drive more than 200 yards to clear the big, yawning waste area. Number 4 is called "Big Bertha," and that name applies here not to a Callaway golf club but to a formidable sand trap located at the left center of the fairway just beyond the waste area. Tough and long, this hole measures 460 yards from the back tees.

While the golf course has been "taking it away," things do get better for the golfer's scorecard. Number Five is a relatively short three par, and #6 is a long hitter's dream. A drive played down the left side will leave a long-iron second shot into a narrow green for a possible eagle putt.

The finishing four holes at Moorland are, to say the least, interesting. Number 15, 593 yards from tee to green, is a definite three-shot hole, and the closer you get to the green, the more narrow the landing area becomes. The green is two-tiered, which leads to tricky pin placements.

The 16th hole is called "Hell's Half Acre," but it is short in length. Only 275 yards from the championship tees and a modest 245 from the regular tees, the green is surrounded by nine very deep and severe bunkers. It is the true definition of risk and reward and dares you to be bold.

Number 17 is different, too. It is an "island green," but the putting surface is surrounded not by water but by sand that runs from tee to green. This green is truly an oasis.

Number 18 is a terrific finishing hole, and it is this green you see when you drive into The Legends complex. This 443-yard par four is a dogleg to the left, with water running from tee to green. A huge mound on the right side of the green blocks the player's view of this green, which is much larger than it appears from the second shot.

All in all, the Moorland course, although a bit sadistic, still is fascinating. It is unbelievable what Dye can conceive while designing golf courses.

Parkland

The Legends Trilogy (three championship golf courses at one location) was completed with the opening of Parkland in the winter of 1992. Taking its place alongside the award-winning Heathland and Moorland courses, Parkland quickly established itself as one of the most exciting courses on the Grand Strand. Popular from the very beginning, it has attracted large numbers of golfers.

Parkland is completely different from the other two Legends courses.

No target golf here. Parkland stands in stark contrast to the wide-open, windswept Scottish look of the other two courses. The natural terrain is both diverse and beautiful, with contoured tree-lined fairways, vast natural areas, deep-faced bunkers, and massive, multilevel undulating greens.

Parkland was designed under the watchful eye of owner Larry Young and his Legends Group. Seeking diversity, Young chose to model Parkland after the style of Alister Mackenzie (Augusta National) and George Thomas (Riviera Country Club). Those are good people to emulate, and the Legends Group did a superb job of borrowing from these eminent golf architects while incorporating some more recent ideas.

Playing the unforgettably challenging fairways and greenside bunkering requires a deft touch from the tee and, for that matter, on every shot from tee to green. Strategy is the order of the day when playing Parkland, and astute management of your golf game is essential.

The two finishing holes (#9 and #18) are among the most memorable holes at Parkland for both men and ladies. Surprisingly, #9 is a short par four, but that doesn't mean it is easy! There are out-of-bounds areas to the left and water on the right, and if the golfer hits the second shot too firmly and goes over the green, there is big trouble.

Play #9 with a short, controlled tee shot and you still have a short iron shot on this hole, which doglegs to the right. A gaping bunker in front of the green often causes golfers to hit the second shot too long in order to avoid this very obvious hazard.

While #9 may be short, #18, described as a great finishing hole, has a lot of length (465 yard from the gold tees and a lengthy 350 for the ladies playing the reds). Water jutting from the left of the tee should not come into play, but most players will be aware of the trees, mounding, and sand on the right—hazards that can cause a natural tendency to pull (hook) the tee shot. Still, the drive should favor the right side of the fairway, leaving a long iron or a fairway wood to a green tucked behind extensive mounding.

Number 18 is very tough, rated as the number-one handicap on the scorecard for both men and ladies. A par four here will win a lot of matches.

However, the par-three holes at Parkland warrant your attention.

Number 16, which is 200 yards from the blue tees, features tall pines that are located all the way up the right side of the fairway and circle the back of the green. Six bunkers guard the green on the left! Again, the mounds in front of the putting surface are substantial, and again the golfer faces a two-tiered green. If you can, play the hole by hitting a long iron or fairway wood to the right side of the green, drawing your shot left.

Once there, the green is very deep, promoting many a three putt.

Number 13, while not as long, is long enough: 175 yards from the blues, 150 yards for the ladies. Pine trees surround the fairway and green, and the golfer must play over a large natural wetland to the green.

Long carries over wetlands and many trees are characteristic of this true "parklands" course, the third jewel in the Legends crown and a Larry Young creation. This creative developer also has installed a series of Scottish-style condominiums that allow the golfer to stay on the premises. (Courtesy Brandon Advertising/Michael Slear)

Aerial pictures of this beautiful hole make it seem as if it were "dropped" into a setting of lush vegetation and gaping sand bunkers.

Parkland's front nine also has two very interesting par-three holes.

Number 3 presents a formidable waste area to the left and front of the green, with bunkers placed between this waste area and the green itself. How to play it? Try a mid-iron to the right center of the large green. If the pin is on the back, you will need more club than you might think.

The par-three 5th hole is a challenge, not only because of the green's depth but also because of how the green slopes from front to back. Water is visible to the right. And, oh yes, don't neglect that water hazard beyond the green. Play your tee shot to the front of the green and allow for a roll. If you hit it past the pin, your golf ball stands a very good chance of taking a swim!

No description of Parkland would be complete without mention of #2, the longest-playing par four on the entire course. The hole requires a good drive and a well-hit fairway wood. Number 2 is a "bust it or be short" hole, 460 yards from the gold tees and 430 from the blues. It is rated—with good reason—as the hardest hole on the front nine.

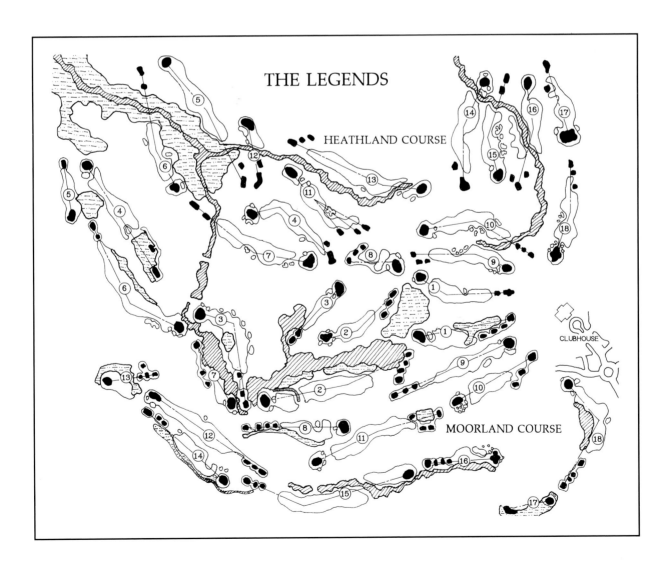

THE LEGENDS

HEATHLAND COURSE

MOORLAND COURSE

CLUBHOUSE

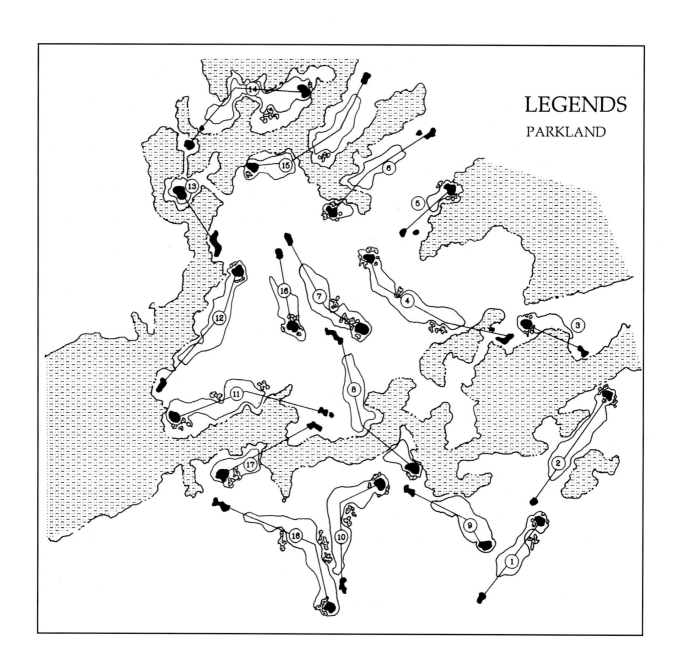

LEGENDS
PARKLAND

Heathland

HOLE NUMBER	1	2	3	4	5	6	7	8	9	OUT	10	11	12	13	14	15	16	17	18	IN	TOT	HCP	NET
GOLD	450	345	210	350	560	460	460	150	405	3390	435	400	165	535	385	345	460	220	430	3375	6765		
GREEN	420	310	195	335	530	385	425	130	365	3095	405	380	145	510	350	315	430	185	375	3095	6190		
RED	370	235	130	285	450	250	390	90	330	2530	330	325	105	475	270	270	385	120	305	2585	5115		
HANDICAP	3	15	13	11	5	1	9	17	7		4	6	18	12	16	14	2	10	8				
PAR	4	4	3	4	5	4	5	3	4	36	4	4	3	5	4	4	4	3	4	35	71		

Moorland

HOLE NUMBER	1	2	3	4	5	6	7	8	9	OUT	10	11	12	13	14	15	16	17	18	IN	TOT	HCP	NET
CHAMPIONSHIP	373	507	404	469	175	494	245	367	469	3503	394	471	459	156	344	593	275/245	194	443	3329	6832		
BLUE	347	484	366	454	162	487	217	337	445	3299	364	454	426	143	326	556	258/227	160	419	3106	6405		
GREEN	301	431	341	426	142	460	183	309	413	3006	296	425	379	115	301	518	240/208	130	397	2801	5807		
RED	254	397	277	352	122	373	130	284	363	2552	269	371	326	79	236	490	220/186	102	294	2387	4939		
MEN'S HCP	11	9	5	3	17	15	7	13	1		8	16	2	18	12	6	14	10	4				
PAR	4	5	4	4	3	5	3	4	4	36	4	5	4	3	4	5	4	3	4	36	72		
LADIES' HCP	11	5	9	3	17	13	15	7	1		8	10	2	18	14	4	12	16	6				

Parkland

HOLE NUMBER	1	2	3	4	5	6	7	8	9	OUT	10	11	12	13	14	15	16	17	18	IN	TOT	HCP	NET
TOURN. GOLD	380	460	175	570	190	440	405	545	340	3505	330	515	470	205	465	580	235	400	465	3665	7170		
GREEN	345	430	165	525	160	380	360	485	295	3145	300	480	430	175	435	520	180	350	410	3280	6425		
RED	320	315	140	470	145	330	305	440	260	2725	245	415	360	150	380	470	160	315	350	2845	5570		
MEN'S HCP	16	2	18	6	12	4	8	14	10		15	17	5	7	3	9	13	11	1				
PAR	4	4	3	5	3	4	4	5	4	36	4	5	4	3	4	5	3	4	4	36	72		
LADIES' HCP	16	2	18	6	12	4	8	14	10		15	17	5	7	3	9	13	11	1				

The "South Carolina" hole at Myrtle Beach National, with traps shaped like an S and a C—fifty-four holes of championship golf. (Courtesy Brandon Advertising/ Michael Slear)

MYRTLE BEACH NATIONAL

4900 National Drive   P.O. Box 1936   Myrtle Beach, SC 29579
(843) 448-2308   (800) 344-5590

Architects: Arnold Palmer Course Design Group (King's North)   Year opened: 1973
Arnold Palmer, Mike Hurdzan (Southcreek)   Year opened: 1975
Arnold Palmer, Francis Duane (West course)   Year opened: 1974

Course rating/Slope rating:
KING'S NORTH
Black - 72.6/136   Gold - 69.7/128
White -68.2/123   Blue - 67/115

SOUTHCREEK
Blue - 70.5/123   Gold - 67.3/112
White - 69.1/118   Red - 66.5/109

WEST COURSE
Blue - 73.0/119   White - 69.0/113
Red - 69.0/109

Bouncing back into the upper echelon of Grand Strand Golf courses with the spectacularly rebuilt King's North course, Myrtle Beach National Golf Club offers three of the most requested courses on the beach—King's North, Southcreek, and the West course—all designed by or in consultation with the "king of golf," Arnold Palmer. Other architects who had earlier influence on this Myrtle Beach National complex also are listed in the heading.

The average golfing enthusiast who visits this "Golf Capitol of the World" would be hard pressed to find a better, more convenient golf resort than Myrtle Beach National. Here, built on a thousand acres near the heart of the city of Myrtle Beach, are three championship courses, each of them different in style, but all of them quality layouts.

Myrtle Beach National has made a strong commitment to the conditioning of their golf courses and, as the $4.5 million King's North project proves, does not skimp on maintenance while also going the extra mile to service its customers both on the course and within the clubhouse. The fourteen employees who staff the pro shop either have or are working on PGA credentials.

The West course is a traditional parkland layout routed through a pristine Carolina pine forest; Southcreek is a finesse course that requires accuracy more than distance; and King's North, which combines elements of both courses, falls into a pattern all its own.

The Myrtle Beach National golfing experience doesn't stop with these three courses at the Highway 501 location. The recent acquisition of Pawleys Plantation on the south end of the Beach is another jewel in the Myrtle Beach National crown, joining the three courses at the Litchfield complex, the twenty-seven holes at Waterway Hills, and the magnificent Jack Nicklaus designed Long Bay Club, all of which are under the direction of this influential company

Ed Bullock was the PGA professional when Myrtle Beach National was opened in 1973. Today's professional, Jerry Cox, has been with the company since 1986.

King's North

Outdoor billboards throughout the Myrtle

"The King Is Back!" and very much in evidence on Arnold Palmer's challenging King's North course. "The Gambler" tempts you to take a shortcut by way of the island.
(Courtesy Brandon Advertising/Michael Slear)

Beach area feature a portrait of Arnold Palmer and proclaim "The King is Back" to recognize the rerouting and redesign of the North course at this well-known Grand Strand landmark by the man who most agree made golf the game it is today.

The all-new King's North features eighteen of the most challenging holes the golfer will ever encounter, including the par-five #6, nicknamed The Gambler, and the par-four #18, called Bulls-Eye because of the accuracy required to avoid the unbelievable forty-two sand traps that line the fairway.

To some golfers King's North is "overkill," but others are literally standing in line to play King's North, firmly believing this surcharge course is the best they've ever played.

Let's begin a closer look at some of these

The 18th hole at King's North is a terrific finishing hole. You can see why it is called "The Bulls-Eye"! (Courtesy Brandon Advertising/Michael Slear)

magnificent holes by turning our attention to #6, The Gambler. There's a plaque behind the tee box to remind visitors that Kenny Rogers of movie and music fame dedicated this hole in June 1996. Aptly named, it is indeed a golf hole that will endear itself to those who are willing to gamble. In nominating the 6th hole for the "Dream Eighteen" of the Grand Strand, golf director Jerry Cox called it one of the finest examples of risk-reward to be found.

The 6th hole measures 565 yards from the championship tee. However, if you choose to play to the island fairway instead of taking the conventional long way home, it plays about 475 yards. Because this island fairway is 100 yards long and 50 yards wide, you'll need a drive of 275 yards to position yourself for the minimum carry (200 yards) over water to the large green that slopes back toward that water you just cleared! Go a little short and you're in the water. Go a lit-

tle long on the left and you're in the water behind the green. Hit it long to the right and you are either in a large bunker or on one of the mounds behind the green. The smart play, of course, is the long way around, and even then the golfer finds himself on a green that does not favor the short stick. Long downhill or cross-green putts are very difficult to get close to the hole because of the slope and speed of the greens.

Taking the conservative route should result in a relatively easy par, but don't forget it is still 575 yards from tee to green. The golfer needs a solid tee shot, a long iron for position within 100 yards, and then a lofted approach over water to a green that slopes from back to front.

Now that you have played the hole, try to forget The Gambler and enjoy some more golfing beauties.

Cox recommends the 14th, a four par that on the left features trees and a large waste

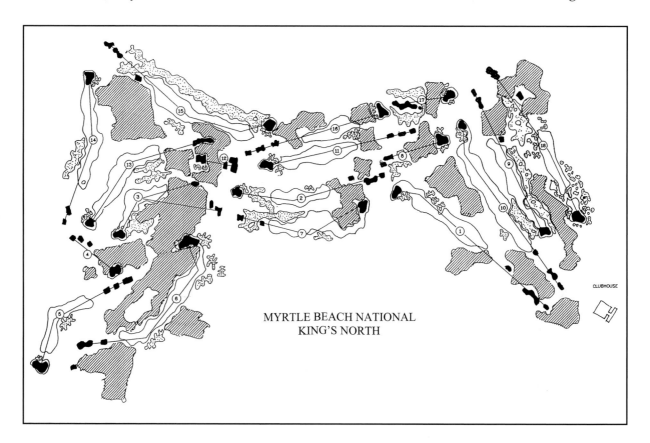

MYRTLE BEACH NATIONAL
KING'S NORTH

Shaped like a boomerang, this 10th hole at Southcreek invites you to be daring and reduce distance by going across the lake. However, your shot had better be accurate, and being a long-ball hitter would help. (Courtesy Brandon Advertising/Michael Slear)

area placed to keep most balls out of that forest. Hit your tee shot to the middle or right side, setting up a middle-to-short iron to an undulating green that slopes from the left rear to right front. The hole features water, a large pond that juts into the rough on the right side starting at approximately 125 yards from the green, but it should not

come into play. Your best chance of making par or better is to keep your approach shot below the hole.

The 16th is a beautiful hole with trees, sand, and water interrupting the fairway. The water comes in the shape of a big pond that completely fronts the green, backed up by a pair of traps. Club selection for the second shot is

A longtime favorite of Grand Strand golfers, the tough three-par 18th on the West course is scenic and has plenty of water. (Courtesy Brandon Advertising/Michael Slear)

critical to position the ball on a small green, and if you're too long with that approach, a pitch shot from the mounds behind the putting surface requires a very delicate touch in order to keep the ball close to the pin.

The other signature hole at King's North is the 18th, the hole that features the incredible set of forty-two sand traps! The left side of #18 must be avoided to have a chance for a reasonable score on this very long par four. The ideal tee shot is down the left side of the fairway, but if you hook or pull your tee shot, one of those many bunkers will certainly catch any shot hit into the rough.

A second shot, played from the left side of the fairway, will allow a ball to be bounced onto this very large green, but a second shot from the right must be carried over a small pond and a bunker that protects the right front of the green.

Short irons to this green are rare. Most players will be hitting long irons or fairway woods to reach the hole in two. Bunkers of every description lie on the left of the green and behind it, and water on the right will catch any stray shots. The green slopes, and the undulations are everywhere.

Forget pin location. Aim for the middle of the green. There is just too much trouble around this green to finesse a shot close to the hole. If you can make par on this one, you will walk away with a well-deserved smile on your face!

King's North has been named by the Golf Course Owners Association as the best course in South Carolina. Golf writers of the world played this course on their way to the Masters in 1996 and had nothing but positive comments. It is pretty. It is hard. It is expensive. It is worth playing.

Southcreek

The golfer who has not played this fine Myrtle Beach National layout since 1990 will have difficulty recognizing it because the Southcreek course was closed that summer and completely redesigned. Operators of Myrtle Beach National, determined to bring the course into the twentieth century, rerouted several fairways, rebuilt the greens, and added a lot more bunkers, sand, and mounds.

Southcreek winds its way through residential areas and becomes quite a challenge, one demanding accuracy. "No question about it," said Jerry Cox, veteran golf director. "You have to hit it straight if you're going to score on this course. However, most people find Southcreek a very enjoyable golfing experience."

Mike Hurdzan, who has designed more than 150 courses in North America and Asia and has renovated more than 200 other courses here and in Europe, was given the assignment to rebuild Southcreek. Hurdzan left one thing intact: the putting surface of the greens. One of the first courses on the Grand Strand to use bent grass, Southcreek has always been noted for its fine greens, which to this day remain in excellent condition.

All eighteen holes were changed, and flat fairways here are a thing of the past. When he began the remodeling project, it was the first complete redesign among the area's seventy courses.

Number 13 is an exciting island hole that is surrounded by sand. Likewise at #9, the vast amount of sand in the waste bunker there must be seen to be believed. Kick-wall bunkers come into play on holes #6, #17, and #18. You'll find another twist at #17: the tee, not the green, is placed on an island.

The 10th is the most exciting and memorable hole at Southcreek. It doglegs around a big pond, daring the long hitter to go for it on the second shot. Of course, this means cutting the dogleg by going over some very big water. Most golfers play it safe, going around the water to leave a third shot of 110 to 150 yards to the pin.

In short, Southcreek's renovations are a great example of making something new out of something that has been around for a while. And the improvement is very, very good, indeed.

The West Course

While the West course certainly is not easy, it is fun to play and is more open than the other two courses at this facility. The layout is good for high-handicap golfers because the fairways are wide, the greens are big, and there are no "out of bounds" except on the three holes that border the neighboring Wild Wing Plantation.

This is a "user friendly" layout, and on a good windless day all of the par-five holes can be reached in two shots. Because these par fives do not penalize the big hitter, you can take out the driver and "let her rip."

If a designer elects to make his par fives reachable in two and the course runs 6,900 yards in length, it is obvious that the other holes must be longer than usual. That's exactly what happened to the par fours at the West course.

Holes #14 and #15, often called the

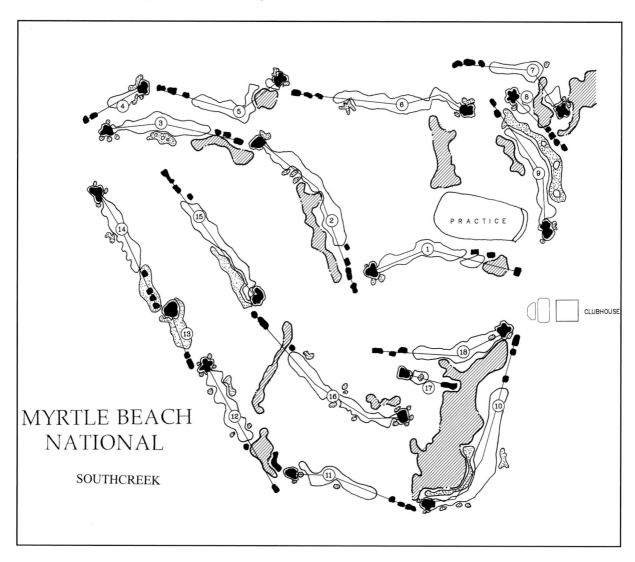

MYRTLE BEACH
NATIONAL

SOUTHCREEK

"essence of the West," are both long par-four holes with water hazards and big greens. As part of the renovations, these greens were converted from Bermuda to bent grass, and the putting-surface sizes were increased as well. Undulations were not changed, but bigger greens made three putts more probable.

Adjacent to Wild Wing, #14 is a severe dogleg left and one of the three holes where out-of-bounds can come into play. The 15th hole really is a straightaway hole, but it plays like a dogleg because of the vast expanse of water on the left. Both of these holes are approximately 420 yards long and rate as two of the three most difficult holes on the back nine. (Number 11, another par four, falls into the same category.)

The finishing hole is spectacular and difficult. It is a three par that demands an awesome 240-yard carry over water.

With these descriptions, don't be fooled into thinking all of the difficulty is on the back side. While #6 is ranked only eleventh in difficulty, some players believe this hole is the toughest of them all. This par five has length (533 yards from the blue tee box), a sloping green that sits below the level of the fairway and is difficult to put on, a trap guarding the left front, and a pond behind the green.

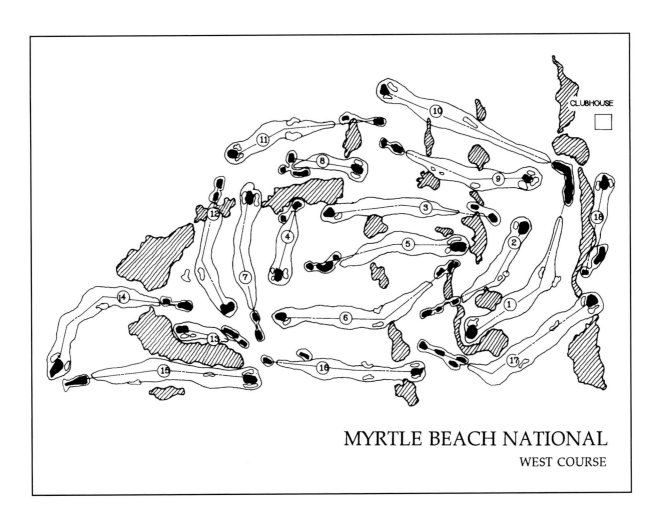

MYRTLE BEACH NATIONAL
WEST COURSE

King's North

HOLE NUMBER	1	2	3	4	5	6	7	8	9	OUT	10	11	12	13	14	15	16	17	18	IN	TOT	HCP	NET
BLACK	502	409	365	180	347	568	423	190	465	3449	517	470	140	407	433	567	410	160	464	3568	7017		
GOLD	483	390	342	130	318	525	377	178	409	3152	504	418	129	396	407	497	397	136	395	3279	6431		
WHITE	459	371	319	107	301	497	357	159	382	2952	481	389	110	379	384	487	370	119	367	3086	6038		
BLUE	437	360	266	97	287	484	342	139	350	2762	461	372	98	363	368	473	347	103	355	2572	5334		
RED	363	310	197	82	267	430	286	107	252	2294	369	334	81	327	391	426	304	85	305	2522	4816		
HANDICAP	4	12	14	18	10	2	8	16	6		3	11	17	13	9	1	7	15	5				
PAR	5	4	4	3	4	5	4	3	4	36	5	4	3	4	4	5	4	3	4	36	72		

Southcreek

HOLE NUMBER	1	2	3	4	5	6	7	8	9	OUT	10	11	12	13	14	15	16	17	18	IN	TOT	HCP	NET
BLUE	421	501	364	165	355	475	335	202	390	3208	523	348	396	166	343	393	507	143	380	3208	6416		
WHITE	382	471	350	149	341	448	325	183	376	3025	525	339	360	154	324	379	490	130	363	3064	6089		
GOLD	362	425	320	133	321	420	310	167	360	2818	503	328	333	139	303	364	458	117	347	2892	5710		
RED	316	365	282	118	248	318	270	154	285	2356	415	275	244	127	246	301	276	103	280	2367	4723		
HANDICAP	3	7	11	17	13	5	15	9	1		4	14	6	16	12	2	8	18	10				
PAR	4	5	4	3	4	5	4	3	4	36	5	4	4	3	4	4	5	3	4	36	72		

West Course

HOLE NUMBER	1	2	3	4	5	6	7	8	9	OUT	10	11	12	13	14	15	16	17	18	IN	TOT	HCP	NET
BLUE	501	360	430	183	421	533	385	194	413	3420	512	422	374	167	419	426	414	491	221	3446	6866		
WHITE	453	302	352	153	393	482	365	156	374	3030	465	384	338	137	361	387	380	466	165	3083	6113		
RED	400	250	321	111	342	416	348	114	323	2625	453	372	244	115	283	344	334	393	144	2682	5307		
HANDICAP	15	17	1	13	3	11	7	9	5		18	4	12	16	6	2	8	14	10				
PAR	5	4	4	3	4	5	4	3	4	36	5	4	4	3	4	4	4	5	3	36	72		

BURNING RIDGE

Highway 501   P.O. Box 3378   Myrtle Beach, SC 29578
(843) 347-0538

Architect: Gene Hamm   Year opened: 1980

Course rating/Slope rating:

EAST
Blue - 72.8/126   Gold - 67.5/113
White - 69.7/124   Red - 65.4/111

WEST
Blue - 71.1/121   White - 69.4/114
Red - 66.5/118

Burning Ridge, a thirty-six-hole championship layout just off Highway 501 between Conway and Myrtle Beach, is a key element of the golfing conglomerate known as "The Links." Burning Ridge joins Sea Gull, Indigo Creek, Indian Wells, the Tradition Club, Quail Creek, Cypress Bay, Island Green, and Colonial Charters in arranging tee times at their highly respected Strand courses using a centralized electronic reservation system.

Burning Ridge is an excellent place to play golf—two eighteen-hole courses, equally demanding, but each as different from the other as night and day.

The West course, opened in 1980, is tight, framed with pines and cypress, and fraught with water perils. The East, opened in 1987, doesn't have as much water, but it does have more sand, smaller greens, and an "Amen Corner" all its own on the back side, featuring three very hard holes.

Greens on both courses are Bermuda, and the West course features some monster-sized putting surfaces, some as much as 60 yards deep.

These courses can be fearsome or friendly, depending on where you want to tee it up. At 4,800 yards from the red markers, the West course can be considered especially friendly to the ladies.

While the five pars are outstanding, golfers on both courses may well go home talking about a signature three par on either course. Number 10 on the West course is 170 yards over water to a narrow green guarded by traps on the right and to the rear. Number 12 on the East course is frightening—247 yards from the back tees with water in front, to the right of, and beyond the green. A tall sentinel pine guards the green on the left and, if you miss the pine, a trap is waiting to grab your tee shot.

East Course

Number 12 is the third in the designated "Amen Corner," a stretch of golf that begins with two very long par fours, both more than 400 yards in length, and if the golfer can match par on these three holes, the chances of a good score are excellent. Many people consider #10, #11, and #12 the key holes on this Gene Hamm-designed course.

They definitely are not birdie holes, but the opportunity to make a subpar score exists on several holes, especially the five-par 15th, which a long hitter can reach in two. Most can forget about reaching #10, #11, #12, and #17 with two shots.

The front side is almost 300 yards shorter than the back, but golfers won't believe it when they play #1, a 571-yard par five with water stretching across the fairway in

Water, water everywhere on the left of the front nine at Burning Ridge West . . . thirty-six holes. (Courtesy Brandon Advertising/Michael Slear)

front of the green. Par here is a good score. There are many good holes, but #2, #4, and #8, while tricky, are only 300 yards in length, and good golfers often will find a wedge in their hands for the second shot.

Nine is a good, tight finishing hole with out-of-bounds markers coming into play both left and right.

The East course winds through an impressive residential development known as "The Commons," which is smack-dab in the middle of the golf course.

It is a challenging golf course, but an accurate player can post good numbers. The course record is 63.

West Course

A mature golf course, this is one that keeps improving with modern innovations.

What a terrific start! Number 1 is 448 yards and rarely fields a birdie. The golfer needs a big drive and must miss a trap on the right side of the fairway. It is a dogleg left with water on the left. There is not much letup on #2 either, as a lake in front of the green prevents golfers from reaching this par five in two shots. The hole is beau-tifully framed with pines, and because of the lake, the third shot usually is a full wedge to a well-bunkered hole. The first four holes are very difficult, but then the golfer can regain some lost strokes, especially on the short par-four 5th and the par-five 8th, which can be reached with two well-placed shots.

The designer took full advantage of water on the front side; therefore the first four holes go straight out with water on the left. As the golfer turns back toward the club-house, he finds those same water hazards still on his left!

Course record on the West course is 64.

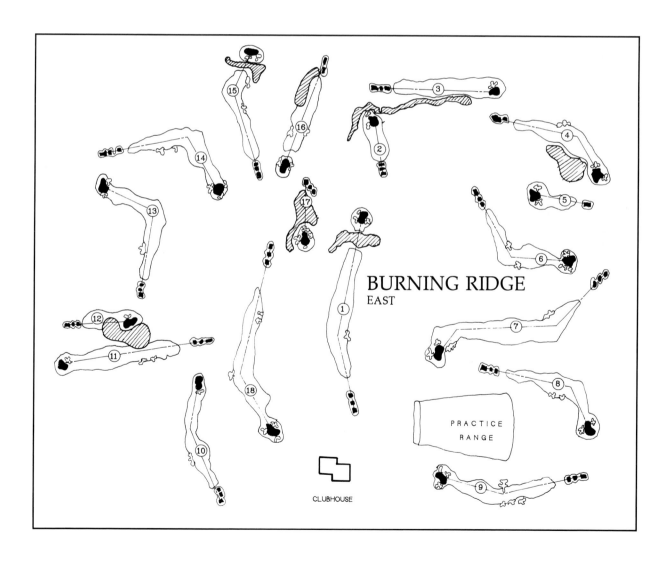

BURNING RIDGE
EAST

PRACTICE RANGE

CLUBHOUSE

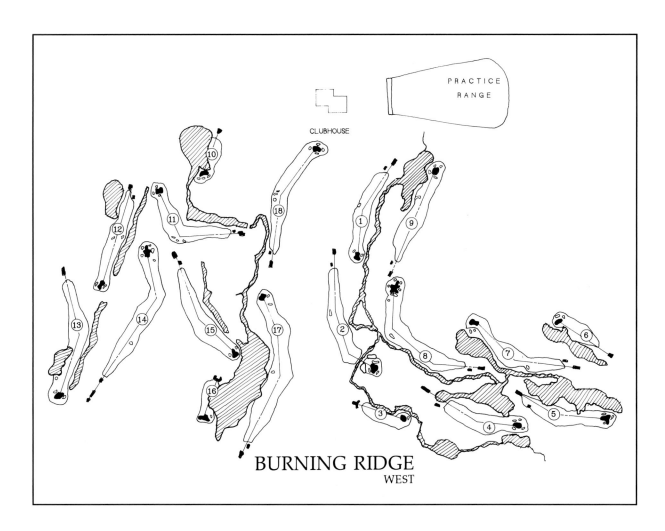

BURNING RIDGE
WEST

East Course

HOLE NUMBER	1	2	3	4	5	6	7	8	9	OUT	10	11	12	13	14	15	16	17	18	IN	TOT	HCP	NET
BLUE	571	185	400	355	209	343	481	352	375	3271	416	450	247	399	413	484	384	187	529	3509	6780		
WHITE	546	153	367	317	175	323	455	305	346	2987	386	427	200	371	377	457	346	164	501	3229	6216		
GOLD	522	131	352	285	165	276	432	291	316	2770	358	403	164	347	346	431	304	134	467	2954	5724		
RED	424	119	287	274	120	215	350	205	241	2235	284	285	108	279	278	330	262	72	391	2289	4524		
MEN'S HCP	1	17	5	11	15	9	3	13	7		8	2	14	12	10	6	16	18	4				
PAR	5	3	4	4	3	4	5	4	4	36	4	4	3	4	4	5	4	3	5	36	72		
LADIES' HCP	1	17	5	11	15	9	3	13	7		8	2	14	12	10	6	16	18	4				

West Course

HOLE NUMBER	1	2	3	4	5	6	7	8	9	OUT	10	11	12	13	14	15	16	17	18	IN	TOT	HCP	NET
BLUE	448	550	202	397	350	168	417	481	397	3410	173	394	382	373	606	381	150	489	356	3304	6714		
WHITE	411	528	167	375	330	149	383	449	372	3164	142	372	359	343	577	361	134	455	330	3073	6237		
RED	300	403	123	291	263	105	311	387	280	2463	112	255	266	327	425	277	121	359	226	2368	4831		
MEN'S HCP	7	3	15	1	13	17	9	5	11		16	6	12	14	2	10	18	4	8				
PAR	4	5	3	4	4	3	4	5	4	36	3	4	4	4	5	4	3	5	4	36	72		
LADIES' HCP	7	3	15	5	13	17	9	1	11		16	8	10	6	2	14	18	4	12				

QUAIL CREEK

Highway 501 West   P.O. Box 2940   Myrtle Beach, SC 29578
(843) 448-7906

Architect: Gene Hamm   Year opened: 1968

Course rating/Slope rating:
Blue - 72.8/119   Gold - 70.4/114
White - 70.3/116   Red - 70.2/112

Wide fairways and huge greens characterize Quail Creek, which is exactly the type of course Gene Hamm was asked to design in 1967 as golf was beginning to flourish on the Grand Strand.

Located just off Highway 501 between Conway and Myrtle Beach, Quail Creek is long and challenging, but the big, wide-open fairways and greens help speed up play.

Construction started at Quail Creek in 1967, and the Gene Hamm design was opened the following year, almost simultaneously with Seagull. It was the eighth course to be opened on the Strand, and ages very well. The very playable course is always in good condition, and you won't lose many balls.

Don't make the mistake of thinking that Quail Creek is easy because it certainly isn't. For more than twenty years some of the best amateur golfers in Myrtle Beach have taken a shot at this course when they come together for the Myrtle Beach Amateur, and only once has a golfer playing in this tournament shot under 70 from the blue tees! It is a long course played from the blues, stretching almost 7,000 yards.

Playing Quail Creek for the first time, golfers are not apt to remember any one hole as much as they are to remember the overall excellence of the course. Number 2 and #6 deserve some attention, however. The five pars are especially good, but none of them are really birdie holes. These holes usually require three shots, even for longer hitters.

Golfers go home talking about #2, a sharp dogleg to the right. This is a relatively short hole, but the tee shot needs enough length to clear a lake while stopping short of trees and rough. From the landing area, it is an uphill shot to a well-guarded green.

Number 6 is a difficult par five, memorable because of a tree posted in the middle of the fairway.

Except for #10, an iron shot across water, the three pars are much longer than the norm, and most golfers would be happy to make par on these holes and go ahead to the next challenge.

There is a feeling of spaciousness at Quail Creek even though some of the holes are played by driving cart paths through resi-

Quail Creek

HOLE NUMBER	1	2	3	4	5	6	7	8	9	OUT	10	11	12	13	14	15	16	17	18	IN	TOT	HCP	NET
BLUE	571	349	416	384	212	531	213	404	402	3482	156	526	440	395	380	203	499	369	362	3330	6812		
WHITE	547	323	391	351	171 145	517	175	381	382	3238 3212	137	490	412	371	348	170	474	351	340	3093	6331 6305		
GOLD	510	264	375	340	135	495	164	360	357	3000	130	475	400	360	335	165	425	340	325	2955	5955		
MEN'S HCP	13	11	9	17	5	1	15	3	7		18	14	2	4	6	16	12	8	10				
PAR	5	4	4	4	3	5	3	4	4	36	3	5	4	4	4	3	5	4	4	36	72		
RED	413	261	310	330	123	467	139	315	330	2688	122	390	313	312	270	135	413	328	316	2599	5287		
LADIES' HCP	7	9	11	5	17	1	15	3	13		14	8	6	10	12	18	2	4	16				

dential areas from green to tee. At only one point could an area be considered as having parallel fairways. Even then, between #1 and 18, there is a large stand of trees separating the fairways and most people will tell you, "It's wide open. No parallel fairways."

Number 2 at Quail Creek, a dogleg right across water. (Courtesy Brandon Advertising/ Michael Slear)

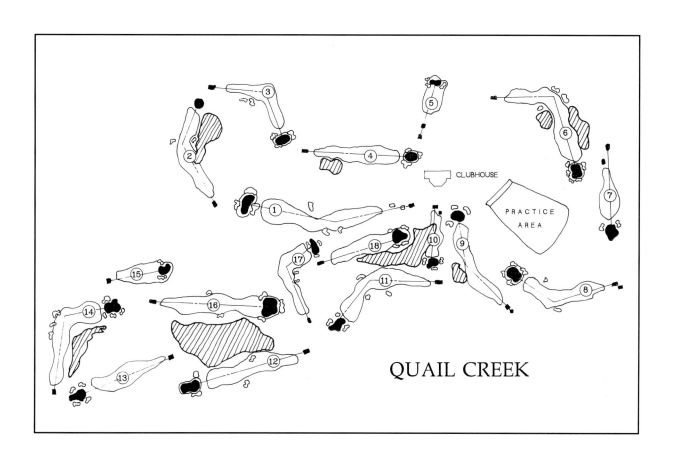

QUAIL CREEK

127

Number 14 at Wild Wing's Wood Stork, first of three courses. (Courtesy Wild Wing Plantation)

Number 5 at Wild Wing's Hummingbird, a Willard Byrd design. (Courtesy Wild Wing Plantation)

WILD WING PLANTATION

Highway 501 North   P.O. Box 647   Myrtle Beach, SC
(800) 736-WING   (843) 347-9464

Architects: Willard Byrd (Wood Stork)   Year opened: 1991
Willard Byrd (Hummingbird)   Year opened: 1992
Jeff Brauer, Larry Nelson (Avocet)   Year opened: 1993
Rees Jones (Falcon)   Year opened: 1994

Course rating/Slope rating:

WOOD STORK
Dark Teal - 74.1/130   Magenta - 71.9/123
White - 69.6/118   Teal - 70.7/121

HUMMINGBIRD
Dark Teal - 73.6/135   Magenta - 70.6/125
White - 68.5/115   Teal - 69.5/123

AVOCET
Dark Teal - 74.2/128   Magenta - 71.4/119
White - 68.5/114   Teal - 70.4/118

FALCON
Dark Teal - 74.4/134   Magenta - 72.3/128
White - 68.7/117   Teal - 70.4/118

One of the most ambitious resort projects on the Grand Strand, Wild Wing has become a destination point within a destination, to wit: Golfers come to the Grand Strand to play golf, and many of them are attracted to this area by the four great golf courses and the fine amenities of Wild Wing.

Termed a "premier golfing destination" by General Manager and Director of Golf Robert Harper, this facility has literally won dozens of awards from publications and organizations throughout America. "When Western Golf Properties, our management identity with headquarters in Scottsdale, Arizona, began this development complex in 1991, they, along with me and golf-course superintendent Dave Downing, made a commitment to bring a new definition of golf to the Myrtle Beach area.

"We have been—and will continue to be—dedicated to providing the utmost in customer service, in quality playing surfaces, and in a customer-friendly atmosphere extended by every member of our staff."

That commitment extends to a 33,000-square-foot imposing, modernistic, brick clubhouse; a superb dining room; and a large and aesthetically pleasing pro shop that offers an outstanding selection of top-quality men and women's wear and the best in golfing equipment of every nature. There's a new addition to delight the golfing enthusiast: Wild Wing, sitting on 1,050 acres of unspoiled beauty, has created a marvelous assortment of freestanding homes, golfing villas, and condominiums.

"Join the Wild Wing Migration" is the message of billboards and other advertising. Many golfers buy a second home for their own individual use and for prolonged stays at Wild Wing, while others are buying these facilities as investments, placing their properties in a rental program supervised by Wild Wing. (Similar programs at the three-course Legends and other facilities are soon to follow.)

Wild Wing has seventy-two holes of championship golf, culminating in the Falcon, a Rees Jones masterpiece that opened in 1994 and promptly was named the best new golf course in America for the year.

Like the other three (Wood Stork, Hummingbird, and Avocet), the Falcon, the fourth course to open at Wild Wing, features the best of bent-green putting surfaces, most of which were produced at Penn State University, where the golf-course superintendent learned the business.

Awards for these Wild Wing courses include a "four star" designation for Avocet to complement its selection as one of the top-ten new courses in 1994 and a designation as one of the ten best in South Carolina each year since it opened.

Larry Nelson, a touring PGA professional, designed Avocet and incorporated some of the newest features in golf-course design, such as a double green and two double fairways.

Willard Byrd was the architect of the award-winning Hummingbird and Wood Stork courses. One of the greatest names in golf-course architecture, Rees Jones, put his signature on the Falcon and calls it one of his best.

Let's look at these four courses on an individual basis:

Wood Stork

When the new strain of bent grass made its first appearance on the Grand Strand on Wood Stork, the first of the four current Wild Wing Plantation golf courses, it was the most discussed feature of this Willard Byrd design.

This new strain of bent is heat resistant, a very important feature because of the steamy summertime of the coastal area, and it is tough enough to withstand heavy traffic.

There is much more to recommend this course than exceptional greens. The Wood Stork has five separate teeing areas on each hole that provide excellent playability to various skill levels. While it measures a tough

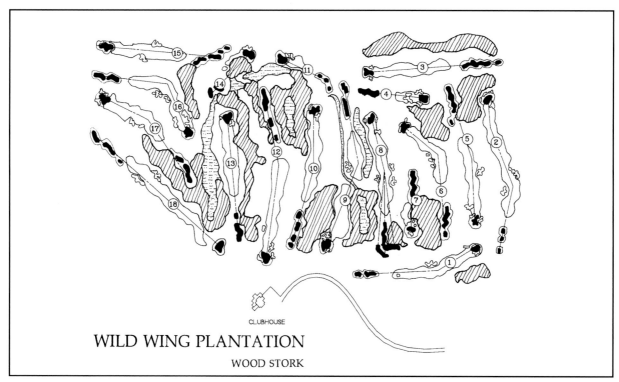

WILD WING PLANTATION
WOOD STORK

7,044 yards from the championship tees, producing a challenge for the professional and low-handicap player, the course scales down to 6,100 yards from the more traditional white tees, providing an enjoyable option and alternate routes for the high handicapper.

Tabbed as a "parkland" type of course (i.e., like Augusta National), the Wood Stork appears to offer wide-open, naturally beautiful, tree-lined fairways. That first appearance can be deceiving. There is an abundance of strategically placed water and natural wetlands that can send scores soaring.

The front nine of Wood Stork is more open than the back side, and the golfer will confront scrub pines and brush. The back is more of a forest type, with much larger trees defining the fairways.

There are some very challenging holes. Number 5, a 433-yard four par from the back, most often plays into the wind and is a good driving hole with wetlands to the left and scrub pines and tall grasses on the right. The trap on the left of the fairway serves as a good directional marker. It comes into play but is not deep, so you can use a five iron there.

Number 7, 178 yards, par three from the back, is pretty and devilish with a lot of water. The hole features a bulkhead in front of the traps to the left of the green, and the mounding is severe.

Number 10, another long par four, displays a two-tiered narrow green. Number 17 is just as long, and the green is surrounded by sand traps. Water in front of the tee and to the left is very much in play, but to get home in regulation you must play to the left, using two fairway traps as directional markers.

Hummingbird

Most golfers will find Hummingbird to be a very difficult course. There are frequent forced carries on this classic links-style course, deep bunkers, hidden traps, and lots of mounding. The course is relatively short at 6,853 yards from the championship markers, but it

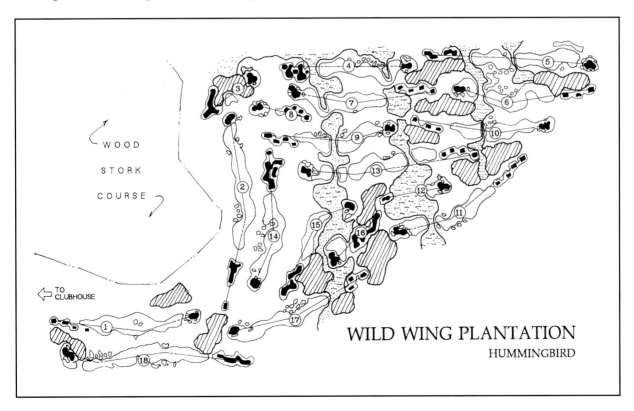

WILD WING PLANTATION
HUMMINGBIRD

Wild Wing has four outstanding courses, and this Larry Nelson design has become one of the most talked about and interesting of any Grand Strand course. Water, sand, tall mounds, trees—all have been used skillfully by Nelson. This tract of land is so large that the resort facility has added upscale golf condominiums. (Courtesy Wild Wing Plantation)

requires a lot good club selection. The golfer must be precise with the irons, and the bunkers frame the grass, set so close to the putting surface that most shots must be played "into the air"—no bump-and-run approaches.

One of the golf director's favorites at Hummingbird is the par-five 5th hole, where water crosses the fairway twice. "It sets up really nice. The first tee shot, for most, is a lay-up short of the wetland. There is wasteland to the left and a series of pot bunkers around a well-trapped, heavily mounded green," he said in describing the course.

Like most of the holes, the green at #5 is smaller than those on the original Wood Stork.

Avocet

The 7,100-yard-long Avocet is the eleventh golf course designed by Larry Nelson, who won the PGA championship in 1981 and 1987 and the U.S. Open in 1983. Most of his courses have been built in the Far East, particularly Japan, and his first design, Coral Ocean Point, opened in Saipan in 1987. One of his best-known courses in the United States is Springhouse Golf Club at Nashville's Opryland.

Perhaps none of his creations are better than Avocet, which is described as a contemporary traditional course with five holes featuring elevated tees and greens. Water comes into play on several holes, and an unusual feature is that all of the par fives and par threes orient to different points on the compass.

There is a double green that serves two holes, the 6th coming in from the east and the 17th arriving on the putting surface from the north.

WILD WING PLANTATION
AVOCET

A memorable hole is #9, which features a double fairway and is considered by many as Avocet's signature hole. Named "Valley of Sin," this hole contains many design features, most of which make the hole more difficult! A line of grass and sand pot bunkers bisects the double fairway. Depending on pin position, you may wish to place your tee shot on either fairway, both of which are a shade under 30 yards wide.

The green features no bunkers and may appear deceptively easy. However, the front left features a re-creation of the famed "Valley of Sin" at St. Andrews. Golfers who choose to hit a longer tee shot to the left fairway must come directly over this, and the penalty for coming up short or spinning back off the deck is a rather unusual putt that is seldom faced. This valley is six feet below the regular putting surface!

The 14th hole invites special consideration. "It looks so easy," said Director of Golf Robert Harper, "but there's a reason we have named it 'Double Dare.'" It offers two tee-shot options, and the safe shot—an iron off the tee and a short iron approach—should yield an easy par. However, the daring man or woman with driver in hand might be greatly tempted to try a drive over the water and the bunkers protecting the green. What an option!

Number 18, an excellent finishing hole modeled after the famed C. B. McDonald hole at MidOcean, dares the golfer to bite off as much as possible on the tee shot to shorten the length of this long (453-yard) par four. The green is two-tiered and angled toward the fairway. It is at least two clubs from front to back, so a combination of distance and direction is essential to get close to the pin. Water and a horrendous bunker (did the bulldozer operator misread the plan?) obviously are not the places to miss.

"I love the Avocet," Harper said, "because of the way it was designed so that every hole seems to lead you directly into the next. Nothing 'funky' about this one."

In many ways Avocet is a microcosm of

A 300-yard sand bunker separates #12 and #13 on Falcon, a Rees Jones creation. Visitors to this fine facility also enjoy a well-appointed, graceful restaurant and an oversized pro shop that earned Wild Wing an award as "Carolinas PGA Merchandiser of the Year." (Courtesy Wild Wing Plantation)

Wild Wing itself, offering great diversity and options.

Falcon

"These may be the best set of green complexes ever built," said designer and architect Rees Jones when asked what makes the Falcon an exceptional course. With that accolade, Jones simply meant the combination of chipping, bunker play, and the putting contours and surfaces are consistently excellent on all eighteen holes and that no other course he has seen can retain that consistency of excellence.

Another plus for the student golfer is the installation of the Pro Shot Digital Caddy, an electronic yardage and course information system that is mounted on the golf carts used on the Falcon. This new tool gives the golfer instant, specific information such as

putting-green and fairway slopes, distances to greens and hazards, and even playing tips from the course professional. An increasing number of Strand courses are embracing this computerized caddy.

The 5th hole on the Falcon is a member of the "Dream Eighteen" selected by a panel of golfing experts for the Myrtle Beach *Sun News,* and the golfer is cautioned to play both #5 and #18 with care because most of the time both of these long holes play directly into the wind.

Number 5 is called "Big Cape," and the challenging tee shot provides a great opportunity to shorten this par five by carrying as much of the lake as possible. Trying to reach the green with two shots requires another well-played and accurate shot. A combination grass-and-sand feature protects the right of the green, and the lake is tight to the

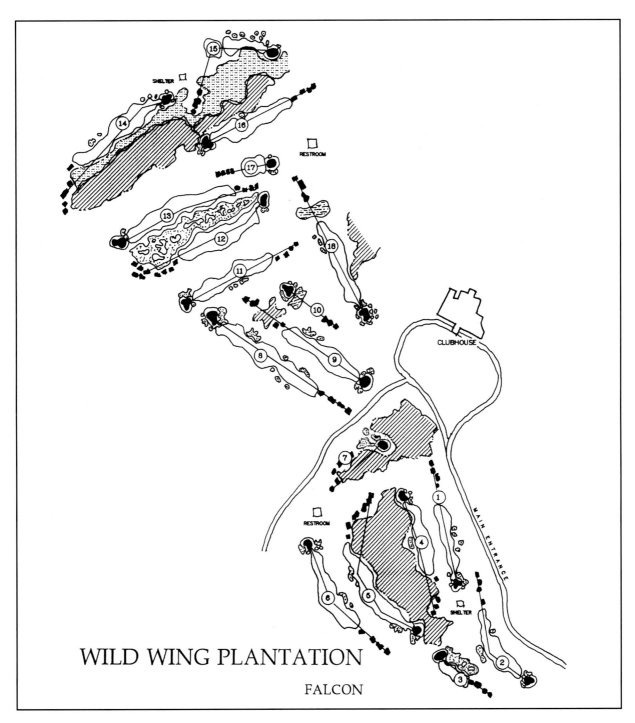

WILD WING PLANTATION

FALCON

green on the left. This hole offers great flexibility and numerous shot options.

Appropriately named the "Falcon's Nest," #18 has become known as one of the strongest finishing holes in the area. Because the hole measures 471 yards, two very strong and accurate shots must be played to reach the green, which is surrounded by thirteen deep oval bunkers carved into an amphitheater-framing berm. The putting surface is contoured into well-defined pin positions that necessitate a long second shot being played to the appropriate area if the golfer hopes to finish the round with a par.

Wood Stork

HOLE NUMBER	1	2	3	4	5	6	7	8	9	OUT	10	11	12	13	14	15	16	17	18	IN	TOT	HCP	NET
DARK TEAL	412	540	431	196	433	394	178	436	524	3544	444	178	512	383	187	398	407	422	549	3500	7044		
MAGENTA	384	513	410	187	401	370	158	409	503	3335	418	162	489	361	170	380	381	393	509	3263	6598		
WHITE	359	476	382	161	376	336	143	371	469	3073	393	139	455	338	149	347	364	367	482	3033	6106		
HANDICAP	13	7	9	11	3	17	15	1	5		2	18	10	16	6	14	12	4	8				
PAR	4	5	4	3	4	4	3	4	5	36	4	3	5	4	3	4	4	4	5	36	72		
TEAL	265	430	355	143	315	310	112	346	425	2701	357	127	399	317	98	319	339	329	423	2708	5409		
TEAL HCP	15	5	3	9	11	13	17	7	1		4	16	10	12	14	18	6	8	2				

Hummingbird

HOLE NUMBER	1	2	3	4	5	6	7	8	9	OUT	10	11	12	13	14	15	16	17	18	IN	TOT	HCP	NET
DARK TEAL	404	542	184	384	528	416	423	154	402	3437	399	449	183	515	389	346	206	420	509	3416	6853		
MAGENTA	371	508	158	353	498	385	394	142	354	3163	356	429	166	478	356	317	180	377	488	3147	6310		
WHITE	346	478	134	320	473	348	362	113	327	2901	325	388	136	442	329	301	148	366	460	2895	5796		
HANDICAP	13	5	11	15	7	3	1	17	9		12	2	14	4	16	18	10	6	8				
PAR	4	5	3	4	5	4	4	3	4	36	4	4	3	5	4	4	3	4	5	36	72		
TEAL	313	425	76	286	442	307	324	86	298	2557	295	327	110	409	291	272	131	340	436	2611	5168		
TEAL HCP	11	3	13	15	1	7	5	17	9		10	8	12	4	14	18	16	6	2				

Avocet

HOLE NUMBER	1	2	3	4	5	6	7	8	9	OUT	10	11	12	13	14	15	16	17	18	IN	TOT	HCP	NET
DARK TEAL	402	422	477	551	183	462	576	176	362	3611	433	510	227	400	308	519	470	196	453	3516	7127		
MAGENTA	380	370	424	526	157	451	553	164	323	3348	398	485	207	364	283	476	446	181	426	3266	6614		
WHITE	348	327	399	501	119	393	494	145	299	3025	375	454	166	344	265	449	418	151	381	3003	6028		
HANDICAP	9	17	3	5	11	1	7	15	13		12	6	8	16	18	10	2	14	4				
PAR	4	4	4	5	3	4	5	3	4	36	4	5	3	4	4	5	4	3	4	36	72		
TEAL	321	277	373	466	100	346	452	96	218	2649	335	414	130	287	221	429	347	143	343	2649	5298		
TEAL HCP	9	17	3	1	11	7	5	15	13		12	6	16	14	18	4	2	8	10				

Falcon

HOLE NUMBER	1	2	3	4	5	6	7	8	9	OUT	10	11	12	13	14	15	16	17	18	IN	TOT	HCP	NET
DARK TEAL	364	414	195	385	525	448	230	537	469	3567	205	380	521	440	560	368	405	165	471	3515	7082		
MAGENTA	343	390	171	365	508	425	211	518	443	3374	180	360	500	430	540	343	380	145	445	3323	6697		
WHITE	313	365	140	349	478	390	142	490	355	3022	150	331	471	385	530	312	353	123	412	3067	6089		
HANDICAP	17	11	15	9	1	5	7	13	3		12	16	10	6	4	14	8	18	2				
PAR	4	4	3	4	5	4	3	5	4	36	3	4	5	4	5	4	4	3	4	36	72		
TEAL	273	322	105	299	406	347	100	449	318	2619	75	298	409	354	436	245	309	112	333	2571	5190		
TEAL HCP	17	9	15	7	5	3	13	1	11		18	14	10	4	2	12	8	16	6				

THE WIZARD AND MAN O' WAR AT CAROLINA FOREST

Two sister courses designed by noted golf architect Dan Maples, The Wizard and Man O' War, located in Carolina Forest just off Highway 501, are widely acclaimed as among the very best new golf courses in the Myrtle Beach area.

The Wizard is located on Highway 501 between Myrtle Beach and Conway, while Man O' War is in Carolina Forest off Highway 501 between Myrtle Beach and Conway. Both are spectacular, not only the links themselves but the surrounding scenery and unusual clubhouses.

THE WIZARD

4601 Leeshire Boulevard   Myrtle Beach, SC 29577
(843) 236-9393

Architect: Dan Maples   Year opened: 1995

Course rating/Slope rating:
Championship - 71.9/128   Regular - 70.1/122
Senior - 67.0/114   Ladies - 70.2/119

Serving as clubhouse for The Wizard is a structure that at first glance reminded this author of a scene from the movie *Lives of a Bengal Lancer.* The sandstone building rises out of the landscape with towers and gables, and a simulated wear and tear displays stones beneath the sandstone. However, you might be as surprised as I was to learn that this architecture is not Moroccan; rather, it has been lifted from a fort in Ireland. "It's a burnt-out Irish fort," explains co-owner Richard Lee, a former PGA Tour player.

"When I play the Wizard—and I play it often—I get the feeling that I'm playing one of the classic courses in Ireland," said Rudy Gatlin, a professional entertainer and one third of the famous Gatlin Brothers Trio, which entertains large audiences more than 100 times each year in their own Gatlin Brothers Theatre in Myrtle Beach. "The stone-castle clubhouse looks like it might have been home to an ancient Celtic wizard.

"As entertainers we've had the privilege of traveling and playing good golf around the world. But the place we choose to call home is Myrtle Beach, and one of the reasons we love it here so much is that it's the home of some of America's best golf. Not only is The Wizard one of Myrtle Beach's finest and most interesting courses, but we think it ranks with some of our country's best layouts."

It took a lot of work and imagination for Maples to create this course. About 1.5 million cubic yards of earth were moved to form The Wizard's intriguing landscapes, and the plantings on the berms and mounds include more than 800 species of plants, flowers, and ornamental grasses. The frequent mounds serve as beautiful frames for many of the holes.

The 1st hole offers a spectacular beginning and an opportunity for the long hitter to begin his round with a birdie. The fairway doglegs right around a massive lake, and the bent-grass green is 560 yards from the tee

The Wizard is the sister course to Man O' War. You'll often find the Gatlin Brothers, nationally famous entertainers who have made Myrtle Beach home, playing one of these challenging Dan Maples courses that are embellished with wide-open spaces, huge mounds, Oriental grasses, water, and sand. (Courtesy Himmelsbach Communications/Bill Woodward)

box, but the adventuresome player can "take something off" by going across a portion of the water hazard, especially when the wind is favorable, as it most often tends to be.

Like most of the others, this green is huge, and the G2 strain is the same selected by Pinehurst #2 for the 1999 U.S. Open.

Number 1 is the favorite hole of Rudy Gatlin, who once was featured in the title role of the Broadway musical *Will Rogers Follies*. "Hole #1 lies along the west side of the lake, with water bordering the length of the fairway. The wind always seems to be a factor out there. If it's favorable, I can reach it in two (don't forget that Rudy plays near scratch and hits long), but if I have to shoot against the wind, it'll take me three. My advice is to play to the left to avoid that pair of bunkers at 272 yards. The green is nice and large, but be careful of the bunker that guards it on the left side."

After some strategic planning on the par-

three second hole, which slopes severely from rear to front, the golfer is confronted with a different challenge at #3 when he first glimpses one of those European-styled *burns* (Americans call them "creeks") that slice through the fairway about 100 yards in front of the green.

Architect Maples again makes this hazard more attractive (but no less dangerous) by installing the banks with riprap (white stones).

The front nine is a good test of golf, but in the opinion of many professionals the back side is more difficult. It is a par 36, while the front side is scaled at par 35. A meandering burn bisects both the 11th- and 14th-hole fairways, and #17 and #18 are consecutive island holes.

"Hole #17 is my favorite," Steve Gatlin said. "When playing The Wizard for the first time, you never know what to expect next, and #17 is no exception. After more than a dozen holes of moving up, down, and around the mounds and hills, this 180-yard par-three brings you back out onto the lake with an island green. Not only does it require a careful shot but also a careful choice of clubs. I've used anywhere from a seven iron to a one, depending on the wind conditions. An awesome hole."

So is the finishing hole: There are two islands on this one! First the fairway and a small expanse of rough are separated from the tee box by a finger of the lake, and then the second shot requires a long play to an island green protected by not only water but also bunkers on both sides.

Larry Gatlin, the headliner of the trio, has a good summation of The Wizard as well as

his own favorite hole. "If you ever thought that golf courses at the Beach lacked elevation changes, wait until you play The Wizard. Dan Maples created a landscape that will remind you of the mountains. Take hole #13, for example. It's a 408-yard par four that plays through a valley surrounded by towering mounds covered with all kinds of flowers, shrubs, and lovegrass. That lovegrass is beautiful, but it's a beast if you get caught in it. The slight dogleg right of the layout is perfect for my left-to-right shot. The second shot is onto a large, undulating green guarded by two bunkers in the front. Shooting par on #13 is a satisfying experience."

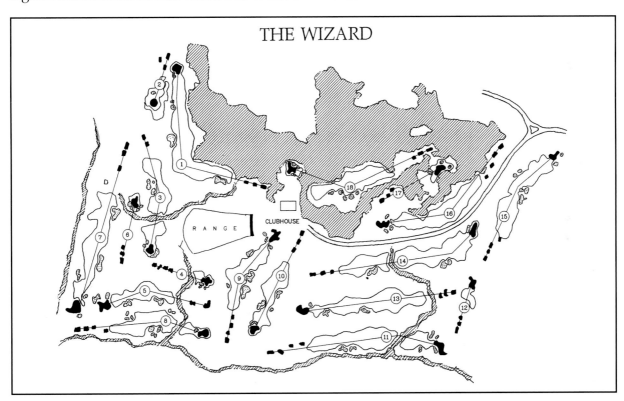

The Wizard

HOLE NUMBER	1	2	3	4	5	6	7	8	9	OUT	10	11	12	13	14	15	16	17	18	IN	TOT	HCP	NET
CHAMPIONSHIP	569	186	405	181	398	208	568	414	392	3321	367	510	167	408	518	405	424	180	421	3400	6721		
REGULAR	534	147	379	149	364	173	534	376	356	3012	338	479	138	372	485	369	396	155	394	3126	6138		
SENIOR	486	128	332	126	342	143	498	335	324	2714	312	442	113	343	458	330	339	138	358	2833	5547		
HANDICAP	1	15	7	17	9	13	3	5	11		14	4	18	10	2	12	6	16	8				
PAR	5	3	4	3	4	3	5	4	4	35	4	5	3	4	5	4	4	3	4	36	71		
LADIES	440	106	300	104	310	123	447	307	287	2424	297	409	94	301	432	296	319	116	284	2548	4972		

One of two course located within the Carolina Forest, Man O' War was developed by former PGA players Richard Lee and Claude Pardue. The spectacular course was created from the depths of a 110-acre lake. (Courtesy Brandon Advertising/Michael Slear)

MAN O' WAR

5601 Leeshire Boulevard   Myrtle Beach, SC 29579
(843) 236-8000

Architect: Dan Maples   Year opened: 1995

Course rating/Slope rating:
Championship - 72.4/130   Regular - 69.5/120
Senior - 67.0/108   Ladies - 71.2/114

The demanding Man O' War golf course is beautifully situated within Carolina Forest and is adjacent to The Wizard. Both are championship courses, and both are designed by Dan Maples. The similarities end there!

Because this course was created from the depths of a 110-acre lake, water is the inescapable element here, your constant companion as you travel from the first tee to the final hole. Don't forget the lake is there—never underestimate it. The water can change from ally to enemy, its sparkling beauty quickly becoming a punishing hazard.

Despite the abundance of water hazards, Man O' War is a uniquely fair playing field (there are four sets of tees), and Maples' own clever strategy of interweaving holes that call for different skills has created a course that rewards golfers of all proficiencies.

After playing this course, many players keep talking about the water hazards, but equally memorable are the back-to-back island greens and an awesome island 9th that is probably is the signature hole of Man O' War.

The entire 9th hole is an island! Bunkers on the left may or may not keep your golf ball dry, but the right side of the fairway is treacherous, too. A berm runs completely down the right side, fronted by two large, grassy mounds designed for beauty and for helping you keep the ball out of that narrow berm or the wide-open lake beyond. After paralleling the fairway for 150 yards, this berm makes a sharp left turn 100 yards in front of the green and completely bisects the fairway. Do you lay up with your second shot or go for the green?

Complicating the equation is the simple fact that the wind has free rein over the wide-open spaces and usually is right in your face. Getting home in three and making a bogey isn't all that bad on #9.

If #9 is difficult, the other homeward-bound hole (#18) is of a more friendly disposition. The lake juts from the left entirely across the fairway, but a big tee shot will put many into position to reach the green. The hole measures 460 yards from the regular tees, and there is plenty of room between the green and that lake in the middle of the fairway. Even a lay-up with your second shot means that you can get home from 160 yards. Golfers have enjoyed many birdies on this hole, which is a good way to complete your round at Man O' War.

Numbers 14 and 15, the back-to-back island greens, are jewels. The 14th hole is a par four, but its tees are designed to let most players get within 100 yards of the island green. The 15th hole is more difficult even though it is a par-three hole. Because there's not much fringe around this one, hit the green or you will find a "watery grave."

In summation, Man O' War rises from a 110-acre lake, and the spectacular course is built through and around that crystal blue lake. The greens are bent grass of the Crenshaw variety, an excellent putting surface. The greens are both fast and huge, and placement of pins can mean the difference of about three clubs' length.

Spacious, large landing areas and friendly placement of tee boxes make Man O' War a golf course that can yield good scores despite all the water that can come into play on every one of its eighteen holes.

Because there are no hidden hazards (even the berms and traps are in clear view) and because it is so wide open, the water does not tend to intimidate most golfers. Man O' War is a fine course and an enjoyable outing.

The marketing-conscious owners of Man O' War and The Wizard extend the ambiance of their golf courses in the clubhouses. Where The Wizard's clubhouse conjures up Old World, leather-chaired luxury and drafts of Ireland, Man O' War's clubhouse

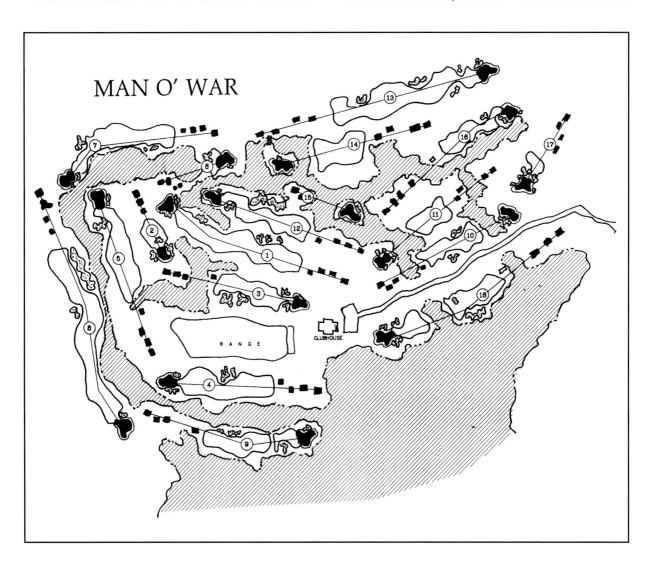

MAN O' WAR

has elected to capture the presence of the water that dominates its course. The clubhouse is actually built over water and comes across with a more casual atmosphere.

They have touched upon the fish-camp-type restaurant. It is very comfortable, pleasing, and with water all around, very restful.

Man O' War

HOLE NUMBER	1	2	3	4	5	6	7	8	9	OUT	10	11	12	13	14	15	16	17	18	IN	TOT	HCP	NET
CHAMPIONSHIP	539	189	400	393	445	189	380	593	433	3561	403	372	423	591	382	173	367	201	494	3406	6967		
REGULAR	503	153	365	376	417	155	354	558	408	3289	374	347	395	547	354	126	329	173	468	3113	6402		
SENIOR	469	121	333	332	376	130	325	503	383	2972	336	286	367	498	302	87	308	131	442	2757	5769		
HANDICAP	3	17	9	11	5	15	13	1	7		8	12	6	2	10	18	14	16	4				
PAR	5	3	4	4	4	3	4	5	4	36	4	4	4	5	4	3	4	3	5	36	72		
LADIES	436	100	257	304	299	113	305	463	336	2613	275	265	329	464	266	70	219	104	360	2352	4965		

An aerial view shows the spectacular beauty of Arrowhead, a twenty-seven hole layout. The course, designed by Tom Jackson and signed by PGA legend Raymond Floyd, flows through gorgeous scenery all the way to the Intracoastal Waterway. (Courtesy Brandon Advertising/Michael Slear)

ARROWHEAD

1201 Burcale Road   Myrtle Beach, SC 29577
(800) 236-3243   (843) 236-3243

Architect: Tom Jackson   Year opened: 1994
"A Raymond Floyd signature course"

Course rating/Slope rating:

Lake/Cypress	Cypress/Waterway	Lakes/Waterway
Blue - 71.4/136	Blue - 71.4/134	Blue - 71.4/132
White - 69.2/124	White - 69.3/123	White - 69.4/122
Green - 67.8/107	Green - 66.3/108	Green - 66.8/109
Red - 71.2/116	Red - 70.9/121	Red - 70.7/118

Just as the statistical data suggests, the three nine-hole courses at Arrowhead are almost equal in degree of difficulty. What the data does not reveal to you is the beauty of this course, which features water on twenty-four of the twenty-seven holes and a vast amount of waste areas.

If the word "versatile" can be applied to a golf course, that word certainly fits Arrowhead, which was designed by South Carolina architect Tom Jackson and signed by the popular Senior PGA professional Raymond Floyd, who has had great his success on both the senior and regular tours. Of his signature courses, Floyd, who has won the Masters twice, the PGA, and the British Open, speaks of only two. In conversation he will tell you how much he likes the results of his input at Doral and the subtle nuances he has built into this Grand Strand course, Arrowhead.

Arrowhead's location is superb. Just off Highway 501, one mile west of Waccamaw Pottery, it is the closest championship course to downtown Myrtle Beach and its exploding motel-hotel facilities. The course, extending to the Intracoastal Waterway, supplies some terrific views and good tests of golf.

Customers love Arrowhead, not only the golf course and the beautiful natural surroundings but the clubhouse as well. The principal owners of Arrowhead have a Western background that quickly is evident. The huge mounted buffalo head and the gracefully carved Indian brave in prayer that grace the foyer speak to that love of the Old West, and the artifacts serve as fitting tribute to the name of this course.

Most golfers tend to appreciate golf courses more than stylish settings and excellent snack bars faithfully attended by pretty Southern girls named Debbie, and the Arrowhead course offers much that you can appreciate.

"For one thing," said Eddie Dennis, head professional since Arrowhead opened, "it is challenging from all four sets of tees; the water is lateral with very few forced carries; and the elevation changes are there, but very gradual. You will find yourself with both uphill and downhill shots—and the need to know how to hit them."

Arrowhead is a gently rolling golf course, much like those you find in the foothills of Carolina, and the drainage is so outstanding that Arrowhead is playable even after heavy rains. The lakes are interconnected, and the water eventually flows into the Waterway. "We're very conscious of the environment and don't even want to use any affluents or chemicals which might damage or cause water pollution," Dennis said.

Let's look at some of the holes through the eyes of Eddie Dennis, starting with #2 at Cypress, one of the most feared holes at Arrowhead:

Cypress

Water is very much in play on #2, a 571-yard par-five hole. A meandering stream begins on the right side of the tee box, cuts in front of the tees, and continues down the left side of the fairway until it changes its mind again and cuts all the way across the fairway in front of the green. The stream continues to be a hazard on the right side and back of the putting surface.

Unique to the Grand Strand area, the Cypress course winds through a natural Carolina hardwood wetland. Taking great care to preserve the natural surroundings, some holes are bordered and even play through these naturally beautiful areas. A canal winds through the first four holes, eventually spilling into the Intracoastal Waterway.

Lakes

This nine-hole course demands precise shot making and daring drives of length and accuracy. Number 9, often your finish of eighteen holes, is one to be remembered. Shaped like a boomerang, it doglegs to the left, with most of the yardage still ahead after you have turned the corner. Water goes all the way down the left, and sand and trees are on the right and around the green. The 9th hole lets the conservative player play three accurate shots to avoid the "big number." A gambler can possibly get home in two, but this approach is fraught with danger, mostly watery graves. Either way,

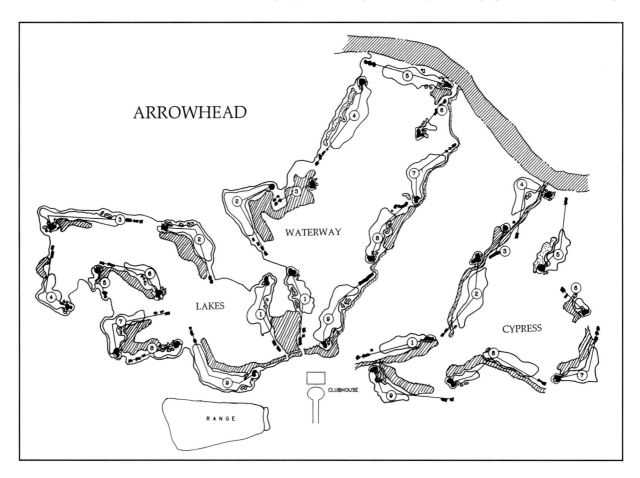

this 9th hole will challenge every golfer's shot-making and course-management skills.

Waterway

This course is the newest of the three nines, completed in the fall of 1995 after another visit to Arrowhead by golf architect Tom Jackson and Arrowhead's signature pro, Raymond Floyd. This classic design features wide fairways, large greens, and elevated tee boxes. Floyd's philosophy of giving the golfer a visual perspective of how to play each hole is very evident on this nine. The most notable holes are #4, #5, and #6, all of which offer breathtaking views of the scenic Intracoastal Waterway.

Lakes

HOLE NUMBER	1	2	3	4	5	6	7	8	9	OUT	TOT
BLUE	392	379	556	363	138	359	411	198	521	3317	
WHITE	373	356	536	336	116	346	379	171	506	3119	
GREEN	331	333	499	305	102	305	347	149	486	2857	
HANDICAP	3	7	4	8	9	6	1	5	2		
PAR	4	4	5	4	3	4	4	3	5	36	
RED	282	294	438	259	78	263	294	120	415	2443	

Waterway

HOLE NUMBER	1	2	3	4	5	6	7	8	9	OUT	TOT
BLUE	376	357	175	520	387	213	410	371	486	3295	
WHITE	341	316	158	497	356	183	387	357	465	3060	
GREEN	300	267	126	463	325	143	354	303	422	2703	
HANDICAP	8	9	5	7	2	6	1	4	3		
PAR	4	4	3	5	4	3	4	4	5	36	
RED	244	230	94	404	297	88	304	239	352	2255	

Cypress

HOLE NUMBER	1	2	3	4	5	6	7	8	9	OUT	TOT
BLUE	381	571	205	355	337	198	391	549	362	3349	
WHITE	368	528	181	339	315	171	363	525	333	3123	
GREEN	332	510	141	322	280	138	335	490	308	2856	
HANDICAP	4	1	3	6	9	7	2	5	8		
PAR	4	5	3	4	4	3	4	5	4	36	
RED	254	417	118	267	206	94	298	443	272	2369	

This view of the Championship course illustrates the design artistry of renowned golf architect Rees Jones. Its contiguous strand of individual sand bunkers leads the golfer from tee to green. (Courtesy Himmelsbach Communications/Bill Woodward)

Championship

HOLE NUMBER	1	2	3	4	5	6	7	8	9	OUT	10	11	12	13	14	15	16	17	18	IN	TOT	HCP	NET
CHAMPIONSHIP	438	199	586	385	182	364	512	463	419	3548	378	503	426	442	161	405	354	206	590	3465	7013		
BACK	419	178	559	359	169	345	489	447	412	3377	364	485	406	426	148	378	336	187	565	3295	6672		
MIDDLE	412	146	546	348	169	326	470	435	397	3249	339	471	388	405	125	359	319	176	537	3119	6368		
HANDICAP	8	16	2	12	18	14	6	4	10		13	5	7	3	17	9	15	11	1				
PAR	4	3	5	4	3	4	5	4	4	36	4	5	4	4	3	4	4	3	5	36	72		
FORWARD	374	125	464	332	145	318	455	418	378	3009	327	375	363	380	101	349	296	155	525	2871	5880		
FRONT	326	104	388	301	111	291	383	406	323	2633	277	330	317	321	81	337	264	63	426	2416	5049		

Rees Jones Par 58

HOLE NUMBER	1	2	3	4	5	6	7	8	9	OUT	10	11	12	13	14	15	16	17	18	IN	TOT	HCP	NET
BACK	126	202	94	304	184	134	145	117	291	1597	179	90	281	150	194	83	139	300	188	1604	3201		
FRONT	108	184	81	276	164	113	120	97	241	1384	140	73	262	132	179	67	126	280	159	1418	2802		
HANDICAP	14	6	18	2	8	12	10	16	4		9	15	3	11	5	17	13	1	7				
PAR	3	3	3	4	3	3	3	3	4	29	3	3	4	3	3	3	3	4	3	29	58		

BELLE TERRE

4073 Highway 501   Myrtle Beach, SC 29577
(800) 340-0072   (843) 236-8888

Architect: Rees Jones   Year opened: 1995

Course rating/Slope rating:
CHAMPIONSHIP
Championship - 74.0/134   Back - 72.2/127
Middle - 70.6/123   Forward - 68.3/113

REES JONES PAR 58
57.8/93

There are two very different golf courses at Belle Terre, but they have one thing in common: Rees Jones designed both of them.

Belle Terre, translated from the French as "beautiful earth," was sculpted from a large tract of land bordering Highway 501. It was cut from pines and makes imaginative use of natural wetlands. Large man-made lakes were constructed with an eye to future golf-course development, and a third course of championship length and design will join the Belle Terre family, occupying much of the 700 acres that still remain.

No residential development is planned. Belle Terre exists for one purpose only: championship golf. And at Belle Terre, championship golf comes in all sizes, all shapes. Not only does the Championship course boast five sets of tees, but—as Rees Jones was designing that par-72, 7,100-yard course—he added a new wrinkle that is extremely popular with golfers: Using similar landscapes, Jones created a par-58 course with fourteen three-par and four four-par holes.

Another reason for the popularity of Belle Terre is that it is a daily-fee golf course that offers the amenities of a country club. "We like for golfers to know that we are their club away from home," said Frank Monk, golf director. "There are lockers for the play-ers, four individual showers, a well-stocked pro shop, and an excellent grill with tasteful decorations."

Imposing in appearance, the red-bricked clubhouse bedecked with columns is nonetheless as handsome on the outside as it is within. The leather desk in the foyer, the English hunt board, the brass lamps, the comfortable dining chairs, the spacious tables, and the display cases of memorabilia furnished by Myrtle Beach golfing legend Jimmy D'Angelo—all provide a sense of well-being and graciousness.

The Championship Course at Belle Terre

Belle Terre's Championship course has five sets of tees, none of which are designated as "seniors" or "ladies." Asked to describe the course, Jones called it "varietal," saying that Belle Terre combines the elements of a links and a parkland course. "Why not call it superb?" said Frank Monk, golf director.

While it is not a well-known fact, golf-course architects have the option of naming any one course they have designed as the "best new course of the year" when talking with golf publications. Rees Jones nominated

The Rees Jones Par 58 course is a "one of a kind" on the Grand Strand, inviting golfers to try their skill with every club in the bag on a well-manicured design. It's a nice bonus addition to the Championship course. (Courtesy Himmelsbach Communications/ Bill Woodward)

Belle Terre's Championship course as the best for 1996, and although it did not win the top honor, many people who truly know golf think it should have won.

The Championship course features plenty of strategically placed water hazards, more than enough sand, big waste bunkers, marshes, environmentally protected wetlands, and enough distance to challenge any player. Exceptional attention to drainage and very good Bermuda greens that are slightly larger than those at most course highlight the attractiveness of Belle Terre. The course record is 66.

First-time visitors are awed by large serpentine sand bunkers that make a lasting impression on three fine golf holes. These traps, snaking their way along the edge of the fairway, traverse the rough and are more than 100 yards long! Making them even more threatening is the fact that some portions are partially hidden, giving the golfer an impression of several traps with safe landing areas in between. Not so!

The 1st hole is a good introduction to the course. The fairway is elevated from tee to green, sloping off on both sides to provide difficult approaches from an errant tee shot. Nor is this a short hole, measuring a lengthy 438 from the championship markers and still formidable at 419 and 412 from the back and middle tees. Like all the holes at Belle Terre, this one is well marked for distance, with posts on either side of the fairway and yardage stamped on sprinkler heads in the fairway.

Number 2 is such a good three par that it was named in 1997 to the "Dream Eighteen" of the Grand Strand by a panel of golfing experts working on the project for the local newspaper, the *Sun News*. Number 2 plays over water and requires a very long shot from the championship tees. Hit it short and you're dead.

While #2 is both very good and very difficult, the other par threes match up well, and many golfers have expressed the opinion that #17 is even harder.

Asked to name *the* signature hole at Belle Terre, Jones disdainfully put his hand to chin and said, "They are all signature holes."

It would be hard to argue with him on this score. Wetlands run down the right side from tee to green on the long par-five 3rd hole, and

it just is not a two-shot hole. You encounter the first serpentine trap on the 4th hole, while #5 is another three par over water.

Both #6 and #7 are dogleg lefts, with water down the left side that comes into play on the approach to the green on both holes, especially if the pin is tucked left. Number 8 is, to put it mildly, a lot of golf—463 yards—and #9 is one of those devilishly dogleg-right holes, requiring a shot to the green over water.

Rees Jones has built a demanding but a fair golf course, giving players the opportunity to "bail out," away from water hazards.

A hole that most golfers will not forget is #16, which is not really the most demanding hole but is visually stunning. A chain of nine consecutive traps on the right side of the fairway guide the golfer to the hole.

"On most courses," Jones said, "traps capture the shorter hitter, and the limber backs—the long-ball knockers—carry over the traps. Not on this hole. They're placed so that anyone who goes to the right gets caught."

The 18th hole falls into the category of great finishing holes, but it can wreck your score, too. Although the green is tucked well to the right of the clubhouse, it is directly beyond some treacherous wetlands. Use the clubhouse front door as your line of flight even though it is well left of the hole, and don't fail to keep your second shot well left, aiming this time at the gazebo where you pick up your golf cart. Even if you carefully manipulate the first two shots like a pro, your troubles still are not over. In the first place, the hole is 590 yards from tee to green, and very, very few golfers even dream of getting home in two. On the third shot you face an elevated green fronted by a large bunker and vast expanse of wetlands.

If you par this one, give yourself a big congratulatory hug!

The Rees Jones Par 58 Course at Belle Terre

This "short" course comes as a wonderful surprise to most golfers, who find that it is anything but a "pitch and putt" layout. Belle Terre management defies anyone, even the top area professionals, to put subpar totals on the scorecard.

"It is good, affordable, and players can walk anytime," Monk said. "The course is a true challenge but is not as demanding as some longer courses. It is a great concept for Myrtle Beach because many people here are senior players or individuals just taking up the game. You can get around the eighteen holes in two-and-a-half, three hours, and it is equally popular with low-handicap players who want to work on their game. On this course they will have the opportunity to attempt all the shots, hit every club in the bag."

The par-three holes vary in length from 90 to 210 yards, and neither of the two par-four holes are shorter than 280 yards. The golfer will be pleased with both #4 and #13, parallel holes, and #9 rivals the best four pars on any course. It is 291 yards from the back tees, with water running the length of the fairway to form a hazard to the left of the green. Attempting to avoid this water, the golfer may very well find himself in trees on the right with large mounding between his tee shot and the green.

When you have finished playing the Championship course, reach in your pocket for a ten-dollar bill and try this one. Or, if you're in a hurry or don't want to be harassed with championship golf, choose this Rees Jones executive-style course, which is both interesting and fun.

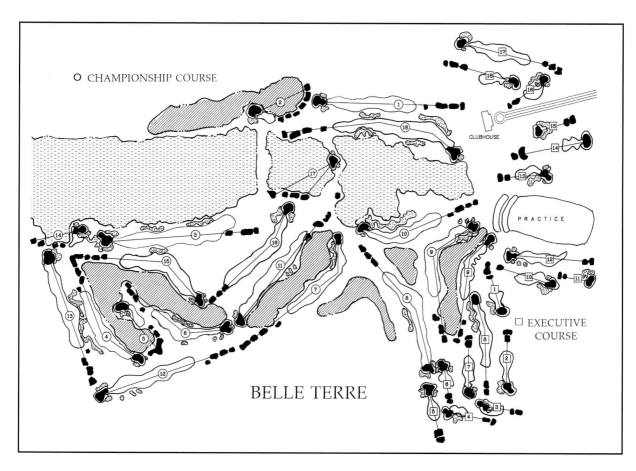

BELLE TERRE

The North Central Section

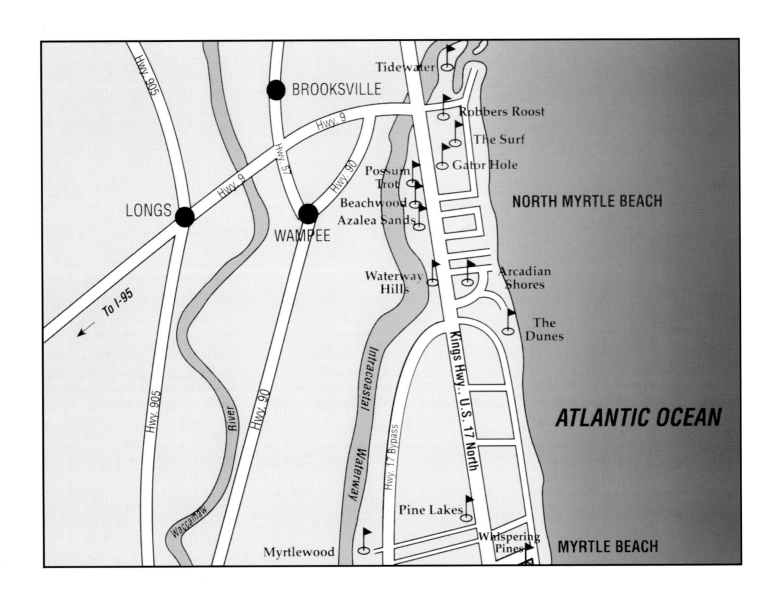

Tidewater

● BROOKSVILLE

Hwy. 9

Robbers Roost

The Surf

Gator Hole

Possum Trot

LONGS ●

Hwy. 9

Hwy. 57

Hwy. 90

Beachwood

Azalea Sands

● WAMPEE

NORTH MYRTLE BEACH

To I-95

Waterway Hills

Arcadian Shores

The Dunes

Hwy. 905

Waccamaw River

Hwy. 90

Intracoastal Waterway

Hwy. 17 Bypass

Kings Hwy. U.S. 17 North

ATLANTIC OCEAN

Pine Lakes

Myrtlewood

Whispering Pines

MYRTLE BEACH

154

ROBBERS ROOST

Highway 17 North   P.O. Box 68   N. Myrtle Beach, SC 29597
(843) 249-1471
Architect: Russell Breeden   Year opened: 1964
Course rating:
Silver - 74.4   Black - 70.2
Blue - 72.1   Red - 70.2

Robbers Roost has one of the best locations on the Grand Strand, with great visibility on Highway 17. Golfers enjoy playing this mature course designed by Russell Breeden and opened in 1964. The back nine may be one of the best on the Grand Strand.

Robbers Roost has successfully withstood the test of time and is a heavily played course despite the fact that the fairways, during the rainy season, are subject to being soft and more apt to hold casual water than some other golf layouts in the immediate neighborhood.

It is a long golf course, measuring an awesome 7,148 yards from the Long John Silver professional markers. Nor is it much easier from the next set of tees—the Blue Beards—playing to a length of 6,725 yards. Most ladies play from the red tees—5,464 yards.

There are a lot of positives about Robbers Roost. The front side is enjoyable and the five-par 4th hole and the three-par 8th have been widely praised. While the first nine compares favorably with most courses, the backside is something else—it is a very, very

good track. Numbers 14 and 16 are excellent, and #16 is one of our picks for the four best five-par holes on the Strand. It is possible that #14 also could make the list of the ten best four-par holes in the area.

The five-par 10th, the four-par 11th, and the four-par 12th also are exceptional, the kind of challenging, pretty golf holes that can "knock your socks off."

At first blush, #10 will remind the golfer of #1, but 10 is much longer and offers more problems. A pond snuggles up to the left side of the green and catches many an errant shot. A fairway trap on the right and greenside bunkers definitely come into play, and Breeden complicated things by positioning a large tree just beyond the fairway trap. That tree can serve as a directional beacon for a second shot, but also can prevent reaching the green.

Number 11 doesn't get any easier. It is a dogleg right and long. This is a very big hole, with woods on both sides and traps fronting the green left and right. The landing area is generous, but it is the exceptional length of this 11th hole (450 yards from the

HOLE NUMBER	1	2	3	4	5	6	7	8	9	OUT	10	11	12	13	14	15	16	17	18	IN	TOT	HCP	NET
SILVER	526	440	192	506	414	428	405	228	420	3559	566	449	400	192	390	196	546	430	420	3589	7148		
BLUE	506	410	175	480	401	398	390	170	398	3328	540	425	382	180	375	185	525	385	400	3397	6725		
BLACK	476	386	155	456	380	385	348	155	390	3131	527	402	366	166	348	166	500	370	380	3225	6356		
HANDICAP	17	1	15	3	9	7	11	13	5		6	2	14	18	4	16	12	8	10				
PAR	5	4	3	5	4	4	4	3	4	36	5	4	4	3	4	3	5	4	4	36	72		
RED	415	323	135	429	332	335	305	107	319	2700	437	355	306	151	286	166	379	327	357	2764	5464		
PAR	5	4	3	5	4	4	4	3	4	36	5	4	4	3	4	3	5	4	4	36	72		

back, 425 from the blues) that makes it so formidable.

Golfers will remember #12, too. A lake in front of the green causes the golfer to consider carefully the club he uses from the tee, but actually the lake is much farther than most golfers think. It takes a drive of 250 yards from the back to reach the water, and the second shot usually is more of a problem than the drive. The green is well guarded by trees left and right and most players are looking at an approach shot of 150 yards through overhanging branches.

Number 14 also plays across water, but has a very different look. The water is 220 to 250 yards from the tee and the green curls around behind the lake. A large oak guards the left front, creating a very narrow entrance to the putting surface.

Number 16 is the signature hole. It is a sharp dogleg left with the green sitting high above a lake, tucked into a corner of the forest. It is the kind of hole that can be reached in two, but requires length, skill, and courage to accomplish such a feat.

Most golfers will attempt to hit it long and straight off the tee, and go straight down the fairway again before attempting to cross the lake. This is a very good hole!

An elevated green beyond a lake—#16 at Robbers Roost.
(Courtesy Robbers Roost Golf Course)

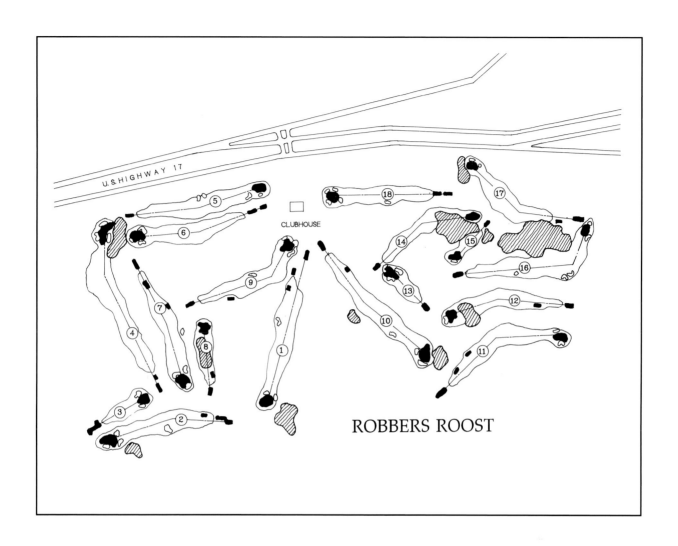

U.S. HIGHWAY 17

CLUBHOUSE

ROBBERS ROOST

The new $2-million clubhouse beyond the beautiful three-par 18th at The Surf.
(Courtesy Himmelsbach Communications/Bill Woodward)

THE SURF

Springland Lane   P.O. Box 47   N. Myrtle Beach, SC 29597
(843) 249-1524   (800) 765-SURF
Architect: George Cobb   Year Opened: 1960
Course rating/Slope rating:
Blue - 72/124   White - 70/117   Red - 69/111   Gold - 69.4/116

If you ask Bill Campbell, the highly respected Surf Club golf professional, about the good things in his life, he might respond with one simple exclamation: "Brian Keck!"

Keck is the golf-course superintendent hired by The Surf's board of directors to implement John Lafoy's remodeling of the course and to install bent-grass greens. "Brian is a genius with grass. You just will not find a golf course in better condition than this one," said Campbell, and he won't find many golfers who take exception to that claim.

Charles Tilghman and members of the Tilghman family built this course in a very pretty setting just off the ocean, and private facilities have even been built alongside the 10th fairway of this beautiful course.

The $2 million clubhouse that was constructed several years ago further enhances the overall ambiance of The Surf and makes it a favorite of out-of-state golfers who enjoy playing in a country-club atmosphere.

Using conditioning, enjoyment, and a fair golf course as criteria, The Surf would rate in everybody's top ten. This eighteen-hole George Cobb layout, one of the forerunners of the golf boom in Myrtle Beach (only Pine Lakes International and The Dunes preceded this course), is not the most difficult layout in the Carolinas, but it is tough enough! Steve Varrick holds the competitive course record of 63, quite an achievement on this very pretty, 6,800-yard, par-72 course.

The three pars are exceptional, and the greenskeeper continues to toughen the course with the blessings of the Greens Committee by making subtle changes on a yearly basis. The three-par 18th is a very good finishing hole; the golfer hits into a wind coming off the ocean and needs to carry a large body of water in front of the green while avoiding traps on both sides of the undulating green. Number 18 is 220 yards from the blues, 179 from the whites, and because of the wind, the hole plays longer than that.

While #18 is the last impression of this championship course, the 3rd hole is regarded by many as the best on the course. It, too, is a demanding test of golf, guarded by trees to the left, a lake to the right, sand traps fronting the putting surface on the right, and another trap on the left between the cart path and the green. The golfer hits into an elevated green that requires a tee shot to carry more than 200 yards from the blues, 180 from the whites. This is not a birdie hole!

The other three pars are also exciting. Number 6 is an island green, and while #13 might be the easiest of the four, it is tight, with trees hanging almost over the green on the right side, shading the trap that is on the right front of the green. Many a golfer, trying to avoid this hazard, will pull the ball into a trap on the left side. And, if the ball is hit too firmly, it could find its way down the slope, across the cart path, and into the lake behind the green.

For most golfers, the front side plays two or three strokes harder than the back, with #7 and #8 being especially testy. Both are more than 400 yards in length, and both are cut between stands of pine. Traps can come into play on both holes, and #8 is elevated.

Not many golfers will reach the par-five 17th with two shots, but the long-hitting daredevil can clear the lake on #10 and go for an eagle putt, and both #1 and #5 can be reached in two by low-handicap and long-hitting players.

It is hard to believe, but that which has been a great golf course just got better! Attuned to the importance of giving the customer the best possible product, officers and professional golf staff of The Surf determined in the summer of 1994 that it was time to make changes in the golf course, some subtle, some dramatic, but nothing that would change the flavor and character of the superb golf course.

The putting surface is much quicker because of remodeling and installation of new drainage, and some fascinating undulations by the greens are very, very true, allowing for much more accurate putting. The Surf switched from Bermuda to bentgrass greens in 1996.

If you're planning a visit to Myrtle Beach, put The Surf on your list. You'll enjoy it!

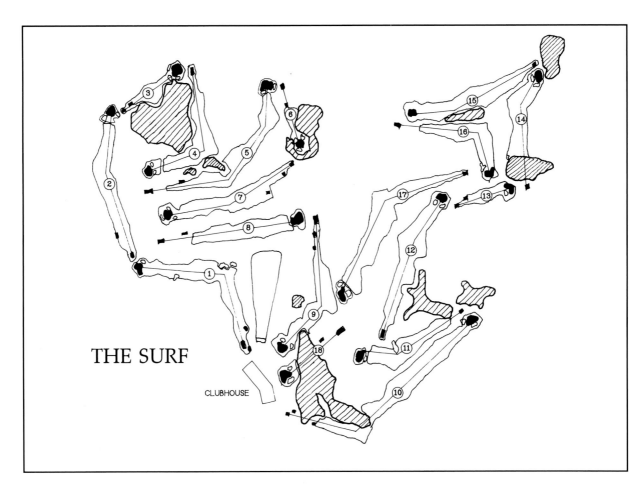

THE SURF

CLUBHOUSE

The Surf

HOLE NUMBER	1	2	3	4	5	6	7	8	9	OUT	10	11	12	13	14	15	16	17	18	IN	TOT	HCP	NET
BLUE	493	432	194	413	532	165	442	430	366	3467	564	317	378	188	362	430	373	561	219	3392	6859		
WHITE	458	415	178	382	517	152	408	419	341	3270	554	277	340	163	334	382	334	539	179	3102	6372		
MEN'S HCP	13	3	11	7	9	15	1	5	17		2	18	8	16	10	6	14	4	12				
MEN'S PAR	5	4	3	4	5	3	4	4	4	36	5	4	4	3	4	4	4	5	3	36	72		
RED	396	318	150	304	449	93	298	340	286	2632	471	225	313	138	244	294	292	457	118	2552	5184		
LADIES' HCP	7	5	15	9	1	17	11	3	13		2	18	8	12	16	6	14	4	10				
LADIES' PAR	5	4	3	4	5	3	4	4	4	36	5	4	4	3	4	4	4	5	3	36	72		

TIDEWATER

4901 Little River Neck Rd.   Cherry Grove Beach   P.O. Box 3707
N. Myrtle Beach, SC 29582   (843) 249-3829   (800) 446-5363
Architect: Ken Tomlinson   Year opened: 1990
Course rating/Slope rating:
Black - 73.7/134   White - 68.7/118
Blue - 71.2/126   Gold - 70.2/132
Green - 67.5/127

Is Tidewater the very best golf course on the Grand Strand? If you listen to the golf professionals (who should know) there can be very little doubt in your mind that this course, named by both *Golf Magazine* and *Golf Digest* magazine as the best new public course opened in the world in 1990, is the *one* course a visitor to Myrtle Beach must play.

In an informal poll of Grand Strand golf professionals, Tidewater was listed on every ballot as one of the three best of the seventy-five courses that dot this area. Many called Tidewater number one.

As you would expect from a course with such lofty praise, there are many exceptional holes on this 7,000-yard par-72 layout, and many features that make Tidewater such a standout. For instance, the course was plotted on a huge 525-acre plot of ground, and there are an unbelievable seven and a half miles of cart paths wandering through this beautiful land. Twice these paths go under paved roads! Imagine the expense of so much paving and the decision to construct tunnels under existing roads.

While these are memorable engineering marvels, the land itself is the glory of Tidewater, and the skill with which owner-designer Ken Tomlinson has blended rolling terrain with the Atlantic Ocean and the Intracoastal Waterway is exciting.

Golf Digest writes, "Any review of Tidewater, our Best New Public Course of 1990, must first spotlight its creator, Ken Tomlinson." Tomlinson is an amateur architect who purchased the property, laid out the course, and supervised every detail. "Tomlinson, believing that nature is the best architect, wanted no special effects on his golf course," the magazine continues. So you won't find any island greens, artificial waterfalls, elevated tees or greens, mounds along the fairways, or steep fairway bunkers. The fairways slope toward the trees, usually without any rough alongside. The terrain is exceptional, bordering the ocean on the northern tip of South Carolina's Grand Strand.

Tomlinson, who once played on the golf team for the University of South Carolina, loves the game and built a lasting memorial. A thorough man, he enlisted Hale Irwin to walk the course and to serve as player consultant. Irwin liked what he saw, made a few suggestions, and Tomlinson built the course.

Tidewater is a real estate development, but the course came first and will remain unspoiled.

Most would agree there is not a bad hole in this course.

Number 13 is a favorite of many, but there are more difficult holes than this 545-yard five par which skirts the Atlantic. It is the fourth-rated handicap hole, and, if the wind is blowing the right direction, the really long hitter can make it a two-shot hole. However, that takes some doing. The cham-

Marsh, Waterway, and the Atlantic Ocean make #4, #3, and #12 especially memorable at Tidewater. (Courtesy Brandon Advertising / Michael Slear)

pionship tee box sits on a peninsula behind the 12th green, and the tee shot must clear a slight rise to find its way into the fairway, which is carved between the ocean on the right and a formidable stand of forest on the left.

The perfect drive will split the two fairway bunkers, leaving a long second shot to a well-protected green. It is heavily bunkered and there is a severe slope north and south through the green. The fairway falls off to the right toward the marshlands that run the entire length of the hole. It is a beautiful view: marshlands, beach homes across the inlet, and a wide expanse of ocean.

Holes 12 and 13 feature ocean views to

162

the right, while their counterparts, 3 and 4, have the ocean on the left.

Number 3 and #12 are very memorable three pars and #4 is one of the most photographed and talked-about holes in America.

A huge trap guards the left entrance to #3 and the green, which slopes severely toward the water, is ringed with five sand bunkers. If you miss the green left, you are out of play.

Number 12 is longer than #3, and plays almost entirely over water and marsh. Between the tee box and the green is nothing but water, a long bulkhead and sand completely circling the entrance to the green.

The 4th hole is a marvelous 420-yard dogleg left with the fairway mounted on a cliff. At the bottom of this elevated expanse of ground, protecting golf balls from a watery grave, is a long half-moon sand trap running the length of the fairway. A golfer

coming from this trap area has the feeling that he needs to knock the ball straight up.

These four ocean holes are sensational, but it doesn't get any easier on most of the other holes. Five are designed with the Intracoastal Waterway in the background, and the 8th hole is an exceptional five par skirting marshland formed by tidal waters that is on the golfer's left from tee to green.

The finishing holes are memorable.

Number 16 is a five par that goes out to the Waterway with the green at a much lower elevation than the fairway as the golfer comes downhill with an approach shot. Number 17 is a wicked three par, deceptively long as the shot is uphill from a seaside-level tee entirely over marsh grass and tall reeds. Number 18 is a demanding four par, 440 yards. The marsh on the right also extends across the fairway in front of the green and the golfer who is wary of hitting the ball to the right finds that he has bought

Boats running up the Waterway behind #16 are a common occurrence at Tidewater.
(Courtesy Brandon Advertising/Michael Slear)

tree trouble. The green is very deep and it is easy to see why #18 is ranked as the toughest hole on the backside.

Since the opening of this superb course no one has shot better than 67. It is a difficult course, but very enjoyable. There are five sets of tees and the course was designed in such a manner that logical landing areas have been created for every tee. Few courses please both the low-handicap player and the short-hitting senior, but Tidewater does just that. Don't miss playing this one.

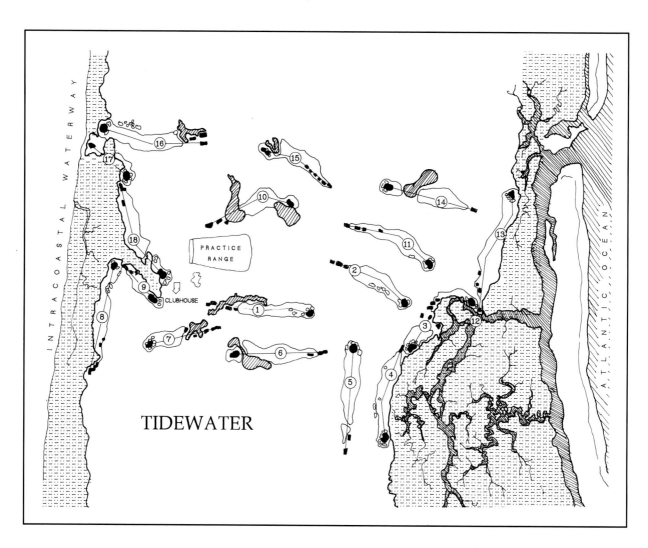

TIDEWATER

Tidewater

HOLE NUMBER	1	2	3	4	5	6	7	8	9	OUT	10	11	12	13	14	15	16	17	18	IN	TOT	HCP	NET
BLACK	525	390	150	420	465	425	360	495	185	3415	410	440	180	545	460	350	570	210	440	3605	7020		
BLUE	490	360	140	385	450	395	315	475	155	3165	390	405	165	480	425	320	540	190	425	3340	6505		
WHITE	470	330	125	365	410	365	295	450	145	2955	385	375	150	440	390	285	465	175	410	3075	6030		
GOLD	400	305	110	305	355	290	245	360	120	2490	335	310	110	390	340	255	375	155	340	2610	5100		
GREEN	390	280	100	275	320	280	235	305	115	2300	320	290	100	380	330	235	335	145	330	2465	4765		
HANDICAP	15	17	13	3	1	9	5	11	7		14	8	10	4	2	18	16	12	6				
PAR	5	4	3	4	4	4	4	5	3	36	4	4	3	5	4	4	5	3	4	36	72		
LADIES' HCP	15	17	13	3	1	9	5	7	11		12	8	14	6	4	18	16	10	2				
LADIES' PAR	5	4	3	4	4	4	4	5	3	36	4	4	3	5	4	4	5	3	4	36	72		

GATOR HOLE

700 Highway 17   N. Ocean Drive Section   P.O. Box 159
N. Myrtle Beach, SC 29597   (843) 249-3543   (800) 447-2668
Architect: Rees Jones   Year opened: 1980
Course rating/Slope rating:
Blue - 69.8/116   White - 69.3   Red - 65.9/112

The Gator Hole golf course and driving range, with great visibility from highly traveled Highway 17, are extremely popular Myrtle Beach golfing landmarks. Featuring three sets of tees and fine Bermuda-grass greens, this championship course was designed by nationally famous golf architect, Rees Jones, and opened in September 1980.

Its easy accessibility and attention to conditioning has enabled Gator Hole to remain one of the most popular golf courses on the Strand. Many people play here and like it so much that they come back year after year for a truly enjoyable golfing experience.

Gator Hole is deceptively long. From the championship tees the course measures 6,045 yards. But this is a par-70 golf course, and it might be the longest 6,000-yard course you ever play. It feels more like 6,500 yards. From the championship tees, the landing areas force you to hit around doglegs.

Built with the resort golfer in mind, this is one of Rees Jones first courses. Gator Holes beautiful, naturally tolling terrain is unusual considering that the ocean is only two blocks away.

Many of the players who try to tame Gator Hole come home talking about the three-par 18th, a difficult finishing hole over water. But the two holes that play around Gator Lake, both five pars, are pretty and tough, too.

The lake borders both holes on the left from tee to green, and both are created as dogleg lefts, which causes many a stray shot to splash. The 12th is especially difficult, with trouble on both sides of the fairway. With the lake on the left, a golfer who is too cautious will find that he has hit a shot into the marsh and woods on the right. The green is elevated and is a long way (565 yards) from the tee.

Number 7 can cause nightmares, too. Although it is very pretty, second shots often go into the lake, and water is perilously close to the green on this 510-yard hole.

The three pars (and there are six of them) are excellent, with two measuring more than 200 yards from tee to green. Number 8, stretching 215 yards, is a particular favorite, featuring a fairway valley and trouble on both sides of the green. If you miss it left, you're down a steep hill into the woods with a very difficult shot. Number 5 is the eighteenth handicap on Gator Hole, but it too can prove difficult, because the golfer must hit onto an elevated green guarded on the left by massive trees.

Gator Hole

HOLE NUMBER	1	2	3	4	5	6	7	8	9	OUT	10	11	12	13	14	15	16	17	18	IN	TOT	HCP	NET
BLUE	390	175	310	385	170	375	510	215	505	3035	475	200	565	370	315	360	165	380	180	3010	6045		
WHITE	350	160	285	360	150	360	485	165	485	2800	440	180	535	350	300	335	150	350	160	2800	5600		
HANDICAP	10	16	12	4	18	8	2	14	6		5	15	1	7	11	9	17	3	13				
PAR	4	3	4	4	3	4	5	3	5	35	5	3	5	4	4	4	3	4	3	35	70		
RED	300	120	240	305	110	305	420	120	460	2380	395	120	420	285	240	310	125	310	100	2305	4685		
HANDICAP	10	16	12	4	18	8	2	14	6		5	15	1	7	11	9	17	3	13				

One of the best known 18th holes, at Gator Hole. (Courtesy Brandon Advertising/ Michael Slear)

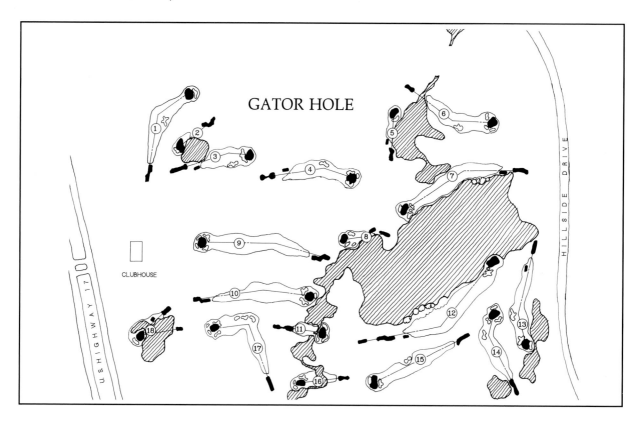

POSSUM TROT

Possum Trot Road   P.O. Box 297   N. Myrtle Beach, SC 29597
(843) 272-5341   (800) 626-8768
Architect: Russell Breeden   Year opened: 1968
Course rating/Slope rating:
Blue - 73.0/118
White - 70.3/113
Red - 69.6/111

Self-titled "The Friendly Course," Possum Trot remains a championship layout that is more comfortable than most, but still a severe test of golf. Lacking the nuances of the Dye-Fazio-Nicklaus courses of the late 1980s, Possum Trot continues to boast one of the most talked about four-par holes on the Grand Strand—#11, "Big Possum"—and is long enough to challenge even the biggest hitter.

Built in 1968, Possum Trot is among the older courses on the Strand. Designed by Russell Breeden, it has matured into a fine test of golf, and is noted for excellent playing conditions year-round.

Open enough to be "friendly" to the high handicapper, Possum Trot also challenges the better player with a blend of length and finesse that is expected from a championship course.

The course has a lot of "guts," stretching to 7,000 yards from the back tees. The holes are routed through stands of pine and oak. Fifty bunkers and nine lakes and ponds keep the golfer honest and distract his attention from the beauty of myriad flower beds and surrounding landscaped areas.

Number 11 ("Big Possum"), while not favored by everyone, certainly is memorable and much discussed by golfers who have challenged this 460-yard par-four monster. A slight dogleg, the hole is almost entirely uphill, and usually plays into the wind. It is a drive and a fairway wood for the very best player, and a three-shot hole for most.

Number 9 is called "No Mercy" and again, the problem is length. A long, uphill par four (438 yards), this hole will have you playing against the ocean breezes.

Hole #13 is a challenging three par which has been named "Analysis is Paralysis." As you stand on the tee and take in the lake, the gaping bunker, the scenic beauty, the wind velocity and direction, and the bulkheads that stop a shot that attempts to skip across the water, try not to think too much about all the danger. Remember, "analysis is paralysis." Choose the right club and get your par!

The finishing hole is also memorable. Many

Possum Trot

HOLE NUMBER	1	2	3	4	5	6	7	8	9	OUT	10	11	12	13	14	15	16	17	18	IN	TOT	HCP	NET
BLUE	533	390	415	530	410	208	360	185	438	3469	500	460	390	203	385	393	205	426	535	3497	6966		
WHITE	500	355	380	485	368	150	340	170	408	3156	471	430	350	163	347	374	168	395	489	3187	6343		
HANDICAP	18	10	4	16	6	8	14	12	2		17	1	7	9	13	5	11	3	15				
PAR	5	4	4	5	4	3	4	3	4	36	5	4	4	3	4	4	3	4	5	36	72		
RED	420	291	293	405	313	130	274	160	310	2596	402	335	283	122	278	305	119	310	410	2564	5160		
HANDICAP	16	4	8	18	2	12	14	10	6		15	1	3	11	13	7	9	5	17				

shots have found a watery grave in the large lake on the right. This is a good one, especially if you can keep your second and third shots out of that lake. Keep the ball in the fairway and a birdie is very possible.

This is an enjoyable golf course, certainly one of the very best of the economical courses clustered in North Myrtle Beach. Green fees and carts are very reasonable.

Pampas grass forms islands in the sand at Possum Trot. (Courtesy Himmelsbach Communications/Bill Woodward)

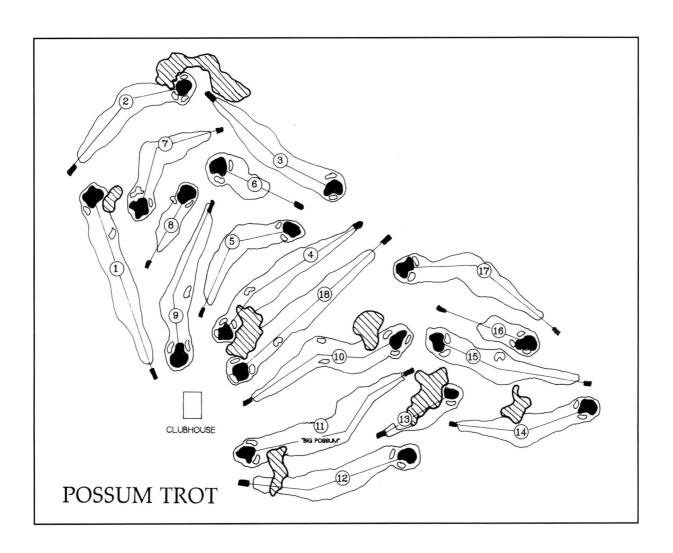

POSSUM TROT

CLUBHOUSE

"BIG POSSUM"

169

The picturesque finishing hole—par three—at Beachwood. (Courtesy Brandon Advertising/Michael Slear)

Beachwood

HOLE NUMBER	1	2	3	4	5	6	7	8	9	OUT	10	11	12	13	14	15	16	17	18	IN	TOT	HCP	NET
CHAMP.	534	389	404	175	402	425	327	191	573	3420	320	411	341	386	581	205 180	410	512	239	3405	6825		
WHITE	513	358	373	145	385	403	318	167	540	3202	294	345	328	361	560	186 173	375	494	199	3142	6344		
GOLD	478	336	351	122	365	320	307	158	501	2938	281	327	306	275	532	158	345	476	179	2879	5817		
MEN'S HCP	15	11	5	9	3	1	17	7	13		18	2	16	14	4	8	12	10	6				
PAR	5	4	4	3	4	4	4	3	5	36	4	4	4	4	5	3	4	5	3	36	72		
LADIES' RED	436	269	277	110	302	313	268	149	413	2537	230	294	294	265	468	150	296	409	109	2515	5052		
LADIES' HCP	3	11	9	15	1	7	17	13	5		16	6	8	14	2	12	10	4	18				

BEACHWOOD

1520 Hwy. 17   Crescent Section   N. Myrtle Beach, SC 29582
(843) 272-6168   (800) 526-4889

Architect: Gene Hamm   Year opened: 1968

Course rating/Slope rating:
Championship - 71.4/120   Gold - 68.3/115
White - 68.8/117   Red - 67.6/111

Beachwood is one of the best-known and most popular golf courses on the Grand Strand, with good reason. The eighteen-hole layout, well located on Highway 17 in North Myrtle Beach with great visibility, was a mid-1960s venture for nine local businessmen who laughingly call themselves "The Wheels." This astute group hired Gene Hamm to design the course and named Hubby Bellamy as their superintendent. Bellamy is still around, and one of the major reasons for the continued success of Beachwood.

"I planted the grass," said the Clemson graduate in one of the greater understatements of all time as he directs a continuing improvement program.

This is a very playable golf course, especially good for women and seniors. And as their ads say, at Beachwood, you can play a premium golf course without paying premium prices.

Indeed, Beachwood keeps getting longer and better. Built in the 1960s, it is not a "tricked-up" layout, but Beachwood has kept itself up to date and mounding has been added to several holes recently.

Beachwood has earned a reputation as being one of the best conditioned courses on the Grand Strand, and the course is wide open—plenty of air and sunshine. The grass just pops up! On the scorecard Beachwood is rated as a par 71 from the blue tees, a 69 from the whites, but that rating will continue to climb. The greens are big, among the largest on the entire Strand, and the

pine trees have matured, standing guard against wayward shots. The Bermuda-grass greens are excellent, and so are the fairways. The roughs are cut short and clean as Hamm felt that the pines are enough of a challenge in themselves.

Water does not come into play at Beachwood as much as it does on some area courses, but there is enough water and sand to make this course a true test of golf.

Number 14 may be the one hole that most golfers remember, but the 18th hole is a great finishing hole, and one of the very best three pars on the Strand. It is Beachwood's signature hole, the one they show in all their advertising, and it is very difficult.

From the championship tees, #18 is 239 yards from tee to green, and even from the white tees it is almost 200 yards, with water to the right and in front of the green an intimidating factor. A long, accurate shot is required to reach this green that is protected by three bunkers.

Number 14 is long and exciting. This is a double dogleg, a par five which demands great accuracy. The big hitter can reach the turn of the dogleg by keeping his drive in the fairway, carrying the shot over a bunker on the left, but the shot must carry 235 yards from the white tee, and this gamble is almost impossible from the blues. Number 14 is a three-shot hole, and the smart play is two shots to the center or right center of the fairway with a pitch to the green.

The four three pars are exceptional, especially #8, #15, and #18, all three 200 yards or longer. Nor is #4 a piece of cake. This hole requires a tee shot that is accurate enough to stay away from bunkers surrounding the green and long enough to avoid the pond that guards the entrance.

There are some very good four-par holes on the front side, and the golfer who can conquer #3, #5, and #6 should be on his way to a good round. The 3rd hole is 400 yards long, with a pond guarding the left front of the green. Numbers 5 and 6 are also memorable and long, playing around a lake that comes into play on the right for both holes. They are the toughest holes on the front; #5 is ranked as the number-one handicap hole, and #6, which is even longer, is regarded as the 7th handicap on the course.

According to the scorecard, #1 is ranked as the second most difficult hole on the front side, and parallels #9, a beautiful pair of five-par bookends. Until 1991, trees separated the 1st and 9th fairways. The trees are still there, but "player friendly" mounds have been built into the right side of both fairways to help golfers keep the ball in the proper fairway.

Don't underestimate #11, one of the two or three toughest holes on the course. The green is very deep, so have plenty of club.

Beachwood is fun, a good golf course in excellent condition. As host of the CPGA Seniors Championship and the prestigious 1989 Carolinas Open, Beachwood has proven that it is an enjoyable challenge.

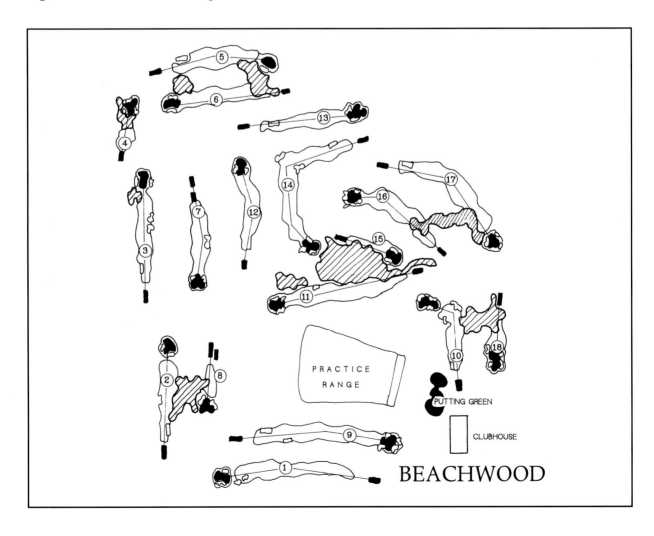

BEACHWOOD

AZALEA SANDS

2100 Hwy. 17   N. Myrtle Beach, SC 29582
(843) 272-6191   (800) 253-2312
Architect: Gene Hamm   Year opened: 1972
Course rating/Slope rating:
Blue - 72.8/119
White - 69.7/113
Red - 70.2/119

Azalea Sands has been a popular destination for golfers on the Grand Strand since Lloyd Bell and some of his friends split from Beachwood and opened this course in 1972. None of the holes at Azalea Sands were ever a part of the Beachwood course, but, because Gene Hamm designed both courses, there are a lot of similarities.

Azalea Sands has been described as "a very good little golf course." It's good all right, and getting better through imaginative renovations, but if a golfer chooses to play the back tees it certainly is not a "little" course!

Azalea Sands possibly entertains more golfers during a twelve-month period than any other course on the Strand. A good reason for its popularity is that this course can be anything you want it to be.

The championship tees play a long 6,900 yards, but when a golfer hits it from the white tees the course is trimmed to 6,200 yards. Azalea Sands has been relatively long for lady golfers, at more than 5,300 yards, but six new ladies' tees shorten the course by more than 200 yards.

The par-three holes are a memorable portion of Azalea Sands. They are long and pretty. Number 5, which parallels the private air field in North Myrtle Beach, is an exceptionally good hole, picturesque and tough from any tee.

This is the hole from which Azalea Sands derives its name, and for three or four weeks

in the spring this one looks like Augusta National—even more so. The azaleas are in full bloom, framed by lush Bermuda grass, tall, flowering pampas grass, and other assorted foliage of every conceivable color.

A stream runs across the fairway halfway between the ladies' tee and green and there is a large trap fronting the green between the stream and the green. It is very pretty and long enough from the championship tees (195 yards) to be quite a challenge.

Golfers who had played Azalea Sands found a different look when they came back in 1992. Several mounds had been added and, with water from a pond at #13, streams were built across #7 and #11 fairways, making both these holes much more difficult.

Number 11 always has been one of the most talked about holes at Azalea Sands. It is a 515-yard five par that could be a two-shot hole for long hitters, except for the pond that fronts the green—making the second shot an extremely long carry. Now the golfer will confront water twice on the hole, the stream in front of the tee and the pond in front of the green!

Golfers will enjoy Azalea Sands from the very first shot. Number 1 is a five par going straight out from the clubhouse to the woods and ditch that separate Azalea Sands and Beachwood. Fairway traps on both sides of the fairway make accuracy a premium, but this is a good hole to start on, with par likely and birdie a possibility.

Holes #2 and #3 parallel #2, #3, and #4 at Beachwood, with out of bounds on the right. Number 3 is especially tough, the number-one handicap on this golf course. In addition to out of bounds on the right, there are woods on the left and a pond lying across the fairway at the 150-yard marker. Club selection is important from the tee and the long hitter cannot use a driver.

Number 14 is another excellent four-par hole, 430 yards in length, turning slightly from right to left and ranked as the most difficult hole on the backside.

Azalea Sands is a golf course where you can have your best round. On the other hand, when Azalea Sands becomes the venue for a serious golf tournament it can be made very tough. Course records are recognized only in competitive rounds and, surprising to some, the record at Azalea Sands is 70. You will find this to be a well-conditioned course with good Bermuda greens, well-manicured bunkers, and excellent fairway grass.

Azaleas frame #5 at Azalea Sands. (Courtesy Azalea Sands Golf Course)

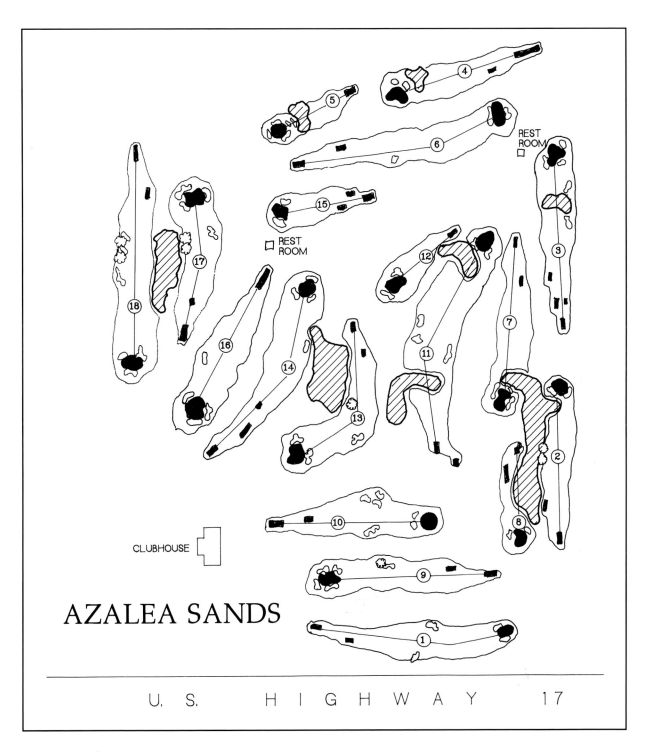

AZALEA SANDS

U. S.   H I G H W A Y   17

Azalea Sands

HOLE NUMBER	1	2	3	4	5	6	7	8	9	OUT	10	11	12	13	14	15	16	17	18	IN	TOT	HCP	NET
BLUE	515	372	435	385	195	535	410	182	420	3449	385	515	207	410	430	221	385	360	540	3453	6902		
WHITE	480	337	390	350	168	501	375	155	385	3141	350	460	190	380	385	199	350	330	502	3146	6287		
MEN'S HCP	7	17	1	13	11	9	5	15	3		16	12	8	10	2	6	14	18	4				
PAR	5	4	4	4	3	5	4	3	4	36	4	5	3	4	4	3	4	4	5	36	72		
LADIES' RED	412	277	320	309	155	421	299	119	321	2633	295	355	163	351	327	178	308	283	429	2689	5322		
LADIES' HCP	3	13	5	11	15	1	9	17	7		14	8	16	4	6	10	12	18	2				

175

Well-trapped greens at Waterway Hills, a twenty-seven-hole layout. (Courtesy Brandon Advertising/Michael Slear)

WATERWAY HILLS

9807 N. Kings Hwy.   P.O. Box 1936   Myrtle Beach, SC   28578
Architects: Robert Trent Jones and Rees Jones   Year opened: 1974

Course rating/Slope rating:

LAKES/RAVINE	OAKS/LAKES	OAKS/RAVINE
Blue - 70.3/123	71.0/119	70.9/121
White - 68.1/114	68.8/115	68.7/115
Red - 69.2/113	68.2/113	67.4/113

A Grand Strand landmark since it opened in 1974, Waterway Hills, owned by Myrtle Beach National Corporation, can be reached only by an aerial tram which carries golfers 100 feet into the air over the Intracoastal Waterway to twenty-seven delightful golf holes.

The aerial transport is part of the charm of this course. Golfers write home about the courteous treatment they receive from the time a be-knickered attendant takes the golf clubs from the car and transfers them to the tram until at the conclusion of the round another attendant, similarly attired, takes these clubs and happy golfers back to the parking lot.

While golfers may remember the aerial tram, there is nothing "gimmicky" about the golf courses at Waterway Hills. The tram exists by necessity, but the golf course was carefully planned, designed by Robert Trent Jones and his son, Rees.

Golfers play three distinctively different nines—The Lakes, The Oaks, and The Ravine. Together these nines form a championship course that keeps getting better. This gives the professional staff at Waterway Hills the option of "triple teeing" golfers during busy periods, and, regardless of course selection, the golfers are going to be pleased.

The Oaks and The Lakes are generally used for tournament play, but The Oaks and The Ravine could be a more challenging test of golf.

The Ravine, even though it is wide open and beautiful, seems to be the most difficult of the three, but it is also the shortest of the three nine-hole layouts.

Holes #3 and #4 are particularly memorable at The Ravine. Number 3 is a five par that has become a signature hole, and is, indeed, the hole for which the course is named. The elevated green is placed directly behind a deep ravine that can give golfers, even the long hitters, pause for second thought before they try to reach this green in two. Most golfers will choose to lay up short of the ravine on this 489-yard hole, and hit a wedge on the third shot across the 70-yard-wide ravine.

That same ravine comes back into play on #4, but is less threatening as the player must drive across the ravine and then hit his second shot uphill to a well-trapped green.

Another favorite at Waterway Hills is hole #6 on The Oaks course. This is a five par that features two lakes between tee and green. There should be no difficulty with the tee shot as the lakes are closer to the green, beginning 155 yards from the front edge. There is a landing area between those two bodies of water, but if pinpoint accuracy is not the golfer's forte, he needs to keep the second shot left and short, leaving a formidable iron approach.

Another good five par is #2 at The Lakes. It is narrow, a "tight" driving hole with woods on the right, and a small body of water some 300 yards from the tee box. The hole is long—527 yards—and the golfer still has a lot of work to do after he reaches the undulating green.

There are some very good three-par holes at Waterway Hills, and a couple of excellent doglegs, particularly #9 on The Lakes and #6 on The Ravine.

The greens are 328 Bermuda and experienced golfers will tell you that the putting surfaces at Waterway Hills, especially in the spring and fall, are as good as any on the Grand Strand.

The best round of golf played at Waterway Hills is a 63, scored over The Oaks and The Lakes by Jim Fellner, but the competitive course record is 65. That number was posted by Bob Boyd.

There are a lot of things to like about Waterway Hills.

The tram definitely is a plus. Golfers exclaim over the great view as they travel over the Waterway. And tourist golfers also like Waterway Hills because it is not expensive. It is not a surcharge course, but its quality compares very favorably with higher-priced courses.

Walking is allowed at all times except for three months in the spring and two months in the fall. Even in those months, walking the course is allowed after noon.

There are three sets of tees on all twenty-seven holes.

When all three courses are in use, play is triple tee with everyone playing the courses on a clockwise basis.

Lakes Course

HOLE NUMBER	1	2	3	4	5	6	7	8	9	TOT
BLUE	356	534	374	346	138	364	526	162	390	3190
WHITE	327	514	354	319	131	349	500	137	370	3001
HANDICAP	7	1	4	6	9	5	2	8	3	
PAR	4	5	4	4	3	4	5	3	4	36
RED	260	470	300	278	94	282	426	96	284	2490
HANDICAP	6	1	3	5	8	4	2	9	7	

Ravine Course

HOLE NUMBER	1	2	3	4	5	6	7	8	9	TOT
BLUE	365	376	483	393	183	372	144	478	352	3149
WHITE	339	353	445	374	169	338	124	463	322	2927
HANDICAP	6	4	1	3	9	5	8	2	7	
PAR	4	4	5	4	3	4	3	5	4	36
RED	260	281	386	301	113	218	99	405	272	2335
HANDICAP	6	4	1	3	9	7	8	2	5	

Oaks Course

HOLE NUMBER	1	2	3	4	5	6	7	8	9	TOT
BLUE	473	186	422	382	370	490	165	390	393	3271
WHITE	458	158	387	363	348	476	148	375	367	3080
HANDICAP	2	8	4	5	6	1	9	3	7	
PAR	5	3	4	4	4	5	3	4	4	36
RED	416	137	308	280	312	388	109	311	318	2579
HANDICAP	2	8	4	6	5	1	9	3	7	

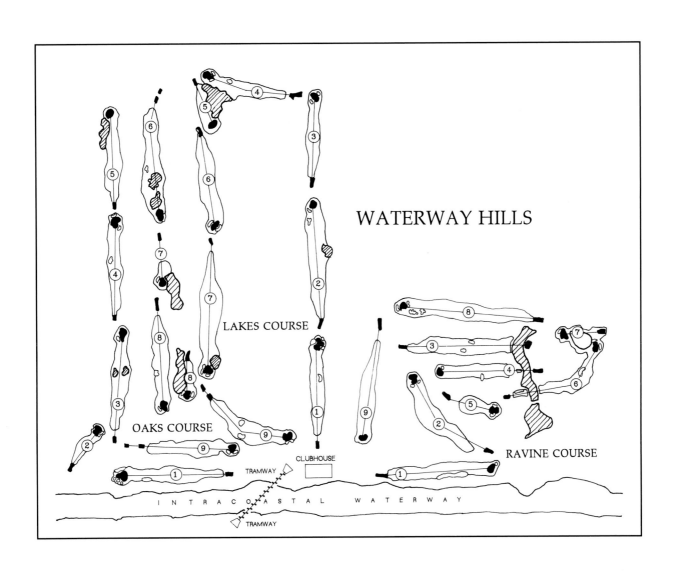

WATERWAY HILLS

LAKES COURSE

OAKS COURSE

RAVINE COURSE

CLUBHOUSE

TRAMWAY

TRAMWAY

I N T R A C O A S T A L   W A T E R W A Y

Number 15 at Arcadian Shores, for years named one of America's top fifty courses.
(Courtesy Himmelsbach Communications/Bill Woodward)

ARCADIAN SHORES

701 Hilton Road   Arcadian Section   Myrtle Beach, SC 29577
(843) 449-5217
Architect: Rees Jones   Date opened: 1974
Course rating/Slope rating:

Tiger - 73.1/137	White - 69.2/126
Blue - 71.5/132	Red - 69.9/117

Arcadian Shores—the golf course located at the Wyndham Resort, formerly the Myrtle Beach Hilton—is not one of the newer courses on the Strand (opened in 1974), but it remains one of the most popular, continually rating among Americas fifty best. Their brochure says it all: "With thousands of outstanding golf courses throughout the South, it takes an exceptional course to remain one of the best tracks, not only on The Grand Strand, but one of the best in the country."

Designed by world-renowned golf architect Rees Jones, the links at Arcadian Shores combine the best of nature with the best of modern golf layout. Sixty-four sand bunkers are strategically placed to make the golfers journey from tee to green memorable and difficult. Natural lakes woven in and out of the fairways add to the challenge.

In another moment of lyricism, the Arcadian Shores brochure states, "The greens are Bermuda and the fairways are manicured and pampered with tender loving care usually reserved for greens."

Few will argue the claim that Arcadian Shores has been an exceptional golf course since its inception, and some might say this course should be in the top five on everybodys list of the "Best of the Beach."

This course measures almost 7,000 yards from the Tiger (professional) tees, so bring your "long" ball as well as your "straight" ball.

There are many outstanding golf holes at Arcadian. Most people consider #2 a signature hole and one of the most difficult in the area. From the back tees, it is 205 yards from tee to green, and length is only part of the problem. This three par is all carry over water. It is virtually an "island" hole except for the left side, where the green is guarded by an enormous mounded sand bunker. Anything short, right, or long is wet, and if you hit it left, par is extremely difficult as this green, like most at Arcadian, has severe undulations and slopes toward the water.

Another test is #11, with a large lake directly in front of the tee box. From the professional tees, the player must hit a drive of at least 225 yards to reach terra firma, and if the tee shot strays to the right, there is still more water!

Another memorable hole is #13, and many call it the most difficult. Again, a good-sized lake fronts the green and catches any ball hit short or to the right on the approach to the green, which sits down on the water in a natural valley. The tee shot is blind, and accuracy is a premium. After topping the hill, the golfer learns that the fairway slopes quickly to the water with a differential of forty feet in elevation from the highest point of the fairway to the lake and the green. Often, the second shot is a difficult downhill approach, and it's a tough green to hit.

Number 18 is a very good finishing hole. It is the longest par four on the course—446 yards from the championship tees and almost 400 from the regular (white) tees. It is a slight dogleg right and uphill to an elevated, two-tiered green that sits just below the clubhouse and is well guarded by bunkers.

All of the five-par holes are more than 500 yards in length from the professional markers, and two of the four three pars are more than 200 yards in length. Arcadian Shores, the site of many professional tournaments, is a championship course in every way.

We talked to those who should know—the golf professionals—and without exception they said that Arcadian Shores has retained its charm and its defenses. Its an aging course that just will not grow old and always will be "a course where you play golf the way it should be played."

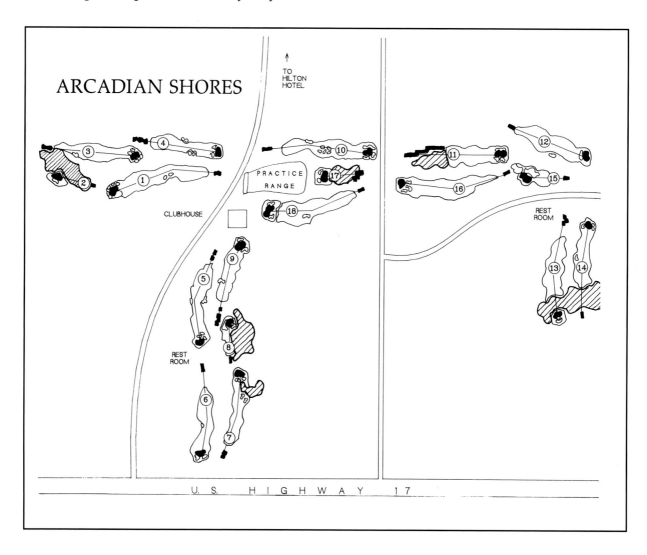

Arcadian Shores

HOLE NUMBER	1	2	3	4	5	6	7	8	9	OUT	10	11	12	13	14	15	16	17	18	IN	TOT	HCP	NET
TIGER	533	205	505	404	415	417	366	187	386	3418	506	424	384	415	409	216	556	164	446	3520	6938		
BLUE	504	178	466	386	392	389	339	153	364	3171	472	394	370	393	395	196	527	141	409	3297	6468		
WHITE	475	156	463	368	368	372	324	147	346	3019	440	364	350	364	273	153	515	116	380	2955	5974		
RED	415	135	418	342	348	355	296	127	307	2743	402	275	309	277	261	120	462	89	356	2551	5294		
HANDICAP	8	4	10	12	2	6	18	16	14		9	3	13	1	11	15	7	17	5				
PAR	5	3	5	4	4	4	4	3	4	36	5	4	4	4	4	3	5	3	4	36	72		

PINE LAKES INTERNATIONAL

5603 Woodside Dr.   Myrtle Beach, SC 29577
(843) 449-6459   (800) 852-6283
Architect: Robert White   Year opened: 1927
Course rating/Slope rating:
Blue - 71.3/121
White - 69.4/115
Red - 71.2/118

Pine Lakes International is more than a golf course—it is an experience, an event, an occasion to be remembered. This is a fine golf course, but you can't separate the course itself from the ambiance of Pine Lakes. This is the first golf course at Myrtle Beach, where it all began. This is where *Sports Illustrated* was born, where Rockefeller played golf with Gene Sarazen, where the Vanderbilts dined with the Roosevelts.

Where else are you greeted at your car by white-gloved, red-jacketed, plaid-knickered caddy masters—or welcomed to the pro shop by courteous men in kilts? The rangers, too, wear kilts, with handsome green jackets and Scottish headgear.

And where else are you offered a cup of clam chowder as you reach the 10th tee, chowder that has been brewed over an open fire by the club chef?

The pretty women in the Grill Room re-emphasize the Scottish flavor, as they wear Scottish kilts and tam-o'-shanters. All of this is a tribute to Robert White, a native of St. Andrews, Scotland, the founding father of golf on the Grand Strand and architect, with Donald Ross, of the Pine Lakes course.

The course was built in 1927, and, yes indeed, Bobby Jones did play here. His score is not recorded, but, at the age of seventy-eight, Sarazen shot 78, which is very good considering the course record, held by John Ross, is sixty-five.

The magnificent clubhouse shows no sign of its age, and the course itself keeps improving with age. The first six holes will severely test the skill of the golfer, whether that golfer is a low- or high-handicap player. The 1st hole is a slight dogleg left, not imposing in looks but made difficult by its demanding length of 565 yards. Then the golfer faces three consecutive four pars, each more than 400 yards long, with water and sand visible and treacherous on every hole. Now it's uphill to a 185-yard three par with a trap stretching halfway across the front of the green, and then back across water to the four-par 6th, which is slightly shorter than its predecessors. This hole is all "guts." You must carry the green with your second shot because of three sandy bunkers that guard the putting area.

As a matter of fact, the golfer cannot roll the ball onto any of the greens at Pine Lakes. This is not a bump-and-run golf course. If there is no sand in front, the architects have supplied a strip of rough cut which effectively curtails a running shot.

There are many outstanding holes, but #3, #13, #17, and #18 are the most talked about par-four holes at Pine Lakes. All are tough! Number 3 runs from the clubhouse, past the home of the course's president, all the way to Business Highway 17. It is beautifully contoured, and the golfer, after maneuvering past woods on the left and a big pond on the right, must hit from a downhill lie uphill to the green.

Number 13 features a hidden green, blocked from the golfer's view by a trap, and it is a dogleg left with a water hazard guarding most of the green. It takes a big, well-placed drive and a strong second shot to reach this one in two!

Even professional golfers regard #17 as awesome. Not only is it very long (442 yards) but there are trees on the left and a pond juts into the fairway, demanding that the golfer keep the ball right into a very narrow landing area. Sand traps further complicate the entrance to the green.

The final hole is deceptively beautiful because it can jump up and grab the unsuspecting golfer. A slight dogleg right, water and a trap can catch a poor first shot, and an oversize pond is strategically placed to the right of the fairway and easily comes into play. Oh, and if you stay away from the water on the right, beware of a fairway trap on the left!

Traditional Scottish golf at Pine Lakes International. (Courtesy Pine Lakes International)

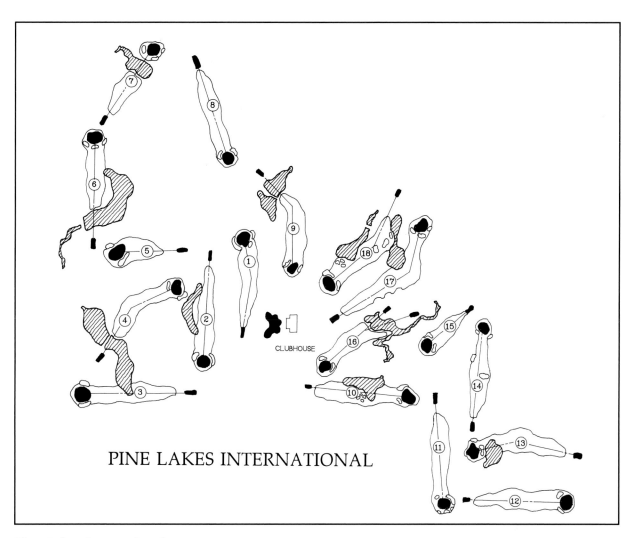

Pine Lakes International

HOLE NUMBER	1	2	3	4	5	6	7	8	9	OUT	10	11	12	13	14	15	16	17	18	IN	TOT	HCP	NET
BLUE	563	432	428	406	185	378	159	367	493	3411	344	185	495	428	355	200	379	442	370	3198	6609		
WHITE	539	411	405	382	153	355	134	349	463	3191	319	164	475	403	328	177	363	407	349	2985	6176		
MEN'S HCP	9	3	1	7	15	11	13	5	17		14	16	18	2	10	12	6	4	8				
PAR	5	4	4	4	3	4	3	4	5	36	4	3	5	4	4	3	4	4	4	35	71		
RED	476	355	363	308	142	294	108	313	423	2782	296	150	421	341	279	162	281	362	302	2594	5376		
LADIES' HCP	5	3	1	9	15	13	17	11	7		10	18	6	2	14	16	12	4	8				

The 18th at Myrtlewood runs along the Waterway. (Courtesy Himmelsbach
Communications/Bill Woodward)

MYRTLEWOOD

48th Avenue N. and Highway 17 Bypass   P.O. Drawer 2095   Myrtle Beach, SC 29778
(800) 283-3633   (843) 449-5134   (843) 449-3121

Architects: Edmund Ault (Palmetto)   Year opened: 1972
Arthur Hills (Pinehills)   Year opened: 1966

Course rating/Slope rating:

Palmetto

Blue - 72.7/135   White - 70.6/132
Gold - 68.9/123   Red - 70.1/117

Pinehills

Blue - 72.0/125   White - 69.5/119
Gold - 67.6/112   Red - 67.4/113

Well-known to golfers, Myrtlewood has been delivering championship golf since the first course opened in 1966, and now it is even better. Both courses—the older Palmetto and Pinehills, the only Arthur Hills design on the Grand Strand—pose considerable challenges and both are rated in the higher echelon of Strand golf courses.

These courses are distinctively different from one another. Palmetto, almost 7,000 yards from the championship tee, features difficult holes and bent-grass greens, with part of the course wandering through residential condominium areas. Pinehills, 6,800 yards from the back tees, also features bent-grass greens and plays through a forest of pines with twenty-six acres of water.

The scorecard points out that Myrtlewood sits at sea level and warns golfers that they might need to adjust to this factor by playing one or two clubs more than they would on their home course. And, if you want to know exactly where you are at this point in time, there is a large directional sign just outside the clubhouse, positioned in front of the Waterway. It reads:

Miami—713 miles
New York—650 miles

To get to Miami, take the boat to your left.

If you're looking for the Big Apple, turn right.

Palmetto

If a golfer playing the Palmetto has any doubt about coming back to play this track a second time, those doubts are dispelled when reaching the championship tees of the 18th hole. The 18th arguably is one of the very best golf holes on the Beach, pretty but demanding. You reach the 18th tee by parking your golf cart some 50 yards in front of the tee, walking across a footbridge, and climbing a small hill to the tee box. From there the view is spectacular and frightening, as the playing area stretches 468 yards to a well-bunkered green. And, despite its length, this is a par five!

The 18th hole is bordered on the left, from tee to green, by the Intracoastal Waterway, and out-of-bound markers shield a row of condominiums on the opposite side of the fairway. The hole is both long and very, very tight.

To reach the fairway (which slopes toward the Waterway) requires a drive that must carry at least 220 yards. The best way to play the hole is to "cut" a drive into a landing area that looks, from the tree, to be the size of a postage stamp.

Like #18, the golf course itself is long. In

one respect it bears a resemblance to many of the legendary layouts in Scotland because, unlike most American golf courses, you don't see the clubhouse except from the 1st and the 18th holes.

The front nine goes away from the clubhouse, with #3 paralleling the Highway 17 Bypass, and the golfer does not begin "coming in" until reaching the halfway house between the 9th green and 10th tee.

Nor do the two nines look alike. Most of the front side is wide open, while handsome homes and condominiums border the final holes of the back nine. The finishing hole on the front (#9) is tough, and the halfway house can be a welcome relief to the players who have just completed this relatively long par four.

At #9 a fairway bunker about 200 yards off the tee catches many golfers who hit the ball to the left to try to avoid the canal that feeds into a lake on the right. Because it is a slight dogleg, the ideal shot is to the left center of the fairway, setting up the second shot to a green that has a lot of undulation. But, if you do follow this advice, don't forget that a sand trap is lurking in that same left-center location. The second shot also calls for accuracy because a bunker guards the right front and another trap is just to the left of the green.

The 10th hole is memorable and unusual because it features a double fairway. At 529 yards, the hole is long, with fairway bunkers strategically placed in landing areas of both the drive and second shot.

Number 14 is an interesting hole, too. A huge lake runs down the right side of the fairway from tee to green, and out-of-bounds markers just beyond the rough to the left again bring accurate shot making into play. A bulkhead guards and supports this green, and the second shot is uphill to an undulating green that can be exceedingly tough with its devilish pin placements.

The par-three holes at Palmetto are good but relatively short. The most memorable and longest is #17 (173 yards), a very pretty golf hole that goes out to the Waterway. You can see the boats go by or watch the sunset if you're playing a late-afternoon round. A cemented canal running clear across the fairway should not come into play because it is located 50 yards in front of the green, but the canal does add another dimension to this hole, which is made more difficult by a big, well-bunkered green.

Pinehills

Pinehills might be one of the best "hidden values" on the Grand Strand. A golfer-friendly course in every way, it costs less to play on Pinehills than on many surcharge courses that are not one bit better, and the aesthetics and challenging golf offered here are very good!

Pinehills, the only design on the Grand Strand by renowned architect Arthur Hills, has had more than its share of national acclaim. In 1994 it was nominated as *Golf Digest*'s best new resort course, and in 1996 that same magazine, writing about "places to play," said "there is no other golf course like this in Myrtle Beach."

Architect Arthur Hills, who has enjoyed great success in the field of golf-course architecture, in 1991 scored a rare "double" award: He designed the two courses that were named "Best New Private Course" and "Best New Public Course." Without a doubt playing golf has become more expensive, but you still can call Pinehills a bargain because it combines excellence and a fair price.

Hills did a magnificent job with a routing that has always been outstanding, and while the routing of the course itself was not changed, few people will recognize Pinehills as the same George Cobb course they played prior to 1993.

We toured the course with Golf Director Doug Hart early in the summer of 1997 and

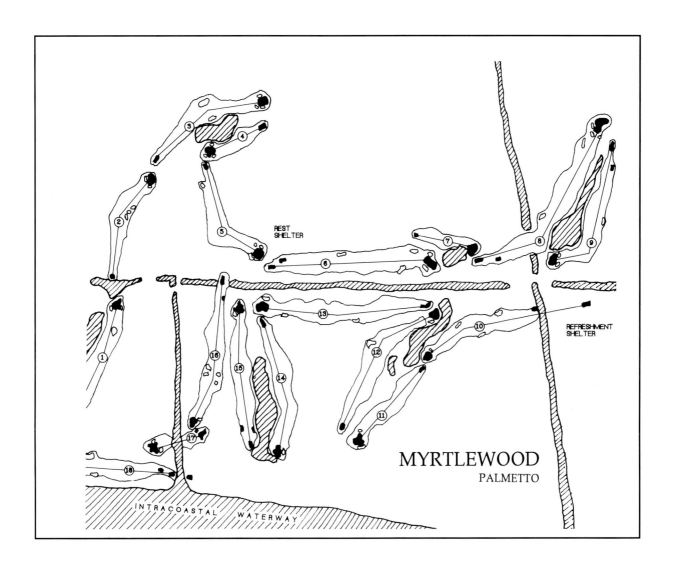

Palmetto Course

HOLE NUMBER	1	2	3	4	5	6	7	8	9	OUT	10	11	12	13	14	15	16	17	18	IN	TOT	HCP	NET
BLUE	414	379	397	195	404	542	178	541	390	3440	529	205	361	529	391	439	422	173	468	3517	6957		
WHITE	387	334	366	175	389	519	166	523	369	3228	503	190	345	511	366	419	394	162	377	3267	6495		
GOLD	347	313	340	150	370	475	153	500	345	2993	484	176	327	493	349	400	373	146	357	3105	6098		
HANDICAP	7	5	13	15	3	9	17	1	11		12	10	18	14	6	2	8	16	4				
PAR	4	4	4	3	4	5	3	5	4	36	5	3	4	5	4	4	4	3	4	36	72		
RED	314	286	305	125	311	439	129	439	299	2647	420	121	306	471	305	309	319	106	301	2658	5305		
LADIES' HCP	11	5	13	17	9	3	15	1	7		2	16	12	4	8	10	14	18	6				

fell in love all over again with Pinehills, especially the back nine. Hills has added a lot of contours and extensive mounding, and he created a sense of serenity with tall fescue grasses that successfully conceal other playing areas and give the golfer a feeling of communing alone with nature in a seemingly untouched setting.

As we visited the front nine, Hart called attention to #4, which is only the 15th-rated hole on the course, but it nonetheless is a beauty. Framed on the left by the well-kept condominiums of Magnolia Place, #4 is a jewel, with water on the right guarding the

Located at Myrtlewood, a convenient midtown destination, Pine Hills is the only Arthur Hill design in the area. It is one of two courses on this site and stands among the very best of the Strand. (Courtesy Brandon Advertising/Michael Slear)

right side and front of the green and with a good-sized sand trap on the left. It is long enough (193 yards from the blues) to be testing.

The par-five #3 is rated as the No. 1 handicap hole, but we liked the par-four #8 even better because it seems more of a challenge. Number 8 is a severe dogleg right, and a large tree is planted at the very corner of that dogleg. Missing that tree is the key to making a good score here.

The green is elevated, but so are most of the putting surfaces at Pinehills, another wrinkle added to the equation by Arthur Hills.

The 9th hole, too, is outstanding. On the scorecard it doesn't look that hard: Straightaway and not overly long. True, it can be a two-shot hole for the golfer who can hit it long *and* straight, but there is water on both sides of the fairway that extends to the green on the right side, which also is bunkered left. What we liked about the hole is the manner in which Hills has framed the green with mounds and plants in a semicircle behind the putting surface. It also is the one hole of Pinehills where the golfer can see the water-

way as he looks to his left nearing the green to get a glimpse of the #1 tee of the Palmetto course and the waterway behind it.

As good as this hole and the front side are, there is no denying that the back is more dramatic. For example, on the front nine you didn't see those tall fescue grasses, the mounds were gentler, and in actuality the holes were not as difficult as those the golfer is about to encounter on the back side.

Number 11, a par three, is shorter than those on the front, but the green is circled with water and sand traps. Therefore, accuracy is a must.

Number 13 has all the characteristics of #8 on the front—and then some! It is a par five, and as though it weren't tough enough, Hart and his staff decided to move the tees forty yards farther back at the conclusion of the 1997 peak season. They had a reason: Because the tees were too close to the big tree that guards the dogleg, the really big hitter could take it over the tree. Now that's history; let's see you do it from this new set of blues!

The difficulty of #13 is compounded for the golfer who tries to stay away from that tree, usually finding himself in a fairway sand trap on the left. Then there are two other bunkers at the green. The 13th hole is not easy, but it is rated second in difficulty on the back to #15, another par five that features water all the way up the left side, a severe dogleg left, and myriad bunkers around the green.

The final two holes are excellent and challenging. Number 17 again is short, so most low handicappers will have little problems with it. However, be aware that water starts about halfway up the right side of the fairway and circles the back of the green. You don't want to be short either because two bunkers guard the front.

When it comes to sand traps, you're talking #18! Big water on the left juts into the fairway and guards most of the front of this green. However, if you try to stay away from the water, there are nine traps on the right, three of which blanket the rear and right side of the putting area.

With all this trouble, how can we say the course is golfer friendly? We say so primarily because it is a spacious golf course and you won't have to hunt for many balls because the rough usually does not come into play. Well, what about the water? OK, but if you hit it into the ponds, you're not going to find your ball anyway!

Featuring Penncross bent-grass greens, Bermuda fairways, scenic beauty, and excellent care by outstanding golf-course superintendents, Pinehills is widely recognized as one of Myrtle Beach's must-play courses.

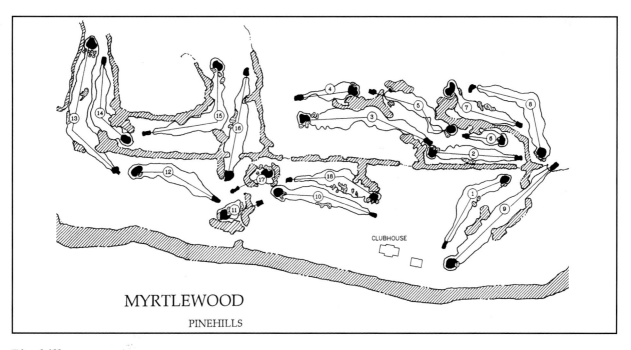

MYRTLEWOOD

PINEHILLS

Pinehills

HOLE NUMBER	1	2	3	4	5	6	7	8	9	OUT	10	11	12	13	14	15	16	17	18	IN	TOT	HCP	NET
BLUE	372	348	505	193	384	190	365	431	503	3291	401	175	400	525	411	498	383	153	403	3349	6640		
WHITE	352	324	482	173	342	165	334	394	485	3051	372	142	360	486	373	469	351	134	374	3061	6112		
GOLD	336	309	470	152	324	143	316	347	472	2869	351	121	334	437	331	438	336	123	352	2823	5692		
MEN'S HCP	9	13	1	15	11	17	7	3	5		8	16	14	4	10	2	12	18	6				
PAR	4	4	5	3	4	3	4	4	5	36	4	3	4	5	4	5	4	3	4	36	72		
LADIES' HCP	9	13	1	15	11	17	3	7	5		8	16	14	4	10	2	12	18	6				
RED	298	277	420	95	254	111	288	315	420	2478	320	96	280	396	288	397	251	104	296	2428	4906		

Atlantic Ocean in background, The Dunes #9 in foreground. (Courtesy Brandon Advertising/Michael Slear)

THE DUNES

9000 N. Ocean Boulevard   Dunes Residential Section near north junction
of Highway 17 and Bypass 17   (843) 449-5914
Architect: Robert Trent Jones   Year opened: 1948
Course rating/Slope rating
Gold - 75.4/141
Blue - 72.1/132
Red - 72.3/132

Talk about prestige!

The Dunes golf course, designed by Robert Trent Jones and opened in 1948, has been *the* premier golf course on the Beach from the day it opened. It continues to be ranked among the very best in the nation, and an invitation to play here is akin—in the minds of golfers—to an invitation from the White House.

For several years now, The Dunes has enhanced its reputation by hosting the year-ending PGA Senior Championship Tournament, proving to the players and to the world through national television that a better golf course just can't be found. While the contract with the Senior PGA Tour continues through 1998, that organization—with Golf Holiday—is building a course of its own on the Grand Strand.

Don't cry for The Dunes—it is a course that every visitor who knows golf wants to play, and if the club management chooses, The Dunes very probably can and will host another major tournament. The golf course is that good!

The Dunes is exclusive, members only, and the membership is proud of the outstanding reputation of the golf course. Ranked number one among Grand Strand courses since its inception, The Dunes in 1992 recognized the influx of excellent new golf courses in the area and took steps to maintain its top-dog position.

The golf committee determined that the excellent Bermuda greens of this eighteen-hole, 7,000-yard championship course had become passé and installed new lightning-fast bent-grass greens.

"This is a course which was a masterpiece when it was created, and it will never grow old. It is simply a classic golf course, carefully designed for a seaside setting, and it is wonderful in every way," said George Hendrix, a golf professional who accompanied the author on a tour of every golf course described in this book.

Elevated greens, carefully manicured sand traps, rolling Bermuda fairways, expertly conceived mounding, and well-defined landing areas are Dunes trademarks that, with the new bent-grass greens, create an awesome golfing adventure.

Many will tell you there are no bad holes at The Dunes, although a few purists may degrade the famous #13, which may well be the most talked about golf hole on the Beach. It is named Waterloo, and many golf balls have found a watery grave in the huge lake that dominates the 575-yard, five-par hole.

We do not agree with those who degrade this one and feel it has withstood the test of time and the efforts of many fine golfers.

"I don't like any golf hole where I can't hit a driver off the tee," said one long-hitting pro. That criticism won't hold true for most golfers, and you wouldn't exactly call #13 "target golf."

True, the tee shot must be hit into a landing area short of the water. Most golfers can go ahead, hit the driver, and not worry about it. Well, they can hit the driver if they can hit it straight.

The hole plays as a dogleg right, with water all the way on the right side of the hole, making it very penalizing to a golfer with a tendency to slice. The objective at #13 is to put the tee shot in play as close to the water as possible because it is a long carry over the lake to the fairway beyond.

There are a couple of options—hit it left and have a shorter carry over water; hit it right and attempt to reach the undulating green in two. The green has been reached in two shots by several players, including PGA Tour pro Leonard Thompson, but it's a pretty exclusive group!

While #13 may dominate the conversation of a golfer playing The Dunes for the first time, golfing aficionados will tell you that it is just one of many fine holes that demand concentration.

Jeff Dotson, golf professional at The Dunes in the late 1980s and 1990, has this to say:

> If you're playing here for the first time, you can expect to find a very good golf course that is ultimately a fair course. If you hit a good shot you are well rewarded and if you hit a poor shot your penalty is in direct proportion to how poor the shot ends up being.

The Dunes is a course that has a lot of

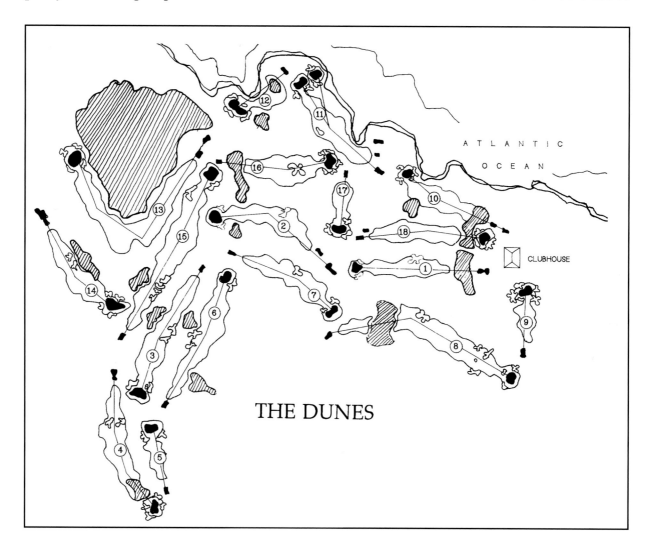

THE DUNES

194

variety. You get a lot of different looks on the golf course, and it fits the terrain very well. If you can drive the ball well on this course, you generally will post a decent score. One of the nice features about The Dunes for a high-handicap player is that he doesn't have to drive the ball particularly straight. The high handicapper will not get into a lot of trouble if he sprays the ball; but on the other hand, he is going to have a lot of difficulty reaching the green in the prescribed number of strokes.

The renovation of The Dunes in 1992 is not the first redesign of this excellent course. In the early 1970s club members invited architect Jones to come back and make a few changes. Number 3, for example, was originally a par five, and the 4th hole was a par four. The green on #11 was relocated, tucked behind a pond.

The changes did not make the course easier. PGA Tour star Ben Crenshaw and the almost-legendary amateur, Billy Joe Patton, share the course record of 67 on the original layout, and another professional, Australian Bob Shearer, shot the same score on the 1970s redesign.

The Dunes has been the site of the Golf Writers of America championship for many years, and that tournament is played the weekend before the Masters is staged in nearby Augusta, Georgia, so that writers can attend both functions. Many writers said the highlight of that busy time is not the famous Masters, but playing golf in Myrtle Beach. If so many writers like The Dunes, you're going to love it, too. It is not easy to get a chance to play The Dunes, but the course may be played with members or by guests of certain member hotels.

If you can get on, The Dunes should be on your preferred list of courses to play on the Grand Strand.

The Dunes

HOLE NUMBER	1	2	3	4	5	6	7	8	9	OUT	10	11	12	13	14	15	16	17	18	IN	TOT	HCP	NET
GOLD	424	422	431	508	203	436	397	535	188	3544	381	358	191	576	455	531	360	178	441	3471	7015		
GOLD HCP	5	9	7	17	15	3	1	11	13		10	12	16	8	2	18	6	14	4				
BLUE	399	391	398	465	176	413	378	491	164	3275	337	325	173	526	411	495	341	162	372	3142	6417		
BLUE HCP	5	9	7	17	11	1	3	15	13		8	10	12	2	4	18	14	16	6				
PAR	4	4	4	5	3	4	4	5	3	36	4	4	3	5	4	5	4	3	4	36	72		
RED	269	291	348	401	134	308	294	394	110	2549	314	290	149	440	292	429	320	137	323	2694	5243		
RED HCP	13	11	3	1	15	7	9	5	17		8	12	14	2	16	4	10	18	6				

Palm trees combine with dense strands of pine to guard the fairways on Whispering Pines, an affordable course located near the Atlantic Ocean. (Courtesy Himmelsbach Communications/Bill Woodward)

WHISPERING PINES

Highway 17 Business at 31st Avenue South   Myrtle Beach, SC 29577
(843) 918-2305

Architects: Dye/Finger/Shelley/Spann   Year opened: 1962

Course rating/Slope rating:
Blue - 73/127   White - 70.6/121
Gold - 66.6/114   Red - 70.6/123

Built in 1962 on the Myrtle Beach Air Force base, Whispering Pines was purchased in November of 1993 by the city of Myrtle Beach, which has operated this popular, economical championship course since then. Described as straightforward, very playable, enjoyable, and challenging, this eighteen-hole layout seems to get better every day.

Carved out of 325 acres of towering pines and mature hardwoods, Whispering Pines is "golf as it should be," said its head professional. "Unlike many courses on the Grand Strand, there are no houses, no buildings, nothing to mar the natural beauty of a very good golf course."

Designated as a wildlife habitat by the National Audubon Society, Whispering Pines is home to various species of Carolina wildlife, and the course's pristine nature delights golfers who enjoy the sense of getting away from it all. Still, the topography of Whispering Pines, which features contoured fairways and large undulating greens, surprises many golfers because the course is located just one mile from the Atlantic Ocean.

Green fees, which here are considerably less than those charged by most Grand Strand courses, make this an exceptionally popular course. Riding carts are available, but budget watchers and exercise seekers may opt for pull carts. Walking is permitted in the afternoon on a year-round basis.

Some have tabbed Whispering Pines as one of the Grand Strand's best-kept secrets,

but more than 52,000 rounds of golf were played here in 1997. While the course caters to "locals," it is estimated that at least 30 percent of the play came from out-of-state visitors who found the location convenient and the course enjoyable. Whispering Pines is reached from the entrance of U.S. 17 and is adjacent to the city's international airport, which comes into view as the golfer winds his way a mile and a half from Highway 17 to the clubhouse and pro shop.

Offering four sets of tees, this course has some fine golf holes. The par-four holes are generally characterized as "more difficult than normal," and one hole in particular, #8, might be slightly lengthened and made into a par five because course operators would like to establish a 36-36 par ratio instead of today's 35-37 with three par fives on the back side.

Number 7 and 8 are consecutive, back-to-back par fours that will test the mettle of any golfer. Both measure in the neighborhood of 400 yards and display an awesome array of trouble. The 7th hole is slightly longer, with water in front of the tee, curving to the right, and stretching all the way to the green. However, #7 does have room around the green, while #8 is narrow and tight around the green and has a water hazard that requires a shot of 160 to 170 yards to carry over the water onto the green.

This hole goes downhill, and although at first glance the water appears to be unreachable, the prudent golfer will take a second look and dig into the bag for a long iron or a four or five wood. If the tee shot hits that downhill slope, the ball can easily roll into the water. Even the host professional, standing on the tee 250 yards from the water, discards his driver on this one because of that downhill roll. The second shot is difficult, too, because the green is small and tight and allows every shot to feed to the right.

Number 16 is another memorable par four. It is a dogleg right, and a pond guards the left side of the green, which affords three different areas for pin placement. Club selection is important because a big hump runs through the middle of the green, forcing the golfer to get his second shot close to the pin or risk a very possible three putt.

While there are four good three pars at Whispering Pines, two stand out. The first three par you come across might be the best—or at least the most frightening. Relatively short, the hole is embraced by water on the left side of the fairway and almost completely around the green. If you bail out to the right, a pot bunker is there to give you trouble. The angle of the green from the tee box makes the pin a small target.

Number 17 is similar but twenty yards longer. The finger of water jutting out from the lake on the right is not the real problem here. Most golfers have no difficulty flying over that watery finger, but the series of pot bunkers between the water and the green offers a more realistic hazard. The two-tiered green doesn't make holing the ball any easier.

Number 12 might be the best par five on the course. It is lengthy, running 538 yards from the white markers, and a long body of water is on the right, but the major problem

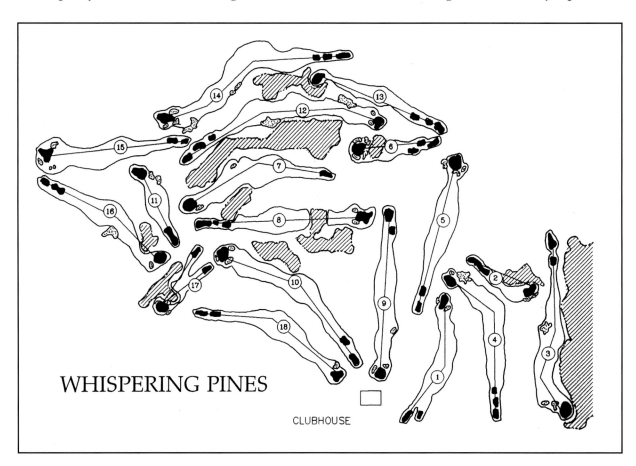

WHISPERING PINES

CLUBHOUSE

is the "late" dogleg to the right that makes a second shot attempt at the green virtually impossible. The dogleg starts inside the 100-yard marker, and the second shot becomes critical for the golfer to get into good position. The green itself is small, with much undulation and many pot bunkers set on the right side.

The golfer who likes to put good numbers on the scorecard will like #10 better. A very realistic two-shot par five, it is wide open except for sand on either side of the green. This hole is the most likely candidate to become a par four in the future to balance the possible changeover of #8 from a four to a five par.

All in all, golfers will enjoy Whispering Pines. They will like the pristine look, the contoured fairways, the elevations, the no-nonsense approach to golf, and the down-to-earth pricing.

Whispering Pines

HOLE NUMBER	1	2	3	4	5	6	7	8	9	OUT	10	11	12	13	14	15	16	17	18	IN	TOT	HCP	NET
CHAMPIONSHIP	355	158	485	404	408	197	413	416	395	3231	497	187	567	320	496	449	405	178	403 441	3502 3540	6733 6771		
MEN'S	353	142	458	366	389	151	398	390	378	3025	480	169	538	288	463	398	381	161	370	3248	6273		
SENIOR'S	348	107	410	323	320	106	338	328	335	2615	434	142	483	276	422	347	331	149	302	2886	5501		
LADIES'	290	95	403	319	300	102	335	322	329	2495	429	130	474	222	416	338	326	132	278	2745	5240		
PAR	4	3	5	4	4	3	4	4	4	35	5	3	5	4	5	4	4	3	4	37	72		
HCP CHAMP.	10	18	2	14	4	16	6	8	12		11	15	1	13	5	7	9	17	3				
HCP MEN'S/SR.	12	18	4	14	10	16	2	6	8		7	17	1	15	5	13	3	11	9				
HCP LADIES'	14	18	4	10	8	16	6	2	12		3	13	1	17	5	7	9	11	15				

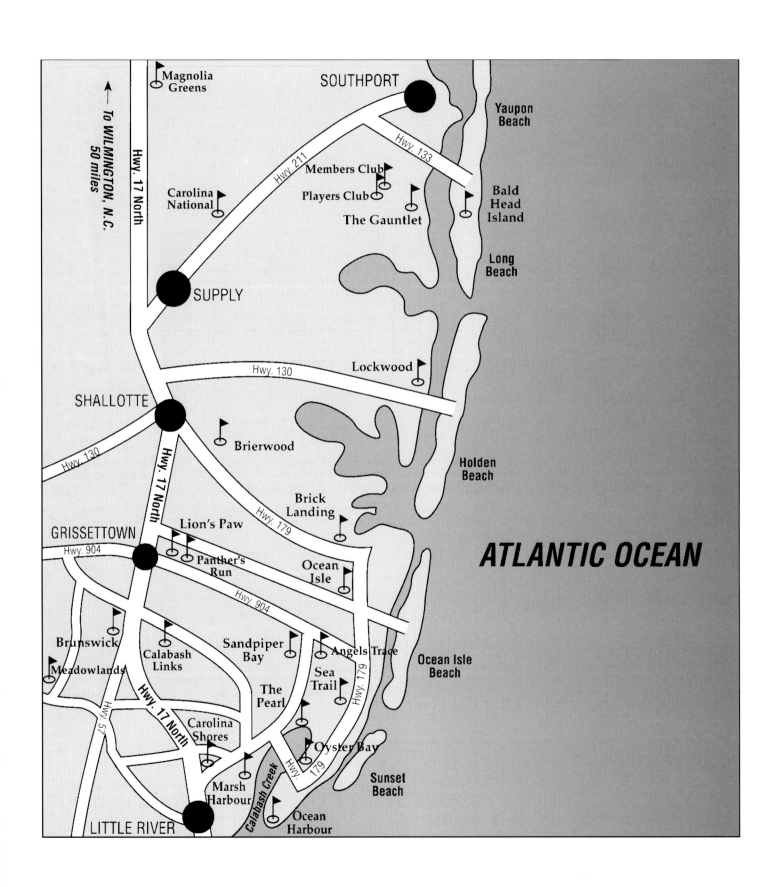

The Sunset Beach Area

Number #18—Lockwood. (Courtesy Lockwood/LHWH Advertising)

LOCKWOOD

100 Club House Dr.   Holden Beach, NC 28462
(910) 842-5666   (800) 443-7891

Architect: Willard Byrd   Year opened: 1988

Course rating/Slope rating
Blue - 73.5/135   Gold - 67.7/121
White - 70.7/129   Red - 70.0/121

Designers of the brochure for beautiful Lockwood invite the golfer to be "nature's guest" and then tell everyone that Lockwood is a golf course that challenges every part of your game and your imagination.

This is a good description of the very scenic, 6,800-yard Willard Byrd design. Byrd has designed many good golf courses, including Atlanta Country Club, the Country Club of North Carolina, and one of the three courses at Sea Trail Plantation, and this one does nothing to damage his reputation.

There are no parallel fairways, so every round affords a feeling of openness. Stroll along the Waterway, scenic lagoons, and Lockwood Folly River. Drive past a cypress island game preserve and a rolling waterfront peninsula. There is plenty of water at Lockwood, and it comes into play on twelve of the eighteen holes.

While not exceptionally long, the course is certainly long enough—even from the white tees, which measure 6,149 yards—to give most golfers a challenge. The course is "tight." It is fun, but can be made extremely diffi-

cult, as evidenced by the fact that the course record from the championship tees is 68, set by Hugh Gill in a Pro-Amateur.

Number 2 and #18 are the signature holes, but every hole will intrigue with its own distinctive character. The meticulously maintained course of bent-grass greens and large, well-sculpted bunkers presents both entertainment and challenge.

Surprisingly, there is little rough at Lockwood, but the fairways are guarded by forests of trees and huge lakes. The golfer just goes straight from fairway to trouble!

From the back tees, #2 is a 200-yard three par over marshland. If the golfer comes up short, the second shot is going to be unplayable. And if his shot strays off-line, chances are good that the second effort will be from woods.

Number 18 goes back to the clubhouse and is an excellent finishing hole. A lake juts almost entirely across the fairway 200 yards from the white tees, requiring a drive of 235 yards to clear the water. If the golfer is successful in getting over the lake, there is a sand trap just beyond the water and

Lockwood

HOLE NUMBER	1	2	3	4	5	6	7	8	9	OUT	10	11	12	13	14	15	16	17	18	IN	TOT	HCP	NET
BLUE	430	200	467	365	389	211	524	405	380	3371	537	180	459	418	374	408	197	357	500	3430	6801		
WHITE	378	157	443	346	372	183	488	335	352	3054	485	157	402	375	341	363	184	335	453	3095	6149		
GOLD	331	131	376	324	335	160	442	288	320	2707	441	130	370	357	315	333	155	293	423	2817	5524		
HANDICAP	4	8	18	16	12	10	2	6	14		7	5	1	9	17	3	11	15	13				
PAR	4	3	5	4	4	3	5	4	4	36	5	3	4	4	4	4	3	4	5	36	72		
RED	300	115	359	295	297	137	393	271	292	2459	408	105	342	324	288	314	128	268	393	2570	5029		
HANDICAP	8	14	12	16	4	18	2	6	10		5	11	1	9	13	3	15	17	7				

another large body of water to the right of the green.

Number 5 is a memorable hole, too. Water cuts across the entire width of the fairway, angling to the left side of the green. This is a four-par hole with a sloping fairway, and the long hitter must be careful not to hit his drive too far. Straight down the middle it is 250 yards from the back cut of the white tees to the water. Most second shots will be anywhere from 130 to 170 yards on this 375-yard hole.

Number 7 and #8 are interesting, too, as Byrd used the same body of water to create two long dogleg holes. The lake forms the dogleg in both instances, #7 going to the right, and #8 back to the left.

There is plenty of trouble on the front side, but the back nine generally is considered more difficult.

Lockwood is a good golf course, created by one of the great names in golf and cared for lovingly. You'll enjoy playing there.

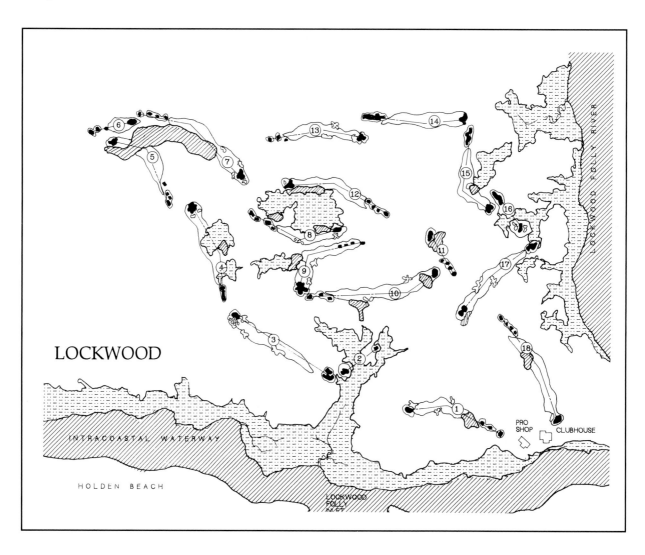

LOCKWOOD

BRIERWOOD

Highway 179   P.O. Box 100   Shallotte, NC 28459   (252) 754-4660
Architect: Benjamin Ward   Year opened: 1966

Course rating/Slope rating
Blue - 71.0/117
White - 69.8/113
Red - 67.0/104

Brierwood is a good golf course which, until recently, had little recognition in Myrtle Beach, but was treasured by Brunswick County residents. This championship course began as a nine-hole layout in 1966 and grew with Shallotte, increasing to eighteen holes in 1974 as 250 homes sprang up alongside the fairways in this 600-acre development.

Designed by the owner, Dr. Benny Brooks Ward, and renowned golf architect Russell

Breeden, the course was built on a plantation owned by the Ward family and fashioned in the style of the mid-1960s—no mounds or swales. It is nothing fancy, just straightforward golf with plenty of water and sand hazards. Although fairly long, measuring 6,700 yards from the blues and 6,200 from the whites, Brierwood is not particularly tough.

There have been many improvements at

Trees in the left of the green frame #17 at Brierwood. (Courtesy Brierwood Golf Course)

Brierwood since Dr. Ward, after leasing his course to outside interests, resumed operations in 1982. Today the course has a full watering system from tee to green and a new fleet of seventy-five golf carts. In 1988 both *Golf Reporter Magazine* and *Golf Links* called Brierwood the most improved golf course in the Carolinas and devotees of Brierwood say it just keeps getting better.

The back nine is the original nine-hole layout, improved with irrigation and imagination. There is nothing wrong with the front side, either, and #9 is a wonderful entrance to the second nine. This is a three-par hole requiring a tee shot of 215 yards over water to a well-manicured, well-trapped

green nestled in the trees by the pro shop.

Number 10 is perhaps the most talked about hole on the course, and as tough as it is pretty. The tee shot comes out of a chute uphill to a dogleg right and the second shot is across a large lake. Underscoring the difficulty is the fact that 20,000 balls are recovered from that lake each year. It is a very hard hole.

There is no letup ahead. Water comes into play on most of the holes, and is particularly vexing on the long, straightaway par-four 11th and the 524-yard par-five 12th which, on most days, just cannot be reached in two. The big-hitting golfer, going for broke, does have an opportunity to gain a stroke

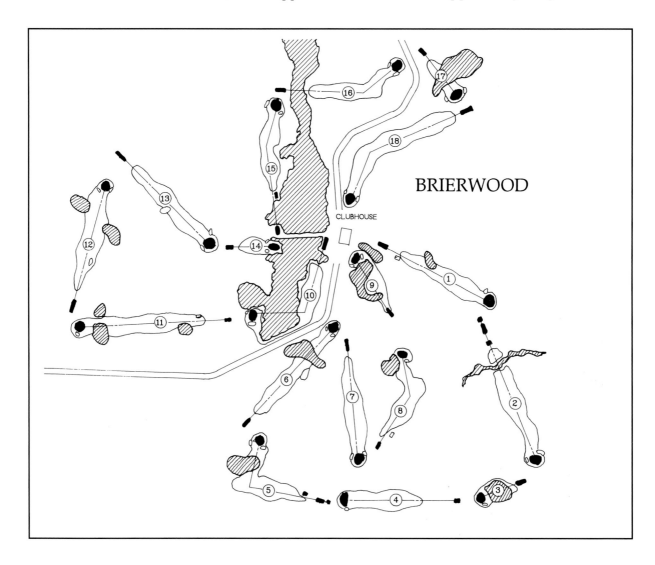

BRIERWOOD

CLUBHOUSE

on par on the par five finishing hole, but needs to draw a long tee shot around or over a tree that juts into the fairway.

Most people enjoy playing this course. It is short enough from forward tees for ladies and the high-handicap male golfer, but can be stretched to championship length and allows the big hitter to bring his driver out of the bag.

Brierwood

HOLE NUMBER	1	2	3	4	5	6	7	8	9	OUT	10	11	12	13	14	15	16	17	18	IN	TOT	HCP	NET
BLUE	389	515	156	373	381	455	387	328	219	3203	389	367	524	417	166	411	427	184	519	3404	6607		
WHITE	375	497	140	328	358	446	376	306	186	3012	366	304	515	400	150	350	393	175	505	3157	6169		
MEN'S HCP	5	3	17	13	11	7	1	15	9		8	16	2	6	18	12	4	14	10				
MEN'S PAR	4	5	3	4	4	5	4	4	3	36	4	4	5	4	3	4	4	3	5	36	72		
RED	273	367	120	240	200	365	276	250	143	2234	245	255	442	322	129	267	274	136	433	2503	4737		
LADIES' HCP	10	4	16	8	18	2	6	14	12		1	9	3	7	17	11	13	15	5				
LADIES' PAR	4	5	3	4	4	5	4	4	3	36	4	4	5	4	3	4	4	3	5	36	72		

The second shot on #18 at picturesque Brick Landing Plantation. (Courtesy Brick Landing Plantation)

Brick Landing Plantation

HOLE NUMBER	1	2	3	4	5	6	7	8	9	OUT	10	11	12	13	14	15	16	17	18	IN	TOT	HCP	NET
BLUE	369	119	345	510	424	365	563	173	456	3324	357	359	153	513	351	501	438	121	365	3158	6482		
WHITE	356	112	332	495	403	338	536	148	431	3151	337	339	145	498	326	481	421	116	346	3003	6154		
GOLD	329	107	319	480	380	301	503	137	408	2964	321	312	134	459	310	459	409	110	314	2828	5792		
RED	255	101	280	428	282	287	449	122	299	2503	257	265	127	379	250	400	292	87	275	2332	4835		
HANDICAP	9	17	11	1	7	13	3	15	5		12	2	16	10	14	4	6	18	8				
PAR	4	3	4	5	4	4	5	3	4	36	4	4	3	5	4	5	4	3	4	36	72		

BRICK LANDING PLANTATION

Route 2 Box 210   Ocean Isle Beach, NC 28469

(252) 754-4373   (800) 438-3006

Architect: Michael Brazeal   Year opened: 1987

Course rating/Slope rating

Blue - 71.0/140   Gold - 67.8/122

White - 69.4/132   Red - 67.8/114

Ask ten people, and you will probably get ten different opinions about Brick Landing Plantation, ranging from "one of the best courses I have ever played" to "I've played it once; that's enough."

Officials of Brick Landing call this "one of the unique golf courses in North Carolina's South Brunswick Islands. Playing through beautiful hardwood forests, along scenic salt marshes by the Intracoastal Waterway, Brick Landing has drawn raves for its challenging design."

This definitely is a shotmaker's golf course.

Professional Ben Hunt, first pro at Brick Landing, wrote and designed a "Golfer's Handbook," which is highly recommended to any golfer playing here for the first time. In the introduction to his detailed booklet, Hunt writes, "You are about to experience one of the most beautiful and challenging rounds of golf you have ever played. Much like the TPC at Sawgrass, course architect Mike Brazeal has designed this to be a shotmaker's golf course with the premium placed on accuracy rather than distance."

Another apt description of Brick Landing would be one offered by the resort's first woman professional, Debra Merritt, who was at this course in 1989 and 1990. "This course takes a lot of local knowledge," said Merritt. "It is short, tight, and wet...."

Water comes into play on sixteen of the eighteen holes.

This course measures 6,482 yards from the tournament tees and 6,154 from the men's regular tees. There are four sets of tees on most of the holes, three for men and one for the ladies, measuring 4,835 yards from tee to green.

Architect Brazeal is proud of his creation.

"Being charged with providing the master land-use plan for Brick Landing Plantation is quite an opportunity in itself, but when added to this is the design and construction of the golf course...well, it's just one of those once-in-a-lifetime experiences."

Brick Landing Plantation consists of 880 acres, and Brazeal can become lyrical about the merits of every acre. "All eighteen holes are individual creations within themselves, painstakingly extracted from this highest caliber of land. The sheer excitement of playing along the Intracoastal Waterway with views of the Atlantic Ocean! The pristine beauty of the Sauce Pan Creek and Marsh, along with the tranquil lagoons and hardwood forest of the interior holes! These are enjoyments you'll simply have to experience on your own."

Holes #10 through #13 are carefully sculptured along Sauce Pan Creek and Marsh, with #11 being particularly notorious. Many publications have cited this hole as the toughest on the course, and one of the most difficult anywhere. From any of the tees a long drive is needed to carry over the marsh to a landing area resembling a postage stamp in size, drastically reduced by the pond on the left of this island-type green. Nor can you "bail out" to the right. If you do, you're in the marsh.

It is a most intimidating hole.

Less intimidating, but very picturesque, golf holes are #1, #17, and #18, which are routed along the Waterway. A long hitter can drive the green from the white tees at #1, but he must be extremely accurate as the Waterway borders the hole from tee to green on the right, and there are two ponds which come into play on the left—plus three sand traps!

"Although it is possible to drive this green from the whites," writes Ben Hunt, "the risks are heavy. I recommend a long iron or fairway wood for safety. This will set up your approach to the green which has water on one side and marsh on the other." A footbridge across the pond by the green affords a picturesque view.

Number 18 has been called one of the most picturesque holes in this part of the country, and goes back to the clubhouse with marsh and Waterway on the right. A good drive must carry the water in front of the fairway and the golfer has the choice of "cutting off" as much of this water hazard as he dares. The second shot can be anything from a long iron or fairway wood to a wedge.

Brick Landing is one of the most challenging courses on the Strand. It is developing a fine reputation as home of an outstanding amateur golf tournament and is being selected for other good tournaments. It is a course you are going to either love or hate—I don't think there is any middle ground. The golfer who is accurate will enjoy the eighteen holes, but the long hitter will find he had better keep his driver in the bag on many of the holes and learn that discretion on Brick Landing is certainly the better part of valor.

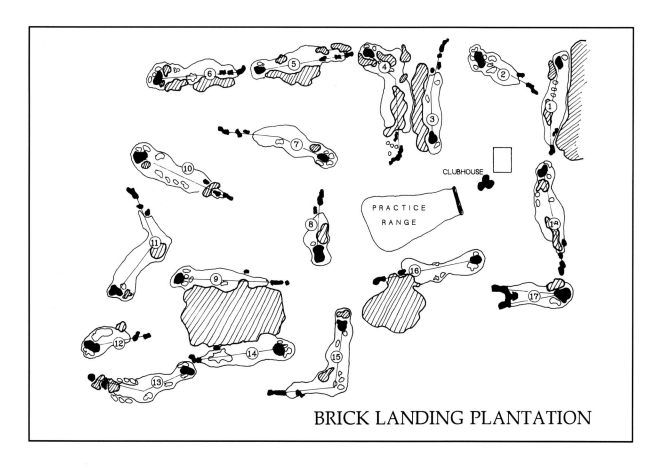

BRICK LANDING PLANTATION

LION'S PAW

351 Ocean Ridge Parkway   Ocean Isle Beach, NC 28469
(Highway 904 East between U.S. 17 and South Carolina 179)
(843) 448-5566   (800) 233-1801

Architect: Willard Byrd   Year opened: 1991

Course rating/Slope rating
Championship - 74.7/130   Senior Men - 68.5/119
Men - 71.6/124   Ladies - 69.3/117

Lion's Paw, a Willard Byrd design, opened in April 1991 and soon became known as one of the premier golf courses on the Grand Strand. Thousands of golfers have enjoyed the challenges to be found at this fine course, located just across the South Carolina border near the junction of Routes 17 and 904 in North Carolina.

Lion's Paw is a "big" golf course, more than 7,000 yards in length from the championship tees, and features a diversity of design that makes it both fascinating and difficult. Byrd has taken advantage of natural rolling terrain on the front side and then turned to wide-open spaces to create a Scottish look for much of the back nine. There is water everywhere and, as you might expect of a Byrd design, plenty of doglegs, elevated tees, mounds, and sand traps.

There are some excellent golf holes, such as #3, a tough three par, and #8, a beautiful five par played from an elevated tee. The 3rd hole measures 204 yards from the championship tees to the center of the green, but length is not the sole reason for citation of this hole. After all, three of the four three pars are more than 200 yards in length and demand an accurate and long tee shot. The feature that makes #3 very special is the bank of oyster shells that forms the "beach" of the lake between the golfer and the green. There is very little room between the oyster-shell beach and the green. The shot is all carry!

The number-one handicap hole on this course, #4, will get your attention, too. It is a very long par four, 428 yards, with water and marsh coming into play if you miss the green on your approach. This hole is long and tight.

When you drive through the entrance of this championship course, the initial impression is that of a wide-open golf course—but that is deceptive. Even the holes "on the plain" force you to hit accurate shots. The five-par 13th is a case in point. The vista is right out of Scotland: no trees, no mounds, flat, fields of flowers. It is one of those "on a clear day I can see forever" types of holes. Sure. Just wait until you play it. With no trees, there is nothing to stop the wind . . . and water runs all the way down the right side of the fairway and then crosses it in front of the green.

But that hole is not more difficult than #15, which also plays through the wide-open spaces and is a "bear." A dogleg left, #15 is a four-par 445-yard hole, very demanding.

There are at least four sets of tees on every hole: championship, men, senior men, and ladies. Some of the holes feature a fifth tee that makes a shorter hole for the ladies. The front side and back nine are very different, and water is in play on every one of the nine holes on the incoming nine. The three-par holes are very difficult, but the five pars can be generous, and the big hitter can come close to reaching them in two-if the wind is in his favor. This is a well-designed course, and the bent grass greens are excellent.

See also Panther's Run (p. 275).

Lion's Paw

HOLE NUMBER	1	2	3	4	5	6	7	8	9	OUT	10	11	12	13	14	15	16	17	18	IN	TOT	HCP	NET
CHAMP.	417	517	204	428	415	228	402	520	386	3517	400	202	383	527	418	445	384	185	542	3486	7003		
MEN	387	477	178	385	399	175	364	495	352	3212	375	188	372	493	396	408	353	154	506	3245	6457		
SEN. MEN	351	433	123	361	366	136	332	478	336	2916	349	172	322	431	393	382	319	131	457	2956	5872		
MEN'S HCP	3	17	7	1	5	9	11	15	13		6	8	10	18	4	2	16	14	12				
PAR	4	5	3	4	4	3	4	5	4	36	4	3	4	5	4	4	4	3	5	36	72		
LADIES'	335	416	108	326	353	125	303	455	305	2726	307	110	300	413	328	366	286	121	406	2637	5363		
LADIES' HCP	3	17	7	1	5	9	11	15	13		6	8	10	18	4	2	16	14	12				

Oyster shells and water at #3, Lion's Paw (Courtesy Himmelsbach Communications/ Bill Woodward)

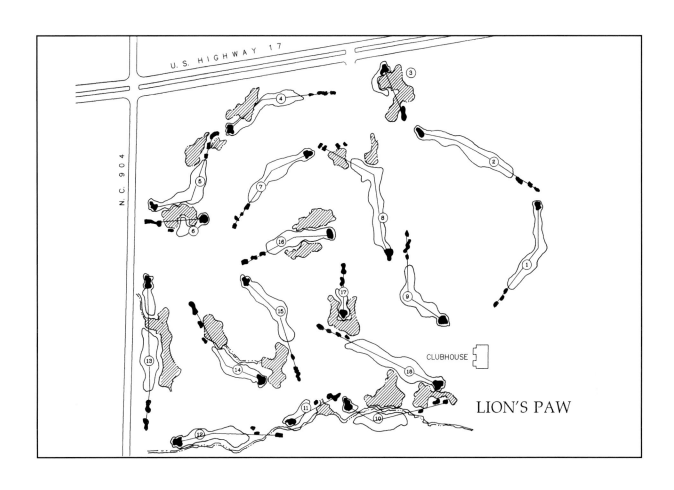

LION'S PAW

You can land your airplane alongside the four-par 8th hole at Ocean Isle Beach.
(Courtesy Himmelsbach Communications/Bill Woodward)

OCEAN ISLE BEACH

Route 6 Box 16   Ocean Isle Beach, NC 28469
(843) 272-3900
Architect: Russell Breeden   Year opened: 1978
Course rating/Slope rating
Blue - 71.0/122
White - 69.5/122
Red - 69.0/116

Ocean Isle Beach is one of the best kept secrets on the Grand Strand—this is a mature golf course with modest green fees and is usually in very good condition. A nice little course, but long enough at 6,700 yards from the back tees, Ocean Isle features well-bunkered greens.

While this is a "comfortable" course, with wide fairways and large landing areas, there are some very interesting holes, and the owner, working with golf architect Russell Breeden, made good use of rolling terrain and stands of pine. While water is not a major factor on this course, creeks and ponds were strategically brought into play when the course was built in 1978, and Breeden designed some severe doglegs, both left and right, creating memorable holes.

Good five-par holes are the norm, not the exception, at Ocean Isle, and a signature of the course.

A local professional is fond of the backside, and cites five-par holes #11 and #17 as his favorites. Both are well over 500 yards in length from the championship tees, and both are played to elevated greens which

defy the effort of most golfers to reach the green with two shots.

Number 7 is another five par that will appeal to many golfers, particularly those who can hit it a long way. This hole is a sharp dogleg to the right, and the green is elevated from a fairway that slopes to a pond on the right. By cutting part of the dogleg, avoiding both a trap and water, a long hitter can put himself in position to try for an eagle putt. The other par five is #1, and a creek bisects the fairway 260 yards from the tee, creating a problem for the long hitter who wants to get home in two and must put his tee shot in play as close to the creek as possible—but not too close! It's even worse for the high handicapper, who will have trouble hitting his second shot across this water barrier.

The course is simplified by the lack of fairway traps, but most of the greens are guarded by formidable sand bunkers.

Ocean Isle is a course that can be tamed, but not without effort, skill, and local knowledge. Jim Campbell, professional at this facility from its inception until 1988, recorded

Ocean Isle Beach

HOLE NUMBER	1	2	3	4	5	6	7	8	9	OUT	10	11	12	13	14	15	16	17	18	IN	TOT	HCP	NET
BLUE	554	177	389	362	157	353	501	396	360	3249	397	561	348	144	392	194	451	532	358	3377	6626		
WHITE	532	163	366	344	140	329	454	367	334	3029	367	540	326	138	371	182	400	468	325	3117	6146		
HANDICAP	2	16	8	10	17	13	4	6	12		7	1	14	18	9	15	5	3	11				
PAR	5	3	4	4	3	4	5	4	4	36	4	5	4	3	4	3	4	5	4	36	72		
RED	463	126	309	269	106	261	354	306	277	2471	327	479	267	95	286	148	331	439	232	2604	5075		

several rounds in the low 60s, and holds the competitive course record of 62.

Ocean Isle may be termed a "good little golf course," but it is really better than that, and a course most people will thoroughly enjoy playing.

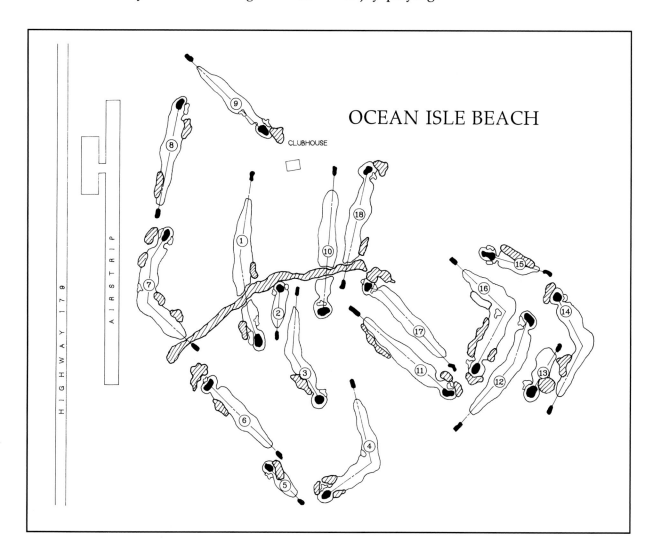

OCEAN ISLE BEACH

SANDPIPER BAY

6660 Sandpiper Bay Dr.   Calabash, NC 28459
(919) 579-9120   (800) 356-5827

Architect: Dan Maples   Year opened: 1987

Course rating/Slope rating:
Blue - 71.6/119
White - 69.0/116
Red - 68.3/113

Sandpiper Bay is a handsome golf course that beckons golfers to the Calabash area. Directly across the old Georgetown Highway from five other resort courses (two at The Pearl and three at Sea Trail Plantation), Sandpiper Bay is one of several excellent courses that adorn a relatively small radius east of Highway 17.

In addition to Sandpiper, Sea Trail, and The Pearl, Oyster Bay, Marsh Harbour, Carolina Shores, Ocean Isle Beach, Lion's Paw, Brick Landing Plantation, and Ocean Harbour are only a hop, skip, and jump away.

However, Sandpiper Bay—a Dan Maples creation—occupies a unique position among these giants. It certainly is a championship course, but unlike most of the others, it was

Aerial view of several outstanding holes on the back nine at Sandpiper Bay. (Courtesy Himmelsbach Communications/Bill Woodward)

not designed to achieve the maximum level of difficulty. Not that Sandpiper Bay is easy for the low-handicap golfer. The course record of 67 indicates this is no "snap" layout from the 6,503-yard par-71 blue tees, but the wide landing areas make it enjoyable and speed up play. Like most Strand courses, there is plenty of water but, for the most part, the water is more decorative than frightening.

Maples did an excellent job here. His design features rolling, contoured fairways, naturally sculptured bunkers, and fast, bent-grass greens. There are three separate teeing areas for each hole, and fifty-seven sand traps add to the challenge.

Esthetically, Sandpiper Bay is very pleasing. The course is located in the center of a National Wetlands Protection Area. No houses can be erected here, and the natural area will stay that way as a sanctuary for birds, animals, and errant shots.

Before visiting this course, we were told by several golfing aficionados, "You're going to enjoy Sandpiper Bay."

They were right.

The bent-grass greens are excellent; the scenery is delightful; golf traffic moves more swiftly than it does on most resort courses; and it is a very good golf course. Don't be lulled into a sense of false security, because the water can jump up and grab you on most of the holes.

Number 1 is straightaway, relatively short,

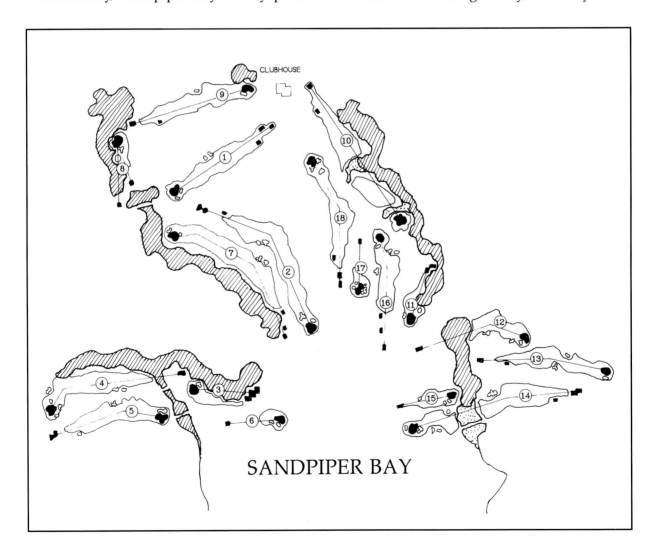

SANDPIPER BAY

218

and it affords the average golfer a good chance to start his round with a par four or, even better, a birdie. However, #2 stretches 577 yards, and the green is strategically bunkered, making a par five a very good score here.

And it doesn't get any easier.

The 3rd hole, from the blues, is a devilish 205 yards, mostly over marsh and water, with very little room behind the green.

At #7, a 524-yard par-five dogleg with water and cypress on the left and traps to the right, try not to bite off too much of the

hole by playing it down the left side. Chances are that you can't reach this one with two blows no matter where you hit your tee shot.

The hole bends around a canal and wetlands. Wild birds are visible in the marsh. This is a very pretty hole, but it's not pretty if you hook the ball. To reach it in two, you would need to cut off a lot of water, an extremely dangerous play.

Officials of Sandpiper Bay are enthusiastic about the reviews of this course, which praise its greens, overall condition, and layout.

Sandpiper Bay

HOLE NUMBER	1	2	3	4	5	6	7	8	9	OUT	10	11	12	13	14	15	16	17	18	IN	TOT	HCP	NET
BLUE	384	577	198	502	374	190	538	191	405	3359	544	173	384	400	553	177	338	159	416	3144	6503		
WHITE	349	534	183	469	349	162	490	160	374	3070	504	142	354	379	514	141	304	129	386	2853	5923		
HANDICAP	11	5	7	13	17	15	1	9	3		6	12	10	4	8	14	16	18	2				
PAR	4	5	3	5	4	3	5	3	4	36	5	3	4	4	5	3	4	3	4	35	71		
RED	300	470	108	406	245	89	424	110	300	2452	448	112	311	319	454	103	258	101	311	2417	4869		
LADIES' HCP	11	3	7	13	15	17	1	9	5		6	12	2	10	8	16	14	18	4				
LADIES' PAR	4	5	3	5	4	3	5	3	4	36	5	3	4	4	5	3	4	3	4	35	71		

Aerial view of finishing holes at The Pearl, a thirty-six-hole golf development of various architectural styles. (Courtesy Brandon Advertising/Michael Slear)

THE PEARL

1300 Pearl Blvd., SW   Sunset Beach, NC 28468
(888) 947-3275

Architect: Dan Maples   Year opened: 1988

Course rating/Slope rating

WEST
Black - 73.2/132
Blue - 72.5/131
White - 71.0/129
Gold - 68.0/123

EAST
73.1/135
72.1/132
70.8/127
68.4/122

Located just north of the border separating North and South Carolina, The Pearl is truly a gem. This showplace of coastal beauty has thirty-six challenging holes to test every facet of the better player, but because there are multiple sets of tees on every hole, it also is gentle to the average higher handicapper.

Golf architect Dan Maples has taken advantage of a beautiful 900-acre tract of ground to construct two championship eighteen-hole courses, both of them good enough to be nominated by *Golf Digest* magazine as the best new courses of 1988, the year they were opened.

Complementing the excellent courses is a magnificent 9,000-square-foot clubhouse, fully stocked pro shop, spacious driving range, convenient putting green, and modern fleet of carts. Everything, including the exterior signs and interior painting and carpeting, is decorated in shades of pink and green. In the wide hallway that leads from the pro shop into the dining area, golfers' attention is arrested by large, full-scale portraits of touring golf professionals who have either in the past represented or now represent

The Pearl. The big black Titleist bag beneath the portrait of Keith Clearwater is a replica of the one carried by Clarence Rose, and the white Ping bag is emblazoned with the name of Cathy Johnston, who not only holds the course record from the ladies tees (70) but represents The Pearl on the LPGA.

The real star of this resort facility, however, is the thirty-six holes of golf.

The public obviously agrees with The Pearl that the two courses are among the best on the Grand Strand, and there is a great demand for tee times here throughout the year.

Dan Maples had a beautiful piece of real estate with which to work. He designed a layout with no two holes alike, perfectly placed bunkers, and 600-yard five pars, taking advantage of the natural roll and plentiful marsh and water.

He considered every element of the property —the weather, the winds, the terrain—and applied those variances in his design. Several holes change daily, so you play a different course every time you go out there.

A unique feature of The Pearl is that it

encompasses in thirty-six holes four totally different looks! Playing the first two holes of the West course, a golfer can be excused if he feels as if he were playing a fine Scottish links course. Then, crossing the highway that leads from the main road into the clubhouse, he begins to play an area that resembles the best of Pinehurst before cutting out of the woods into a windblown fairyland with the flavor of the Florida Everglades.

The East course is built more in the line of a traditional great coastal course, wide fairways cut through a forest of pine, moving onto rolling terrain and finishing with marsh and water.

The last five or six holes on both courses are world class, giving you the chance to go for birdies.

The West Course

On the West course, #15 offers different elevations. The tee is set more than three hundred feet above sea level and the golfer drives downhill into a ravine, then plays a dogleg right back up a steep incline to the green, usually playing into a stiff wind. When a minitour event was played at The Pearl in 1989, this was a pivotal hole. Most of the golfers approached #15 with extra caution, and stroke average was considerably more than its four-par rating. There is trouble on both sides, and a hazard down to the right that does not come into view from the tee box. Then, too, the green itself is two-tiered, and from the middle of the green slopes to the right.

Number 16 is an extremely tough, very long five par. Tee shot is crucial because of a well-positioned sand trap to the right. If the golfer carries his drive over this trap, he is flirting with the marsh, and if he hits it right of the trap he definitely is in the marsh. Hit it too far left and his second shot is blocked by the trees. The second shot is just as important. Hit it too far and you have a

downhill lie. This is a "thinking man's par five," and the chances of reaching the green in two are very poor. The green itself is long, and pin placement can make a three-club difference from front to back. Well bunkered, it is a classic par five.

Number 17 is not a long par three, but it is very deceiving. Completely circled by trees, it looks much shorter than it actually plays.

The Calabash River borders these last four holes, and the golfer needs to play a shot across it on #18. It is a gambler's hole requiring a crucial tee shot. It is possible to put a driver in your hands and try to cut the corner, making it possible to reach the green in two, but it is much safer to use a three wood on the tee and play it as a three-shot hole even though you encounter a tree in the fairway for your third shot.

The East Course

Number 18 on the East course parallels #18 on the West, but they are entirely different in character.

The last three holes on the East are tough, and will make or break your round. They will make a lasting impression, beginning with the four-par 16th, which is relatively short but a very severe dogleg to the right. You use a long iron or three wood off the tee to a small landing area guarded by a trap and woods on both sides, leaving no room for error as you hit into a green that is well below the fairway.

Number 17 may be the best hole on the East course. The Calabash River again is on the left, along the entire length of the hole, which is a long dogleg par four with a tremendous bunker at the bend of the dogleg. Hard to believe, but even at sea level there are drastic changes of elevation, and a downhill lie to an elevated green is very possible for the golfer who has elected to clear the trap...if the drive goes right, the ball could find itself surrounded by strategic mounding.

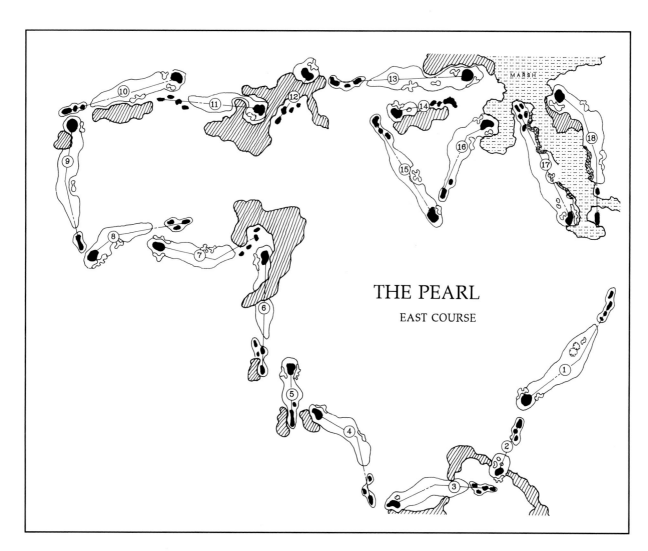

THE PEARL

EAST COURSE

West Course

HOLE NUMBER	1	2	3	4	5	6	7	8	9	OUT	10	11	12	13	14	15	16	17	18	IN	TOT	HCP	NET
BLACK	391	205	556	167	431	358	579	215	458	3362	394	358	401	147	614	443	604	151	534	3646	7008		
BLUE	364	190	546	157	411	349	568	195	425	3207	367	349	390	138	605	436	584	139	523	3531	6738		
WHITE	359	180	531	148	386	336	551	183	391	3065	349	338	356	135	571	407	556	134	508	3354	6419		
GOLD	336	145	485	125	360	318	512	169	358	2808	320	313	315	122	507	370	475	124	467	3013	5821		
PAR	4	3	5	3	4	4	5	3	4	35	4	4	4	3	5	4	5	3	5	37	72		

East Course

HOLE NUMBER	1	2	3	4	5	6	7	8	9	OUT	10	11	12	13	14	15	16	17	18	IN	TOT	HCP	NET
BLACK	533	200	349	416	208	394	412	353	510	3375	398	324	185	521	177	421	358	418	572	3369	6749		
BLUE	523	186	339	405	195	381	399	340	501	3269	385	311	171	506	166	415	352	406	562	3274	6543		
WHITE	506	171	327	381	185	357	384	322	481	3114	361	294	152	485	155	402	341	396	550	3136	6250		
GOLD	476	145	315	346	165	326	351	292	463	2879	329	271	120	442	142	361	316	369	527	2877	5756		
PAR	5	3	4	4	3	4	4	4	5	36	4	4	3	5	3	4	4	4	5	36	72		

223

From the green, #5 on the Jones course at Sea Trail Plantation. (Courtesy Himmelsbach Communications/Bill Woodward)

SEA TRAIL PLANTATION

Clubhouse Road   Sunset Beach, NC
(843) 272-2185   (800) 624-6601

Architects: Rees Jones   Dan Maples   Willard Byrd

Year opened: 1986
Course rating/Slope rating:

MAPLES	JONES	BYRD
Blue - 71.7/121	72.4/132	72.2/128
White - 70.1/117	70.4/126	70.4/126
Gold - 68.1/112	67.7/118	66.1/110
Red - 68.5/108	68.5/115	67.9/111

Sea Trail Plantation makes the claim that it is the "hottest new golfing destination on the East coast," and few will argue that it is, indeed, unique, pretty, and an excellent test of golf.

Nothing about Sea Trail is minor league.

Not only does the resort feature fifty-four holes of championship golf, but it also boasts two separate clubhouses with fully equipped pro shops, restaurants, and lounges.

To create a memorable and award-winning resort, the owners of Sea Trail started the project by engaging proven winners to design fifty-four signature holes of championship golf. The names of those golf course architects—Dan Maples, Rees Jones, and Willard Byrd—are enough to make any golfer want to visit this 2,000-acre playground.

The Dan Maples course was the first eighteen-hole layout opened at Sea Trail in 1986, and it may well be one of his best ever. *Golf Digest* certainly thought so, nominating it as one of the most outstanding new resort courses in the country in 1986. The par-72 course has four sets of tees, ranging from 6,751 yards from the blues to 5,090 yards from the reds. It is a "sporty" course, a fitting companion to other Maples designs such as Oyster Bay and Marsh Harbour, both ranked by *Golf Digest* maga-

zine as two of the top fifty public courses in America.

The Rees Jones course, opened in the spring of 1990, is a great course; many professionals consider it to be the best on the Strand. Among the courses designed in the Myrtle Beach area by Jones is Arcadian Shores, selected four times by *Golf Digest* as one of "America's 100 greatest golf courses." The Jones course at Sea Trail seems much longer than its 6,761 yards from the blue tees, with elevated greens, many of them surrounded by water hazards.

Opened in the fall of 1990, the Willard Byrd course is a great favorite of visitors to the Strand, and is built around several large, man-made lakes, each ranging in size from fourteen to twenty acres. This course, too, measures 6,750 yards from the blue tees and enhances Byrd's reputation, earned as architect of Heather Glen here on the Strand and courses at Atlanta Country Club and the Country Club of North Carolina. He is a prolific architect and his firm has participated in more than nine hundred projects.

All three courses are exceptional, and many visitors elect to rent facilities at Sea Trail and play them again and again. Oyster Bay, another prizewinning course, is also located within the Plantation.

The Maples Course

Good players find this course not overly difficult, but everyone seems to agree that this is an innovative, fun course worthy of *Golf Digest*'s label as one of the most outstanding resort courses.

Maples likes it and one of his signature traits—a tree in the fairway—is visible on several holes. The course is fairly short, and gains its length of 6,332 from the white tees primarily because all of the five-par holes are more than 500 yards from tee to green.

The average player, if he can hit the ball straight, gains confidence on the first two holes, as #1 usually plays slightly less than 300 yards, and #2 335 yards.

However, there is water all the way down the right side with a stand of trees bordering the fairway on the left. This is typical of the problems golfers will find on all of the holes on this course with each shot requiring precision in length and accuracy.

Number 7 is a particularly memorable hole on the Maples course. It is a sharp dogleg left and the approach to the green must carry a sizeable lake. Medium but accurate drives set up a short iron over the water to a well-guarded green. It is necessary for the golfer to hit his tee shot past trees on the left into the dogleg, and not let that shot drift too far right. Traps on the right of the fairway serve to direct the tee shot.

Dan Maples built this trap around a tree at #15 at the Maples course, Sea Trail.
(Courtesy Himmelsbach Communications/Bill Woodward)

Number 7 on the Byrd course at Sea Trail. (Courtesy Brandon Advertising/Michael Slear)

Have you ever seen a 400-yard-long sand trap that extends almost the entire length of the fairway? You will if you play #15. Number 17 is perhaps one of the most photographed holes in the Southeast, a par-three, 177-yard layout with bunkers on the left and right guarding an elevated green.

While the 18th hole is short, reaching the green is only the beginning of your adventure. If the pin is near the front, a putt from the middle or beyond is almost impossible to hold and, if the golfer plays it too cozy, the entrance to the green is well trapped.

The bent-grass greens are fast and there is danger everywhere for the golfer who loses concentration. This is a course where a golfer thinks he can shoot low numbers, but the slope rating says "no."

The Jones Course

The Jones course is exceptional—elevated greens, good bent-grass greens, water on eleven of the eighteen holes, lots of sand, 6,761 yards in length.

Golfers will remember #5, which is one of the premier par threes on the Grand Strand. Almost 200 yards over water from the blue tees, your shot must be long and accurate. A bulkhead defines the front of a tremendous green, with large, inviting pot bunkers guarding the rear.

Another good hole is #10, bordered by a beautiful freshwater lake along the entire fairway. It is a sharp dogleg right with a string of sand traps punctuating the right side of the dogleg approach to the green. It is a par-four, 345-yard hole which certainly deserves your attention and your concentration.

The 18th is a very good finishing hole requiring three accurate shots to a well-trapped green. However, the trouble begins before your third shot, as a pond to the left threatens the tee shot and the fairway curves around a large lake on the right from landing area to the green. It is a spectacular hole.

First-time visitors also will remember the finishing holes on the front side of the Jones course. Rarely will they find two five pars in succession, but both #8 and #9 are devilishly tempting five pars, giving the golfer a chance to lower his score or zoom into the stratosphere. Both are doglegs and both holes afford the golfer a chance to "get wet" with a lake crossing the fairway on #8 and guarding #9 on the left side and rear.

The Byrd Course

If you are driving northeast on the Old Georgetown Highway, past The Pearl on your right and Sandpiper Bay just ahead to the left, the golf holes you are seeing are #13 and #5 of the Willard Byrd course.

It, too, is an outstanding golf course, and fun to play.

Number 13 is an exceptionally fine five par, long and straight but "tight" as the architect narrows the landing areas with a battery of fairway traps.

The 14th hole features tees that have been elevated more than normally found on a hole of this design to give the golfer a commanding view of the fairway. Unfortunately for many, the golfer also gets a good view of a wide, meandering lake that runs all the way down the left side from the tee box and continues around the back of the green. "This is a great golf hole that must be played with finesse," advises Byrd.

That advice extends to the entire course, which emphasizes doglegs, water, and sand. Bring your thinking cap with you when you play The Byrd.

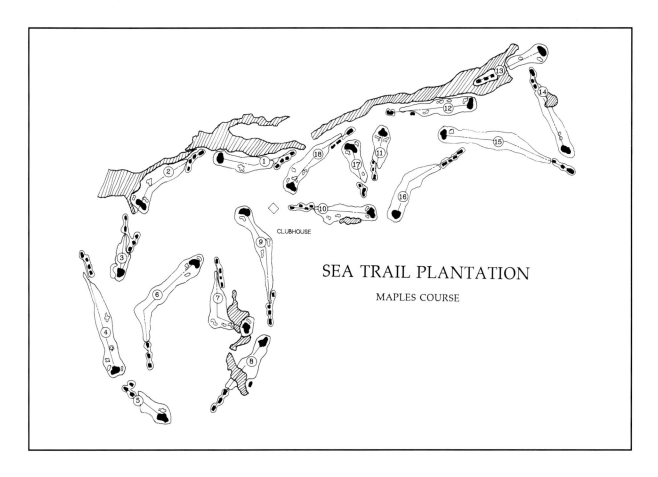

SEA TRAIL PLANTATION

MAPLES COURSE

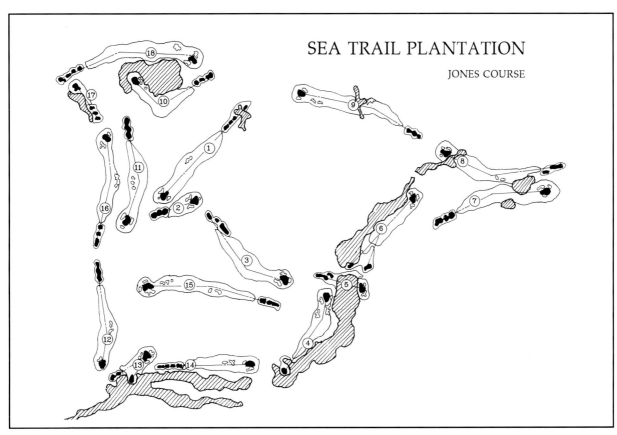

SEA TRAIL PLANTATION

JONES COURSE

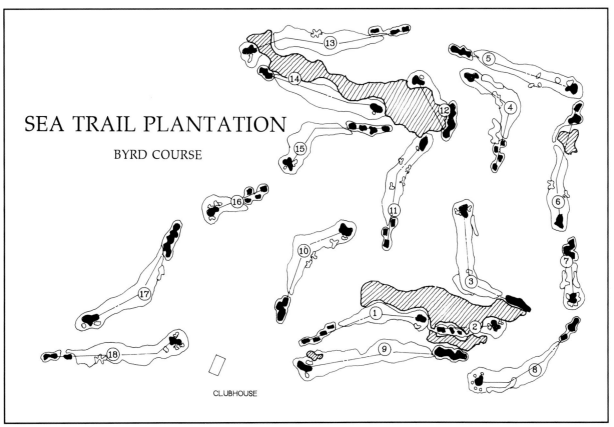

SEA TRAIL PLANTATION

BYRD COURSE

CLUBHOUSE

Maples Course

HOLE NUMBER	1	2	3	4	5	6	7	8	9	OUT	10	11	12	13	14	15	16	17	18	IN	TOT	HCP	NET
BLUE	315	350	185	545	180	555	410	410	455	3405	420	178	550	345	365	575	360	198	355	3346	6751		
WHITE	295	335	150	525	170	535	375	380	445	3210	400	155	490	325	345	555	345	177	330	3122	6332		
GOLD	275	315	120	510	160	520	365	365	420	3050	385	140	475	315	325	540	330	160	315	2985	6035		
MEN'S HCP	13	11	17	9	15	7	5	3	1		4	18	8	16	10	2	14	6	12				
PAR	4	4	3	5	3	5	4	4	4	36	4	3	5	4	4	5	4	3	4	36	72		
RED	245	275	100	465	145	475	330	235	360	2630	345	105	420	225	245	485	275	110	250	2460	5090		
LADIES' HCP	13	11	17	9	15	7	5	3	1		4	18	8	16	10	2	12	6	14				

Jones Course

HOLE NUMBER	1	2	3	4	5	6	7	8	9	OUT	10	11	12	13	14	15	16	17	18	IN	TOT	HCP	NET
BLUE	445	198	365	407	189	400	440	500	530	3474	345	418	398	144	340	555	420	157	510	3287	6761		
WHITE	405	178	350	365	155	375	385	482	510	3205	328	395	385	127	320	535	405	144	490	3129	6334		
GOLD	385	160	327	300	115	330	327	458	488	2890	305	355	347	110	298	455	367	134	455	2826	5716		
MEN'S HCP	1	17	13	9	7	5	3	15	11		10	4	14	18	12	8	2	16	6				
PAR	4	3	4	4	3	4	4	5	5	36	4	4	4	3	4	5	4	3	5	36	72		
RED	275	140	292	285	60	310	288	435	440	2525	220	305	310	100	250	392	288	117	405	2387	4912		
LADIES' HCP	13	15	7	9	17	5	11	3	1		14	4	6	18	12	10	8	16	2				

Byrd Course

HOLE NUMBER	1	2	3	4	5	6	7	8	9	OUT	10	11	12	13	14	15	16	17	18	IN	TOT	HCP	NET
BLUE	387	174	525	407	412	396	190	391	542	3424	400	368	186	528	404	387	202	382	469	3326	6750		
WHITE	350	163	468	378	392	365	167	365	517	3165	379	342	163	493	380	364	167	368	442	3098	6263		
GOLD	315	139	455	323	375	321	142	326	464	2860	353	278	126	454	340	345	155	333	346	2730	5590		
MEN'S HCP	15	11	18	3	1	7	9	5	13		8	16	12	17	2	4	10	6	14				
PAR	4	3	5	4	4	4	3	4	5	36	4	4	3	5	4	4	3	4	5	36	72		
RED	300	106	407	305	326	222	102	285	380	2433	310	216	99	382	250	271	126	309	321	2284	4717		
LADIES' HCP	13	11	5	3	1	17	15	7	9		4	8	18	2	10	6	16	12	14				

OYSTER BAY

614 Lake Shore Drive   Highway 179   Sunset Beach, NC
P.O. Box 65   North Myrtle Beach, SC 29582
(800) 552-2660

Architect: Dan Maples   Year opened: 1983

Course rating/Slope rating:
Championship - 71.6/134
Men - 69.7/125   Ladies - 68.0/118

It's hard to believe that Oyster Bay is fifteen years old. This Larry Young golf course wears well.

Opened in 1983, recognized by *Golf Digest* magazine as the best resort golf in the country that year, and consistently ranked among the top-fifty public golf courses every year, Oyster Bay is beautiful, diversified, and tough.

Designed by Dan Maples for Larry Young, who also built and operates the three golf courses at The Legends and the Heritage Club, Oyster Bay is located at Sunset Beach only five minutes away from the first Maples-Young design, Marsh Harbour.

With two beautiful island greens and some well-designed golf holes, Oyster Bay certainly is one of the most popular courses on the Strand. It often is 80 to 90 percent sold out for its spring season by the preceding fall. It is one of the "toughest tickets in town," and golfers who want to play this one are advised to call well in advance for tee times both here and at the other Larry Young operations.

The course is well named. By design, there are oyster shells everywhere—in the driveway to the clubhouse and even used to construct walls for some of the greens.

Variety and innovation are the name of the game at Oyster Bay. Consider severe marsh-oriented holes, two island-green par threes (one a near-perfect copy of the famous hole at PGA Players' Course), beautiful freshwater lakes, long holes, and short holes. Oyster Bay is long—6,700 yards from the back tees—but is a par 70!

Emphasizing the oyster trademark, the beautiful par-three 17th hole is played from oyster-shell-walled tees to an island green built on a mountain of shells. Another signature hole is the short par-four 13th hole, which is played along a lake that skirts the entire right side, then across a cavernous bunker to a wickedly undulating green resting on an oyster-shell wall rising starkly out of the lake below. These two holes in particular graphically illustrate this unique and innovative concept of oyster shells on a golf course.

Oyster Bay is difficult, with water affecting fifteen of the eighteen holes. At 6,700 yards, the course may seem short. The five par threes are short, but that makes the other thirteen holes even longer than average.

There are so many good holes on this course that it is difficult to pick and choose.

Holes #3 and #6 will remain in a golfer's memory. The 3rd hole originally was a par five, then was modified to a four. A sharp dogleg left, #3 requires a big drive if you're going to get it to the green over the water protecting the front and right side of the green. It is another picturesque hole, and the golfer reaches the green by driving the golf cart over a bridge.

The three-par 6th features a gigantic sand trap running from tee to green on the left side of the fairway. The distance is short (165 yards) but deceiving. The bunker on the right appears to be green-high but actually

Number 14 green at Oyster Bay is supported by a wall of oyster shells. (Courtesy Himmelsbach Communications/Bill Woodward)

is short of the green. Trust the scorecard—not your eyes!

Number 16 must be regarded as one of the best four pars on the Strand. It not only is long (470 yards from the back tees!) but, being on low ground, often is soft enough that the player gets little roll. Add water on the right and in front of the green and the result is a very difficult hole.

It is one of a group that course designer Maples calls four great finishing holes. Number 15 can play anywhere from a driver to a short iron depending on tee markers and wind conditions. The Intracoastal Waterway is in the background, and this

means that the wind is usually in your face.

Number 17 is the signature hole. It truly is an island green. There is the tee box, then 170 yards of water to the green. That's it—hit a good shot or you're swimming.

The Oyster Bay people who designed the scorecard have this admonition concerning #18: "Don't have a mental let-down after that island hole because you still have one terrific hole ahead. It is 400 yards in length, a great finishing hole as marsh extends across the fairway in front of the green." The golfer needs a good drive down the right side or will need to lay up. Even then, it still is a "pretty far piece" to a very deep two-tiered green.

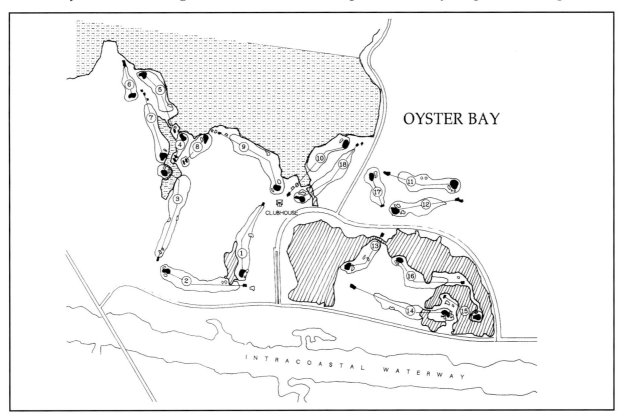

Oyster Bay

HOLE NUMBER	1	2	3	4	5	6	7	8	9	OUT	10	11	12	13	14	15	16	17	18	IN	TOT	HCP	NET
GOLD	390	450	470	190	550	165	390	160	560	3325	440	450	370	330	535	210	470	165	400	3370	6695		
BLUE	380	420	420	180	530	155	380	150	550	3165	430	430	360	320	525	205	450	165	385	3270	6435		
WHITE	340	385	365	160	510	125	370	135	490	2880	395	415	315	300	510	135	375	100	365	2910	5790		
RED	265	320	285	135	380	95	275	100	450	2305	250	360	260	230	410	85	360	75	295	2325	4630		
MEN'S HCP	7	1	3	11	9	17	13	15	5		4	6	18	14	16	8	2	10	12				
PAR	4	4	4	3	5	3	4	3	5	35	4	4	4	4	5	3	4	3	4	35	70		
LADIES'HCP	11	7	5	15	1	17	9	13	3		2	4	18	10	12	14	6	16	8				

Number 5, regarded as one of the most difficult holes on the Azalea nine at Brunswick. (Courtesy Brunswick Plantation)

BRUNSWICK PLANTATION

(Twenty-seven holes: Magnolia, Azalea, Dogwood)
Highway 17, P.O. Box 4778, Calabash, NC 28467
(800) 848-0290   (910) 287-PUTT

Architect: Willard Byrd   Year opened: 1992

Course rating/Slope Rating:
Black - 72.7/131   Blue - 70.2/124
White - 68.1/118   Red - 70.4/115

* Magnolia and Dogwood are used for yardage and ratings.

Brunswick Plantation is rapidly growing into one of the premier golfing resorts of the Grand Strand, and the twenty-seven-hole Willard Byrd course is the heart of the enterprise.

With much foresight, developers of Brunswick bought a 4,000-acre tract of ground fronting U.S. Highway 17 just north of the South Carolina border. Nine holes were added to the original eighteen in early 1998, but that's only the beginning. There's plenty of room for another three or four courses on this magnificent site, which already includes a large, columned clubhouse, seventeen condominium buildings, and six hundred taps for individual housing.

The condominiums borrow from low country (or Charleston) architecture and are picturesque and colorful, painted in hues of blue, green, yellow, beige, and coral. Many of the homes are statuesque, large, and brick, but others are designed to individual taste.

Golfers, of course, don't come to the Grand Strand to admire housing developments, although many are so enchanted with the area that this building explosion does get their attention. They are here, first of all, to play golf, and Brunswick is a quality facility, challenging but enjoyable.

Those who have played here before are going to find Brunswick familiar but different—that's because the original back nine has been intermingled with a third nine. However, while there are nine new golf holes, these holes are not strung together in a straight line. Seven of the new additions are to Dogwood, and two have been placed squarely in the middle of Azalea. Golfers will want to play all three of the nines because each is different from the other in look, style, and nature.

The original front side, Magnolia, has not been changed. Except for three holes that are bordered with tall pines, it remains wide open, exuding a distinctive Scottish flair. Dogwood has been built around the meandering Caw Caw River (the sound a crow makes) to create a shot-maker's delight that requires both thought and accuracy. Azalea is best described as a "big" traditional course, not big in terms of length but in spaciousness. The fairways are wide, the mounding is extensive, and every green is framed with beautifully sculptured and carefully manicured sand bunkers. This green, and indeed every green at Brunswick, is composed of Crenshaw bent grass.

Now we'll look at some of the great holes of the three nines on an individual basis:

Magnolia's #2 has water on the right side of the fairway, and the bunkers on the left serve as a guide for your tee shot. This par five is not exceptionally long, but the

235

configuration of the hole makes it difficult to reach in two shots. While it doglegs to the right, the dogleg doesn't begin until the golfer is within 150 yards of the elevated green, which is well guarded by sand. Furthermore, the series of pot bunkers to the left front of the putting surface are a subtle hazard that can add strokes to the scorecard.

The very pretty 5th hole at Magnolia is a long par four with a sharp dogleg to the right that leaves most golfers a second shot of 200 yards or more. An attempt to reach the green by going over the trees on the right is a risky maneuver and often results in disaster, with the golf ball disappearing into the water on the right. An innovative approach to golf-course creation is very visible here in the chipping area that slopes from the green on the right side. It looks like an extension of the green that requires an uphill putt, but upon further examination the golfer finds this area to be a swath of very short rough cut between deeper strands of grass that forces the golfer to "hack" at the ball. Golfers will like this chipping area because it provides an opportunity to become more selective in their club and shot decisions.

Number 9 at Magnolia is a good finishing hole—not spectacular, but interesting and requiring forethought. Hole #9 plays slightly uphill and is a slight dogleg left. With the clubhouse in the background and a large fairway bunker on the left, many golfers attempt to "draw" their second shot, hooking it to the left. Don't do that. Hit it straight away onto the elevated green that slopes to the left.

Much of the Dogwood course was still under construction as this book went to press, but this newest addition looked destined to be both difficult and beautiful, thus bringing Brunswick to a new level of golfing quality and sophistication. The first two holes of this nine are very pretty, cast in a traditional style as the Caw Caw begins to come into play.

Here the flat open spaces and the pines give way or mingle with hardwoods to create an entirely different look. Number 6 is an exciting island green, and the par-five #7 may well become the signature hole. The Caw Caw streams the length of the fairway on the right and is very much in play around the green. The golfer also must negotiate a centuries-old cypress tree, regal and undaunted by age, located on the right side of the fairway.

Azalea is a typical Byrd traditional design, but maybe more so. Every hole is framed with sand, and Byrd has not placed any hazards directly in front of the greens, as is his wont. You don't have to "fly" the pin; you can hit it short and let the ball roll on even though the Crenshaw bent-grass greens hold very well and are conducive to lofty approach shots hit to the flag.

Number 3 is memorable because of three deep grass bunkers. From the fairway approach these bunkers don't appear threatening, but once your golf ball has disappeared in this lush and very deep grass, you become frustrated and will do everything possible to avoid them. These bunkers are "much more difficult than sand, and every bit as bad as water. You may need two or three shots to get out," said Howard McMeekin, golf professional.

Although the 4th hole at Azalea intimidates most golfers, it shouldn't. This island green is more aesthetic than it is dangerous. The green is 20 yards beyond the far edge of the lake, and there is room short and on both sides for errant shots.

For golfers needing a birdie, the opportunity presents itself on #5, especially for the long-ball hitter. It is possible to hit the tee ball through the fairway into a lake, so the best advice is to keep the ball in play to the right. You'll get a better roll, and if you should hit the cart path, the ball will jump forward and give you a much shorter shot to the green.

Watch out for #8. That fairway sand trap on the left is "sneaky," jutting farther into the fairway than is apparent from the tee.

All three nines are good tests of golf, and you should have ample time to play them all, going eighteen in the morning, stopping for lunch at the fashionable Jasmine's Club House restaurant, then going back out for the course you haven't played or an entire eighteen, for that matter. There is only a nominal charge for replays, and you will enjoy the Willard Byrd layout.

Brunswick Plantation

HOLE NUMBER	1	2	3	4	5	6	7	8	9	OUT	10	11	12	13	14	15	16	17	18	IN	TOT	HCP	NET
BLACK	409	521	388	180	425	510	204	357	401	3395	398	409	400	154	392	197	518	414	502	3384	6779		
BLUE	384	489	358	150	385	492	170	325	370	3123	365	380	359	140	372	152	484	380	460	3092	6215		
WHITE	360	451	335	126	365	455	151	290	346	2879	348	350	345	118	350	135	471	353	442	2912	5791		
MEN'S HCP	7	1	15	13	3	9	17	5	11		14	10	12	16	18	8	2	6	4				
PAR	4	5	4	3	4	5	3	4	4	36	4	4	4	3	4	3	5	4	5	36	72		
RED	310	425	315	102	325	403	122	258	316	2576	310	315	320	102	322	94	437	329	405	2634	5210		

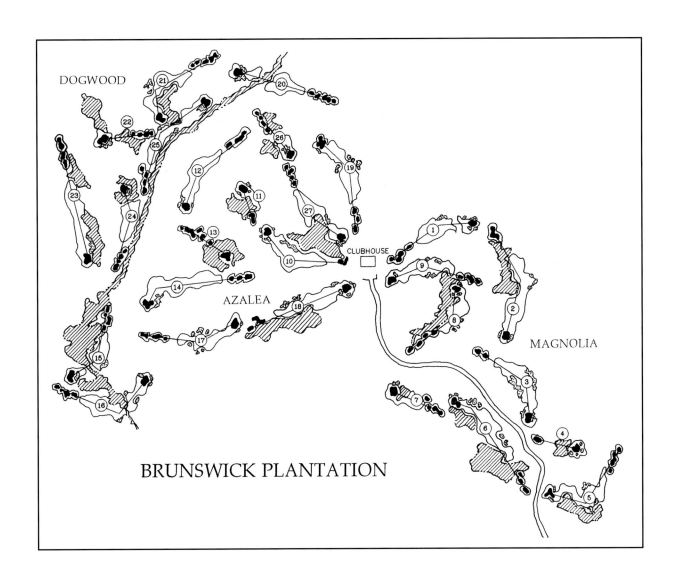

DOGWOOD

AZALEA

CLUBHOUSE

MAGNOLIA

BRUNSWICK PLANTATION

BALD HEAD ISLAND

P.O. Box 10999   Southport, NC 28461
(919) 457-5000   (800) 443-6305

Architect: George Cobb

Course rating/Slope rating:
Blue - 74.2/143   Yellow - 68.1/124
White - 71.3/136   Red - 69.5/121

Playing the challenging eighteen-hole Bald Head Island course is a unique and pleasant experience. For starters, it is impossible to drive to Bald Head Island because it is exactly as it sounds—an island sitting in the Atlantic Ocean some four miles from Southport, North Carolina.

Nor is Southport itself near major population areas, located seventeen miles east of heavily travelled Highway 17, which connects Myrtle Beach and Wilmington.

When you do reach Bald Head Island, via a picturesque fifteen-minute ferryboat ride, you still can't drive to the golf course!

Or at least you can't drive a conventional gasoline-powered automobile. Kent and Mark Mitchell, developers of Bald Head Island, wanted the island to "retain its innocence," and the only means of transportation is the electric golf cart. If you own or rent a home or condominium on Bald Head, an electric cart goes with the deal and that's the way you get around. There are no high rises here except Old Baldy, North Carolina's oldest lighthouse, built in 1817.

Because more than three-quarters of the island's 13,000 acres have been donated by the developers to the state of North Carolina as a wildlife refuge, this is a sparsely inhabited island and, in the spring of 1991, there were exactly fifteen permanent residents. However, it's not that difficult to get to Bald Head, and, in our book, the little bit of trouble and extra time you might need to play golf at Bald Head is worth the effort.

This is one whale of a golf course.

At first you're going to be enchanted with the windswept look and the tropical atmosphere, complete with palm trees, giant live oaks, and many, many oversize alligators, wild foxes and graceful shorebirds, but when your attention focuses on playing golf, you will realize this is one handsome—but tough—golf course.

The new rating of Bald Head Island from the professional tees is 74, and there is water on sixteen of the eighteen fairways. Once upon a time a professional golfer—Tom Plankers—shot 67, but no one else has ever seriously challenged that mark.

Bald Head has two very different looks—the front nine plunges into the lush interior of the island, and you play six holes carved from an ancient maritime forest. The backside more closely resembles the very best links courses of Scotland and Ireland.

Some of the holes are spectacular. Both #8 and #16 are three pars played from an elevated tee with the green set well below the teeing area. There is water in front of the 16th green and a quaint red footbridge that allows the golfer who has elected to hit short of the water to walk up. This definitely is one of the very best three-par holes in the Carolinas.

The most difficult holes at Bald Head Island, however, are the four-par finishing holes, #9 and #18.

Number 18 is beautiful, paralleling the Atlantic Ocean and playing every inch of its

Bald Head Island, a lush tropical setting for golf. (Courtesy Bald Head Island)

460 yards from the championship tees. There is water on both sides of the fairway and three palm trees on the right, strategically placed to catch the long driver or to form a barrier for the shorter hitter. Getting to the green is only the beginning—this is the deepest green of our memory, and position of the pin can make a four-club difference!

Number 9 is equally difficult. Coming back toward the ocean after a delightful tour through the manicured jungle, the golfer, most of the time, will find himself playing into a stiff breeze. There is a tremendous lake to the left of the fairway and another on the right, hidden by cedars blocking the lake from the tee. If that isn't enough to defeat most golfers, there is another lake in front of the green, which means you have to hit the drive 250 yards to have a 200-yard carry to the green with your second shot.

In the opinion of this writer, there's not a bad hole on this course, which measures 7,000 yards with no parallel fairways.

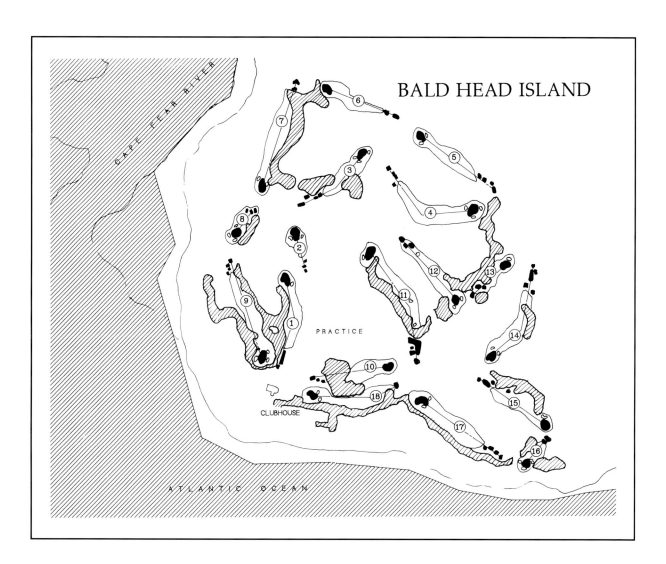

BALD HEAD ISLAND

Bald Head

HOLE NUMBER	1	2	3	4	5	6	7	8	9	OUT	10	11	12	13	14	15	16	17	18	IN	TOT	HCP	NET
BLUE	380	190	370	505	420	390	500	170	440	3365	410	510	410	215	420	385	195	485	460	3490	6855		
WHITE	342	180	320	470	385	370	470	147	410	3094	390	455	375	170	390	350	185	450	380	3145	6239		
RED	213	110	245	385	330	310	370	110	327	2400	310	360	300	100	315	230	120	380	295	2410	4810		
MEN'S HCP	15	17	5	3	7	11	9	13	1		12	16	6	10	2	18	4	14	8				
PAR	4	3	4	5	4	4	5	3	4	36	4	5	4	3	4	4	3	5	4	36	72		
LADIES' HCP	11	17	13	3	7	9	5	15	1		2	6	8	18	4	14	16	12	10				

241

Looking back from the 18th green at The Gauntlet, the tee box is over the marsh and far, far away. (Courtesy Brandon Advertising/Michael Slear)

ST. JAMES PLANTATION

Already known for its challenging P. B. Dye course, The Gauntlet, this area of great golf has expanded its reach to become the anchor facility for the golfers who prefer an upscale experience and are willing to drive half an hour or so to get there.

Ten miles toward the ocean and Southport from U.S. Highway 17, drive down 211 past the new Fred Couples signature course at Winding River and into the gates of St. James Plantation. You'll find your dream world of golf on this spacious expanse of ground, beautifully manicured and conscious of the local ecology. You'll even get a lesson in horticulture as signs identify the various types of trees and grasses.

There are three courses, three clubhouses (one to serve each course), miles and miles of concrete cart paths, imaginatively detailed and sculpted bridges, and—most importantly—breathtaking golf-course designs. The Gauntlet was the first one, followed by the Hale Irwin-designed Members Club and now The Players Club, which was created by Tim N. Cate and has been hailed by builders and construction workers as perhaps the best golf course they have ever seen.

Whether or not you agree with that assessment, you will agree that each of the three courses is different from the other and that all three are worth your time and effort. Villas, patio homes, town homes, and condominiums are under construction, and in the near future rental programs will be available on the site. Many of these will become permanent residences, joining the fine upscale homes the visitor will see along the fairways of these three fine golf courses.

As this second edition of *Golfing the Carolina Grand Strand* goes to press, the motels and hotels, for the most part, are thirty to fifty miles away. Still, if you've got the stamina for it, arrange a morning tee time at one course and play another in the afternoon. It will be difficult to find better golf than this.

And golf isn't the only fine amenity at St. James. There's a private beach club, tennis courts, swimming pools, easy access to the ocean for boating and fishing, and hiking and cycling trails.

On the next few pages, we'll take a closer look at St. James, especially the three championship golf courses.

THE GAUNTLET AT ST. JAMES PLANTATION

Highway 211   Southport, NC   P.O. Box 10040
Southport, NC 28461   (800) 247-4806

Architect: P. B. Dye   Year opened: 1991

Course rating/Slope rating:
Gold - 75.9/143   Silver - 69.9/126
Black - 72.5/134   Red - 70.8/119

Visitors returning to the Grand Strand golfing area will find that nationally famous golf architect P. B. Dye has thrown down the

gauntlet again, issuing a challenge to master another of his creative designs. This time, however, the gauntlet (a symbolic mailed fist from the bygone days of knighthood) holds a rose and becomes the advertising trademark for an affordable, first-class golf course tucked within the confines of St. James Plantation, an upscale residential development.

Golfers familiar with the Grand Strand-area Dye designs such as DeBordieu Club, Prestwick, and Moorland at The Legends will want to play this course, which incorporates many characteristics of those magnificent layouts while retaining the ambiance of island living.

There are four sets of tees, and while the championship markers make the course play almost 7,100 yards and deserve its 75 rating (almost exactly the same as the Dye design at DeBordieu), the other tees provide a course similar in length and difficulty to many others on the Strand.

The Longview Golf Corporation, builder and operator of St. James, had an imaginative marketing plan offering "a resort-level golfing experience in a country club setting without the high cost normally associated with such facilities and service."

To accomplish this aim, the corporation opened play with a 9,000-square-foot clubhouse with restaurant and pro shop adjacent to a pool and four tennis courts, and it spared no expense in building the golf course.

"The Gauntlet features the bulkheads, pot bunkers, multilevel fairways, variated grasses, and multiple tee placements that are Dye trademarks and normally seen only on private or surcharge courses. The ball can be rolled onto most greens, and the landing areas for the tee shot are extra large," says the corporation.

To give even more character and to make it even more memorable, each of the eighteen holes has been named, and The Gauntlet has instituted caddy service. "To our knowledge, no other course on the Grand Strand has caddies," said a Gauntlet official. "As a matter of fact, I don't know of many anywhere in this country who have caddies available to the fee player, other than Pinehurst #2."

The medieval names affixed to the eighteen holes are descriptive, especially the mind-boggling #12, "The Moats," which features multiple bodies of water; #17, "The Moor," which is played over and alongside a salt marsh running the length of the hole; and #6, "The Labyrinth," which is played straight uphill to a green guarded by huge, randomly placed mounds and bunkers.

Want more? Some names are quickly obvious, such as #1, "The Quest," signaling the beginning of a quest for par. Number 18 is the equally understandable "Camelot," as the majestic clubhouse is visible from tee to green.

Gauntlet officials remind that:

> In Scotland, historic home of golf, and elsewhere throughout Europe, the naming of holes and even some bunkers has long been a tradition. On some, hole designations are so old that their origin and meaning are obscured. For the most part, hole names reflect an outstanding feature, hazard, or playing characteristic of the hole, such as "The Road Hole" at St. Andrews in Scotland.

With eighteen holes laid out to play beside and in view of salt marshes, ponds, and the Intracoastal Waterway, Dye calls The Gauntlet "one of my most challenging yet." First-time visitors probably will carry home a stronger impression of the back nine, which is more picturesque, but it is unlikely they will forget the green at the three-par 5th, which is in excess of 12,000 square feet. It is probably the biggest one ever built, humongous, and if you're on the

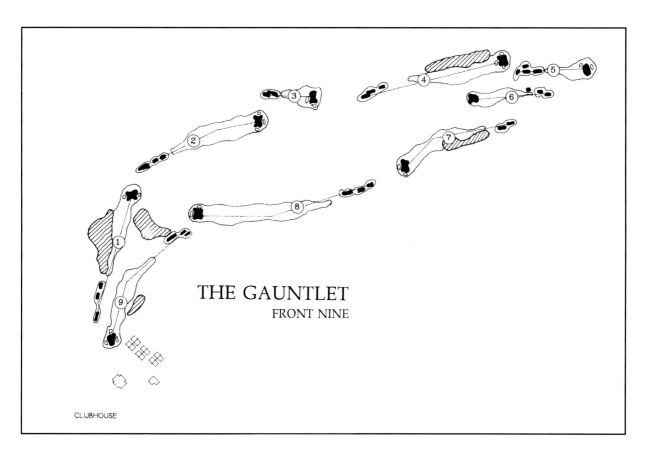

THE GAUNTLET
FRONT NINE

CLUBHOUSE

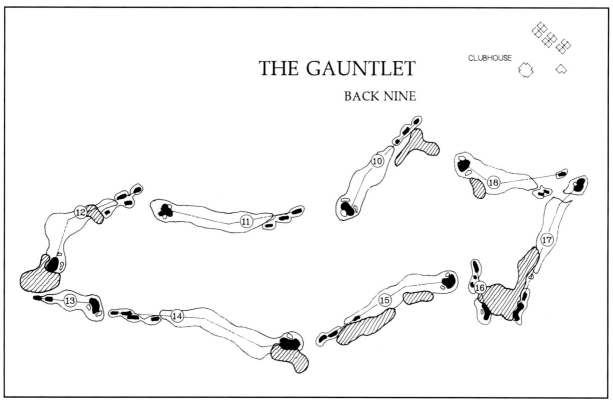

THE GAUNTLET

CLUBHOUSE

BACK NINE

wrong side, you might never get in the hole!

The Labyrinth (#6) certainly is different, and the long four-par 7th ("Devil's Garden") is a tough test of golf with a marsh bisecting the fairway near the green.

The finishing holes are exciting.

Number 14 is indeed a "Crusade," measuring 585 yards from the championship tees, and #15, "Highlands," stretches into a very demanding 466-yard par four. While the golfer may feel he or she has been given a temporary reprieve on the short "Lady of the Lake," reality returns on the final two holes.

The green at #17, "The Moor," is set into the marsh and requires a very accurate second shot. The home hole is a dogleg right that invites the long hitter to see just how much of the marsh he can "bite off." While the silver and red markers on this hole afford a very short carry over the marsh, even the longest-hitting low-handicap player should use caution and keep his shot to the left on this one.

Visitors to the Grand Strand, particularly those making their headquarters in Myrtle Beach or North Myrtle Beach, will find that traveling to the Gauntlet is worthwhile. Like the other two championship courses at St. James Plantation, it is a memorable course, easily reached by a four-lane highway that measures twenty-seven miles from the bridge over the Waterway in North Myrtle Beach to Highway 211, and then fourteen miles to the gates of St. James. If you like Dye courses (and they are good), you are going to like this one, which offers beautiful scenery and a greens fee lower than most in peak season.

THE MEMBERS CLUB AT ST. JAMES PLANTATION

3779 Members Club Boulevard #160, Southport, NC 28461
(800) 474-9277   (910) 253-9500

Architect: Hale Irwin   Year opened: 1996

Course rating/Slope rating:

Gold - 73.5/127   Black - 70.9/123
White - 68.8/118   Teal - 70.5/121

The Members Club can best be described as a handsome, good-looking golf course reminiscent of Pinehurst and certainly designed in a parkland style with wide, rolling fairways cut through pines and live oaks.

The first two holes can lull the golfer into a sense of false security, but if the wide fairways make the trees less menacing, both holes are long and, as throughout the course, the sand traps are strategically placed to trick players into using the wrong club. Number 1 might be a two-shot hole for some, but if you are going to try to reach the green in two, you have to hit two mighty wallops and be aware of the three bunkers on the right, which are placed exactly where most will hit their second shot, something like 75 to 80 yards short of the green.

Number 2 is a dogleg, and again it is a long way home, 400 yards from the most frequently used tee box. Then, too, there are grass traps on both sides of the green and three large sand traps behind the green. While it's true that more players come up short than too long, keep in mind that Irwin designed these greens to slope gently away from the shot. Therefore, your ball can hit beyond the pin, keep rolling, and trickle into one of those traps.

On the scorecard, #3 and #4 look much easier than the starting holes, but professional Mike Beverly says #1 and #2 are favorites of his. A marshy area crosses the fairway on the par-three third hole, but it shouldn't come into play. However, that long, snakelike trap on the left of the green certainly does, and the green itself has some huge undulations. One good thing about that sand trap is that it might keep you out of the water that runs all the way up the left side from tee to green.

Number 4 is a short par four, but my, oh, my: Water and wetlands are everywhere; the narrow green looks like it was created in another area and gently placed among the pines, sand, and water; two oaks are in your line of fire from the tee box. Are you going to slice it or draw it around those trees? The right side actually is preferable because the landing area is bigger. Why the small green? If you're going to be hitting wedges and nine irons on your second shot, you should be accurate, so why shouldn't the green be smaller?

On the 5th hole you meet those dreaded bunkers again, placed in the very center of the fairway so they can catch many drives on this 400-yard hole. The golfer who can call his or her shot will draw it to the left.

Each hole is good, and you must think about your shot if you are to score well on the Members Club. One of the prettiest vistas is from the tee box on #9 as you hit uphill toward the new 20,000-square-foot clubhouse that has everything a player would love. There is a sports bar on the

This picture shows the green at the 16th hole and a large portion of the beautiful 15th hole at The Members Club. (Courtesy Brandon Advertising/Michael Slear)

ground level, fine dining on the second floor, and a fitness center to the right. Majestic yet retaining a low-country, coastal look, the clubhouse is as upscale as the golf course, which features expensive, curving, concrete cart paths and granite markers on each tee inscribed with bronze descriptions. Each tee-box marker weighs six hundred pounds!

The very memorable back nine features a 472-yard, par-four 11th hole; and a haunting par-three 12th, with each tee box placed in descending order to create a tiered theater effect to a well-trapped hole. The hole is anywhere from 230 to 100 yards from the tee boxes, depending on pin placement and your choice of tee box.

Numbers 13 and 14 give the golfer some

breathing room and possible birdies. The breathing room is very nice, because the last four holes—or at least #15, #16, and #17—are very difficult. There is big-time water on the right off the tee of #15, a narrow landing area with ponds on both sides, and a green that is guarded by still more water. Unless you are well left with your tee shot, you can't get to this green without going over the water. This is a relatively short par five, but it's not really a two-shot hole because of the accuracy it demands from the tee.

Number 16 is dubbed by this course's professional staff as a "great par three." Well, it all depends on your interpretation of "great." If that word is synonymous with water, "great" is a good description. Water starts behind the tee box and runs up the left side of this long par three to a green protected by bunkers of sand and grass.

Number 17 is pretty and has a very natural look, but getting to the green requires two long shots that are confined by narrow fairways and sand traps around the green. This hole might be *too* natural for most golfers. It is a dogleg right, but be advised to keep your first shot to the left. Don't be concerned about the water in front of the tee. Unless you top your drive, it doesn't come into play. Don't be intimidated. Although tough, the 17th hole is pretty and does yield pars to the accurate golfer.

Irwin has designed #18 so you won't feel so bad about your golf game. The hole is straight, and when you hit it past the top of the rise facing you from the tee box, the fairway is level and unencumbered with sand. Many golfers get home in two, so you should lower your score here.

At The Members Club, Hale Irwin has put his signature on a very pleasant, playable course that can jump up and bite you if you don't give every shot careful concentration. It looks like the kind of course Hale Irwin would play well, but then he plays every course well!

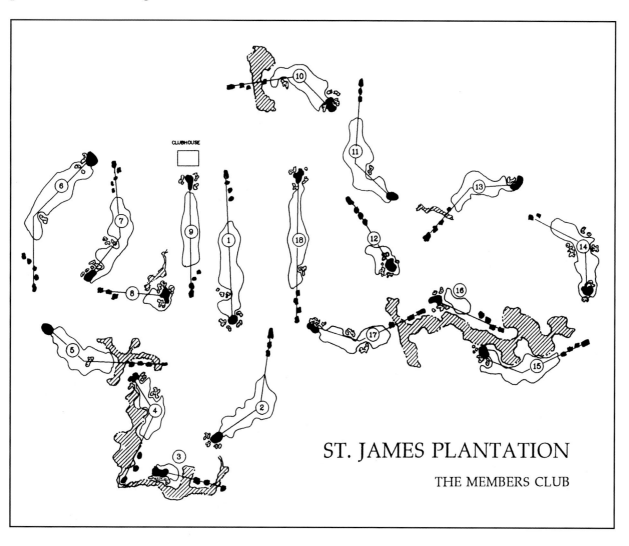

CLUBHOUSE

ST. JAMES PLANTATION

THE MEMBERS CLUB

Every hole is a masterpiece at The Players Club. Pictured here are #4 and #17.
(Courtesy Brandon Advertising/Michael Slear)

THE PLAYERS CLUB AT ST. JAMES PLANTATION

3640 Players Club Drive, Southport, NC 28461
(800) 281-6626   (910) 457-0049
Architect: Tim N. Cate   Year opened: 1997
Course rating/Slope Rating:
Gold - 75.1/149   Black - 71.7/135
White - 68.1/120   Teal - 69.6/121
Teal (front) - 66.6/113

Anyone talking about a golfing facility such as St. James Plantation and aware that the first two courses were designed by high-profile and highly respected golf-course architects such as P. D. Dye and Hale Irwin would have to be very courageous to say The Players Club is the best one yet. However, that's what many people who are the insiders of the golf-course-design world have said about this Tim N. Cate creation—even before it opened for play.

A visual delight, The Players Course is as unusual as it is stunning, and as difficult as it is entertaining. "I am very proud of this golf course," Cate said. "Just look how it flows from one hole to the next."

Developer Wade Coleman was even more exuberant. "What a beautiful conception. The design is excellent. We have been involved in building good golf courses all over this country, and I don't know of any better than this."

Seven strains of ornamental grasses are used throughout the course, and the greens are bent grass, L-93. Zoysia is used for the banks of sand traps, and native flowers abound on almost every hole.

Because this course adjoins wetlands throughout the eighteen-hole stretch, building the holes without transgressing on the environmentally protected areas took plenty of imagination. Leaving the wetlands in their natural state provided some beautiful vistas but also some very difficult shots.

On hole #17, no matter how you get across the wetlands, they are exactly 100 yards across, so you might want to get your shot as close to the edge as possible before choosing your club.

At one time, Cate thought #4 might be the weakest hole on this course, but others have changed his mind. "Heck, there isn't a weak hole on The Players Club, and actually #4 might be a truly great hole," Cate said. It certainly is spectacular, with two wetland areas coming into play; both completely bisect the fairway, one near the tee, the other in front of the undulating green.

It seems there are memorable surprises on each hole. There is nothing but sand and more sand on the par-three #3, all the way to the two-tiered green. The water is big and imposing to the right side of #5, and the second shot dictates a long carry of 200 yards or more. Number 6 displays great-looking grass bunkers and a big marsh directly in front of the green. Number 12 has split tees. Do you want to play it left or right?

Two live oaks growing from pure white Carolina sand in a large waste area make #18 a dramatic finishing hole, but #10 may be the best of all. Number 10 is one of those delights that make you step up to the tee and say, "Wow. Wham-bam!" The two oaks extending into the fairway on the right dictate the layout of this one, but that's just a portion of the difficulty.

An unusual aspect of the entire course is the visibility of sand bunkers and ponds. What's so unusual is that they are so clearly defined. You know where they are, and if you find yourself in the sand or have discovered a "watery grave," there is no one to blame but yourself . . . and, of course, your wayward shot.

Ladies will find something else different about The Players Club, and they'll like the difference. To help golfers stay away from the hazards and the long carries over wetlands, water, and sand, Cate has created "Pinkie" tees on several holes, building them on pilings in the ponds and bulwarking these tees against the encroachment of nature. Not only do these "Pinkies" make the holes much more playable, but they are pretty, too. Par is 72 from most sets of tees and 70 from the "Pinkies."

Architect Cate wanted to be certain that golfers would find this course in a very natural, unspoiled state. "Even though we may have moved 600,000 yards of dirt, I defy you to tell me what was there and what wasn't," Cate said.

If a good golf architect is handed a great piece of sandy ground like this low-country layout spiced with wetlands and water, he is going to build an exceptional golf course. That's exactly what Tim Cate has done here, creating a marvelous companion piece to The Gauntlet and The Members Club.

Gauntlet

HOLE NUMBER	1	2	3	4	5	6	7	8	9	OUT	10	11	12	13	14	15	16	17	18	IN	TOT	HCP	NET
GOLD	396	448	186	519	235	295	453	592	449	3573	371	485	403	198	585	466	152	448	387	3495	7068		
BLACK	351	420	162	470	220	255	415	524	439	3256	362	444	352	178	543	424	138	434	358	3233	6489		
HANDICAP	15	3	11	13	7	17	9	5	1		16	4	8	10	6	2	18	12	14				
PAR	4	4	3	5	3	4	4	5	4	36	4	5	4	3	5	4	3	4	4	36	72		
SILVER	308	385	145	444	183	235	374	494	411	2979	324	401	333	137	506	379	109	379	351	2919	5898		
RED	277	367	121	375	150	188	307	443	376	2604	266	346	275	103	457	338	97	332	297	2511	5115		
HANDICAP	11	3	15	13	9	17	7	5	1		16	12	6	18	2	8	14	4	10				

Members Club

HOLE NUMBER	1	2	3	4	5	6	7	8	9	OUT	10	11	12	13	14	15	16	17	18	IN	TOT	HCP	NET
GOLD	587	441	160	324	404	542	367	173	403	3401	375	472	201	374	393	531	214	419	507	3486	6887		
BLACK	559	421	151	296	381	522	346	144	384	3204	353	436	176	352	360	493	186	411	476	3243	6447		
WHITE	508	393	129	274	354	496	327	136	363	2980	330	407	148	321	331	435	162	394	440	2968	5948		
TEAL	473	331	116	250	287	436	281	112	320	2606	267	378	124	286	307	406	137	282	413	2600	5206		
HANDICAP	1	5	15	7	9	3	13	17	11		8	2	18	14	12	4	16	6	10				
HANDICAP TEAL	1	5	15	11	9	3	7	17	13		8	4	18	12	14	2	16	6	10				
PAR	5	4	3	4	4	5	4	3	4	36	4	4	3	4	4	5	3	4	5	36	72		

Players Club

HOLE NUMBER	1	2	3	4	5	6	7	8	9	OUT	10	11	12	13	14	15	16	17	18	IN	TOT	HCP	NET
GOLD	364	176	424	369	506	417	204	420	543	3423	426	192	416	450	182	539	449	396	569	3619	7042		
BLACK	332	151	388	339	483	380	176	381	488	3118	374	173	362	407	148	510	423	374	498	3269	6387		
WHITE	280	120	343	293	387	345	151	349	471	2739	331	124	296	361	108	432	379	331	461	2823	5562		
TEAL	231	109	304	222	351	313	142	324	403	2399	303	89	250	307	92	412	329	302	426	2510	4909		
HANDICAP	17	15	9	7	13	1	11	5	3		14	18	10	2	16	6	12	8	4				
HANDICAP TEAL	13	17	7	15	9	1	11	5	3		12	18	14	4	16	10	8	2	6				
PAR	4	3	4	4	5	4	3	4	5	36	4	3	4	4	3	5	4	4	5	36	72		

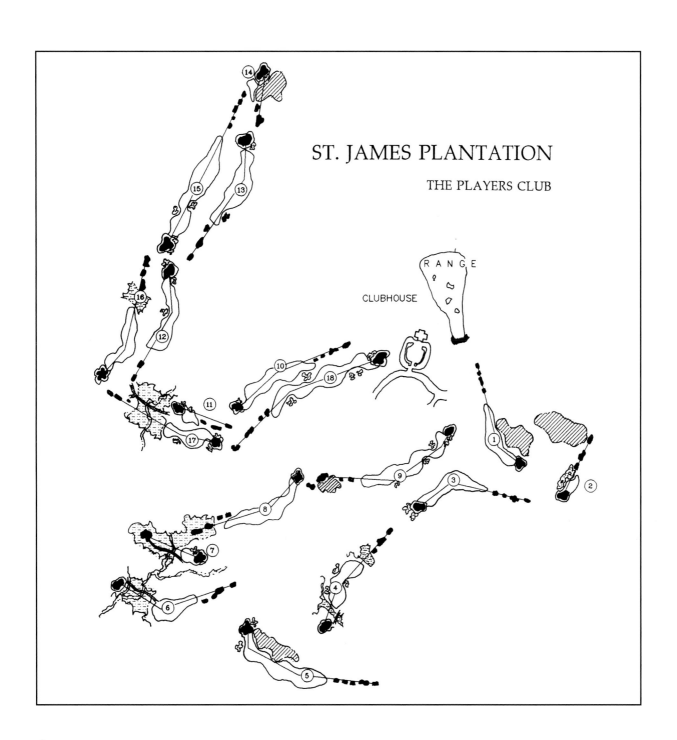

ST. JAMES PLANTATION

THE PLAYERS CLUB

RANGE

CLUBHOUSE

Number 18 at Ocean Harbour winds its way back to the clubhouse, Waterway, and Atlantic Ocean. (Courtesy Brandon Advertising/Michael Slear)

OCEAN HARBOUR

Highway 179   Calabash, NC   #2 Causeway
Ocean Isle Beach, NC 28459   (843) 448-8398
Architect: Clyde Johnston   Year opened: 1989

Course rating/Slope rating
Pink - 74.2/138   White - 70.4/127
Blue - 72.4/134   Red - 71.9/126

Spectacular is the best word to describe Ocean Harbour.

When the golfer turns off Highway 179 between the large white entry gates, the first impression is that this must be a pretty special place. By the time he has driven 1.9 miles through pristine forest, catching occasional glimpses of the well-manicured Clyde Johnson designed course and perhaps sighting deer, squirrel, raccoons, foxes, and ducks, he is certain that this is, indeed, a marvelous setting for a championship course.

That opinion is reinforced when the first-time visitor steps into a spacious, opulent clubhouse with wide expanses of window looking over the Intracoastal Waterway to the Atlantic Ocean. The pink carpeting and the light wood decor is soothing and impressive, and the clubhouse mirrors the excitement of the course itself.

Ocean Harbour is not an easy golf course.

The first golf course to bear the name of Clyde Johnson, golf architect, may be the best he will ever build! Ocean Harbour, on a spit of land between the Calabash River and the Intracoastal Waterway, is built on more than 500 acres of ground, and has everything anyone could ask of a championship golf course.

It stretches 7,004 yards from the professional tees, and encompasses sand, water, and marsh.

The four-par 4th hole, 436 yards in length from the professional tees, may be the best hole on the Strand. A photogenic corridor of centuries-old water oaks lines the entire left side of this hole, which borders the Intracoastal Waterway. You play this hole in the state of North Carolina, but the border that separates the two Carolinas is directly behind the green. The Waterway comes into play, but golfers also can get a glimpse of the ocean by standing on one of the hillocks that are located on the right side of this large wraparound green.

Spectacular as it may be, this hole might not cause as many memories as the controversial #7, or the group of finishing holes, which are played through and around the marsh areas from #14 through #18. These holes may fall into the category of "target" golf, but they are long enough to demand superior golfing skills.

Number 7 is a five par, 532 yards long,

Ocean Harbour

HOLE NUMBER	1	2	3	4	5	6	7	8	9	OUT	10	11	12	13	14	15	16	17	18	IN	TOT	HCP	NET
PINK	512	416	166	436	409	175	532	434	414	3494	434	402	181	404	578	165	400	534	412	3510	7004		
BLUE	483	402	153	411	390	164	504	415	388	3310	411	373	160	373	562	142	369	511	381	3282	6592		
WHITE	466	386	135	388	371	151	482	395	366	3140	393	353	131	351	483	132	344	466	355	3008	6148		
RED	410	341	114	320	329	129	400	333	346	2722	325	318	101	303	434	119	316	411	309	2636	5358		
HANDICAP	3	7	15	5	9	17	1	13	11		10	12	16	14	2	18	6	4	8				
PAR	5	4	3	4	4	3	5	4	4	36	4	4	3	4	5	3	4	5	4	36	72		

and features a breathtaking view of marsh and the Waterway. Each shot on this hole must clear marshland, and the green appears to sit on an island. This is a photographer's delight, but can become a golfer's nightmare. The long-hitting daredevil might reach it in two, but designers of the course and those who play it most often think that such an approach is risky to the point of being suicidal, and strongly recommend a drive, a long iron, or four wood for the second shot, and then an eight or nine iron over the final section of marsh.

Number 16 is spectacular, too. It is a sharp dogleg right with marshland intersecting the fairway. The golfer needs a big, well-placed drive, and then an accurate shot to the green, which is completely separated from the rest of the hole with a pretty, but dangerous, marsh.

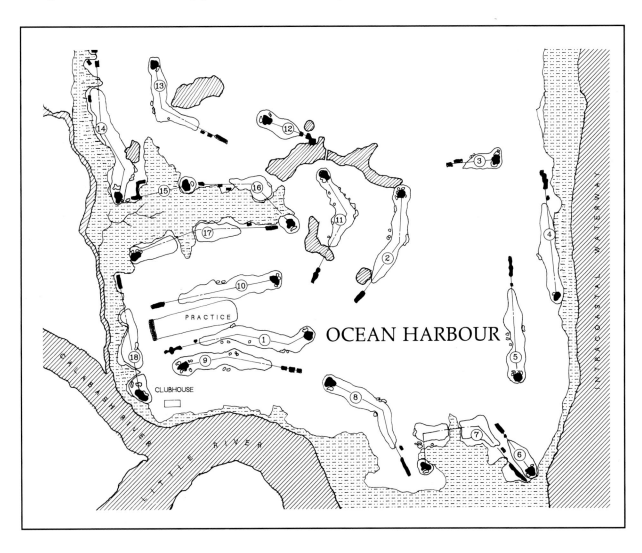

MARSH HARBOUR

Highway 179   Calabash, NC   P.O. Box 65   North Myrtle Beach, SC 29597
(843) 249-3449   (800) 552-2660
Architect: Dan Maples   Year opened: 1980
Course rating/Slope rating
Blue - 72.4/134
White - 69.3/121
Red - 67.7/115

One of six spectacular golf courses on the Strand operated by Larry Young, Marsh Harbour was opened in March 1980 and rapidly became one of the most renowned golf courses in the Southeast, appearing again and again in *Golf Digest* ratings as one of the twenty-five best public courses in America.

All of the Young-operated courses have earned high ratings, and the golfer who comes to the Strand will feel he has discovered golfers' paradise if he can play Marsh Harbour, Oyster Bay, the Heritage Club, and the three courses at The Legends. Best of all, he really can do this. Young has a central telephone system that covers reservations for all six courses, and one call to any of these great courses can set up play on all six!

Marsh Harbour was the first Larry Young course on the Strand, and it is as popular and highly regarded now as it was when it opened in 1980. Lying along beautiful salt marshes adjacent to the Intracoastal Waterway, Marsh Harbour has the unique distinction of sitting on the North and South Carolina borders less than a quarter-mile south of Calabash, North Carolina.

The course has the rare combination of elevated ground skirted by low-lying marsh. Natural vegetation outlines the tee boxes (a lot of wiry love grass) and landing areas. Wildlife abounds.

Dan Maples was the golf-course architect, working closely with Young to create a design that offers the ultimate in beauty while demanding the utmost in shot-making ability.

There are many very good golf holes at Marsh Harbour, but the 17th hole is of particular interest and generally named as one of the four five-par holes on the Dream Eighteen of the Strand. This hole has been billed as the "most beautiful and exciting hole on the Grand Strand."

That's a legitimate claim, but #17 also can be frustrating. It features three distinct targets or landing areas. Facing the golfer off the tee are trees along the left and large bunkers sloping toward the marsh on the right. Assuming a successful tee shot (between 220 and 260 yards), the second shot must carry across the marsh to a landing area surrounded by water on three sides. From this point the golfer must cross the marsh again en route to a green precariously perched on the side of the marsh.

Oh yes, forgot to tell you that the prevailing wind usually is in the golfer's face. A score of five on the 17th at Marsh Harbour is one to be cherished!

Now that #17 is behind the golfer, he must not go to sleep. He might be lulled by the lack of distance on the 18th, but this is a great finishing hole that requires a very accurate tee shot; and the second shot, often a wedge or short iron over water to a narrow green, is testing.

The front side of Marsh Harbour is a little

shorter than the back but no less difficult. There are three three pars on the front, making this nine a par 35, and it is complicated by a very good five-par 9th hole. The left side of this 540-yard hole is defined by marshland. Golfers are urged to favor the right side with the tee shot and the left side with the second shot. Still, the pitch shot is difficult because this is the narrowest green on the course.

Number 8 is also frequently mentioned as a memorable golf hole. It is a very long par three and seems even longer because it usually is played into the wind. With the Intracoastal Waterway as a backdrop, the 8th is one of the most picturesque holes at Marsh Harbour.

There are golfers who have had the opportunity to hit a ball from one state, or even from one country, to another. But on the 10th hole at Marsh Harbour, the golfer can hit the ball from North Carolina to South Carolina and then back again to North Carolina, all on the same hole! From the 10th tee, a good drive with a fade will go from the Tar Heel State across a historic boundary marker into the Palmetto State before landing safely on the fairway . . . back in North Carolina.

Number 11 in our book is a terrific three

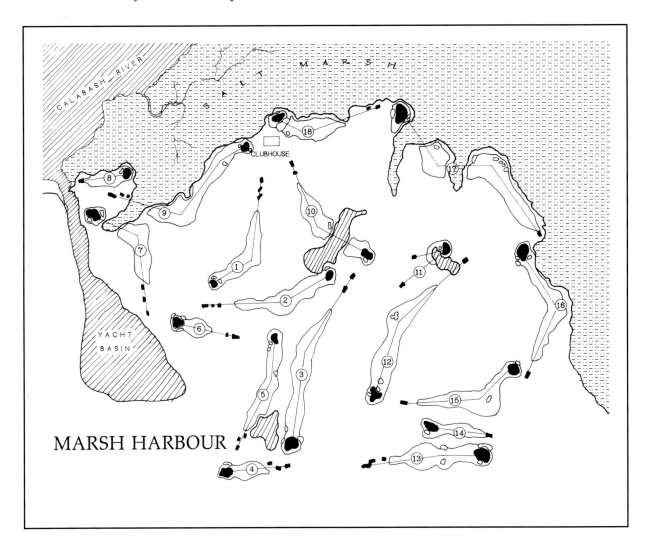

MARSH HARBOUR

par. Carved into a hill, this hole also has a pond short and a deep bunker left. Both accuracy and distance are needed.

It's not often you will find a golf course with no bad holes, but many will describe Marsh Harbour as that kind of golf course. It is a course that should be on every golfer's "must play" list when visiting the Myrtle Beach area.

Marsh Harbour

HOLE NUMBER	1	2	3	4	5	6	7	8	9	OUT	10	11	12	13	14	15	16	17	18	IN	TOT	HCP	NET
BLUE	370	375	520	240	370	210	390	210	540	3225	410	190	500	390	220	420	435	570	330	3465	6690		
WHITE	325	320	475	190	330	175	360	170	510	2855	365	155	475	365	180	385	400	510	310	3145	6000		
RED	310	270	415	120	270	150	300	145	460	2440	325	70	350	300	130	350	300	330	200	2355	4795		
HANDICAP	14	16	18	6	12	8	10	4	2		9	11	17	15	5	7	3	1	13				
PAR	4	4	5	3	4	3	4	3	5	35	4	3	5	4	3	4	4	5	4	36	71		

Number 17 at Marsh Harbour requires three well-placed shots to carry over two water hazards. (Courtesy Brandon Advertising/Michael Slear)

Aerial view of Carolina Shores—90 sand traps! (Courtesy Brandon Advertising/ Michael Slear)

CAROLINA SHORES

Highway 17   99 Carolina Shores Dr.   Calabash, NC 28459
(800) 579-8292

Architect: Tom Jackson   Year opened: 1974

Course rating/Slope rating
Blue - 72.6/128
White - 69.8/122
Red - 72.7/122

Carolina Shores, a well-established and popular course located on the border of North and South Carolina in the Calabash area, was developed by professional golfer Jim Stoffel, and is affectionately known by natives as Carolina "Sands." This nickname is not entirely facetious.

If you can't play sand shots—or, if you don't hit the ball exceptionally straight—you're going to put up some big numbers at this championship layout which is owned and operated by American Golf. This national organization owns, leases, or manages more than one hundred courses across the country. (River Oaks, in the center of Myrtle Beach, also is operated by American Golf on a lease basis.)

Sand is not the extent of your problems at this course designed by Tom Jackson. Carolina Shores was one of the first courses designed by Jackson, who has become extremely popular, and it is still considered to be one of his best. The greens are Bermuda, overseeded with rye, and measures 6,783 yards from the championship tees.

Carolina Shores boasts 100 hazards: 90 sand traps and 10 lakes. But the course is not overly difficult. The hazards simply add to the beauty of the course. From the white tees it is relatively short.

But golfers should be warned that three of the holes at Carolina Shores were among the thirty-six most difficult holes on the Grand Strand when former sports editor Willie Binette conducted a poll for the Myrtle Beach *Sun News*. Those three are #1 ("Genesis"), #2 ("Duffers Dread"), and #15 ("Gamblers' Choice"), but as the names of several other holes imply, these three are not the only ones that can rise up and take a bite out of the unsuspecting golfer.

Number 5 is called "Monster," 6 is "Waterloo," and the 11th is hailed as "Devil's Bend." The tough finishing hole, the 18th, appropriately enough, is tabbed the "Last Mile," and it plays every one of its 570 yards!

Even the shorter holes are devilish at Carolina Shores. The 16th is named "Crater Lake," and the natural lake to the left of a green which slopes that way catches many a

Carolina Shores

HOLE NUMBER	1	2	3	4	5	6	7	8	9	OUT	10	11	12	13	14	15	16	17	18	IN	TOT	HCP	NET
BLUE	567	403	155	396	377	373	532	150	386	3339	390	390	177	542	381	430	170	394	570	3444	6783		
WHITE	528	386	125	374	360	353	512	128	346	3112	361	355	140	510	343	372	145	372	521	3119	6231		
HANDICAP	2	8	16	10	12	6	4	18	14		17	7	13	1	15	3	11	9	5				
PAR	5	4	3	4	4	4	5	3	4	36	4	4	3	5	4	4	3	4	5	36	72		
RED	498	240	109	352	320	312	471	107	296	2705	329	307	123	469	258	291	115	332	456	2680	5385		
HANDICAP	2	14	16	6	10	8	4	18	12		9	11	15	1	13	3	17	7	5				
PAR	5	4	3	4	4	4	5	3	4	36	4	4	3	5	4	4	3	4	5	36	72		

wayward hook or pull. Number 13 is named "Lucky," but that's not what many golfers call this tough par five. Even the brochure says, "After playing this one you may have the feeling you have played in The National Open. Would you believe it took 1,000 tons of sand to fill the traps on this one hole?"

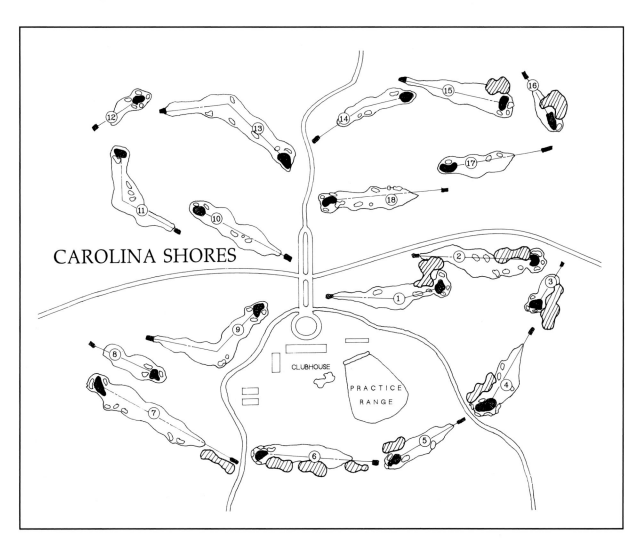

CAROLINA SHORES

MEADOWLANDS

Calabash Road NW   P.O. Box 4159   Calabash, NC 28467
(888) 287-PLAY (7529)   (910) 287-PLAY (7529)
Architect: Willard Byrd   Year opened: 1997
Course rating/Slope rating:
Raven - 74.8/136   Heron - 72.6/127
Egret - 69.8/123   Cardinal - 72.4/124
Cardinal - 67.0/119   Hummingbird - 64.8/115

The Meadowlands, one of the newest golf courses on the Myrtle Beach area of the Grand Strand, came to life late in 1997 and should be an extremely popular layout. The course is conveniently located: Simply go north toward Wilmington on Highway 17, turn left one mile past the state line onto Calabash Road, and proceed 1.2 miles to the main entrance of this Willard Byrd creation.

Golfers who know Willard Byrd golf courses will be surprised with this one. "For one thing, a lot of dirt was moved to create Meadowlands," said Tom Heyward, who is the only Master PGA professional in the area, a rating panelist for *Golf Digest* since 1983, and a frequent contributor to the special golfing section of the Myrtle Beach *Sun News*.

Best be described as a classic course, the Meadowlands has more natural roll and elevation than many area courses, with differentiation of 48 feet on the course. Owners of this new course have been so considerate of environmental features that Meadowlands currently is only the seventh course in America designated as an Audubon International Signature Status Wildlife Sanctuary.

For example, drainage pipes from both bunkers and greens carry wastewater into specially created drain fields rather than into lakes or ditches, thus eliminating pollution of the lakes. Of the six other courses designated as Audubon sanctuaries, two are in Canada and four in America, Pinehurst being one of those four.

Although considered for the most part to be "player friendly," the course is subtle, a sleeping giant that you don't want to awaken with careless play. Only one of the twelve par-four holes (#17) is less than 400 yards in length from the championship gold tee. The presence of water on fifteen of the eighteen holes and the seventy-two bunkers and waste areas further complicates this course!

On the bright side, three of the four par fives can be two-shot holes, and birdies are very possible.

Number 3 probably will become the signature hole at Meadowlands. It is awesome in length, actually longer than one of the par fives (#4) and almost as long as two other par-five holes (#14 and #18). But it's not just the length of #3 that makes it "perhaps the hardest par four I have ever played," in the eyes of Heyward, who as a *Golf Digest* panelist has played some of the toughest golf courses in America. Standing at the blue tee, the golfer can see the Shingletree Canal cutting across the fairway and knows he must hit the tee shot 205 yards to carry over that slim body of water.

Once across the canal, the choice is either a 100-to-120 yard lay-up or a full-fledged swing with a fairway wood to a two tiered green at least 225 yards to the nearest point—and the green is elevated!

In designing this Audubon course, Willard Byrd was instructed to do everything possible to give this long, tough course a "natural" look. He has done better than that, and the owners have capitalized on the feel by building the pro shop to resemble a vintage 1900 farmhouse. (Courtesy Meadowlands)

Even the fairway is two-pronged, with the lake splitting it all the way up to the green. To get home in two, the shot has to go over the lake, but most will choose the fairway on the right (for positioning) and then chip on, hoping for a one-putt par.

Number 6 is an unusual hole and one you won't forget. The landing area of this par four is a plateau 100 yards long, 55 yards wide, and elevated 40 feet above the fairway. From this plateau the golfer looks down to the green for his second shot, knowing he must carry the lake in front while being aware of the water behind the green.

Three consecutive holes—#11, #12, and #13—are the heart and soul of the back nine at Meadowlands. The 11th hole features not one but three waste areas, one just off the tee

on the right side of the fairway, another to the right of the green, and the third halfway down the left side. This par three really isn't difficult, but it certainly is memorable.

The 12th hole, a long par four, has water off the tee on the left and bunkers to the right of the fairway. Byrd has left an elm tree standing as a sentinel in the fairway 150 yards from the green, and the tree's strategic placement can cause golfers problems with their second shot. To compound the difficulty of #12, two bunkers guard the front left of the green.

Number 13 is a beautifully picturesque hole that doesn't appear to be too difficult. However, as on most holes at Meadowlands, #13 has sand bunkers placed to the right front and right center of the green. The bunkers are the primary reason the hole can cause problems. It slopes *4 feet* from right to left for a substantial drop-off. This hole can make you feel like you've hit the right shots and are looking for a birdie, and then—wham—you have a three putt!

Although the tiftway dwarf greens are average in size, they are the centerpiece of the golf course because of the many contours and mounds that cause subtle rolls.

Primarily because of the greens, Meadowlands can be described as a course subtle by nature and design, one that can yield good scores but also can cause heartaches and bogeys.

The course is golfer friendly because of the five sets of tee boxes (four for men and one for ladies and juniors), but we don't believe scores will be consistently low.

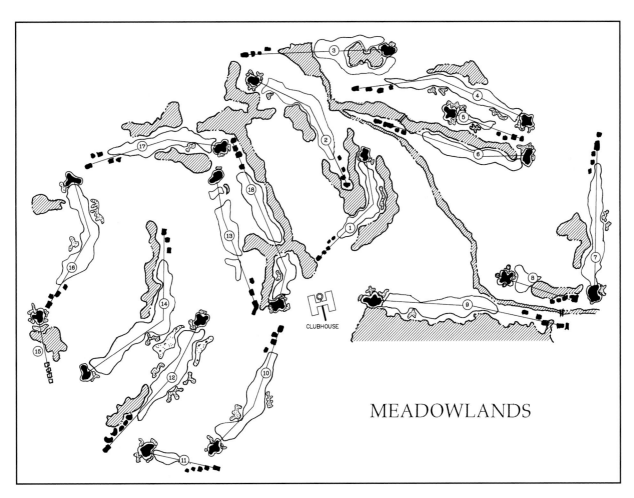

MEADOWLANDS

Meadowlands

HOLE NUMBER	1	2	3	4	5	6	7	8	9	OUT	10	11	12	13	14	15	16	17	18	IN	TOT	HCP	NET
RAVEN	416	430	480	484	198	432	410	189	566	3605	402	206	449	426	519	160	403	382	502	3449	7054		
HERON	400	411	455	474	173	409	388	173	519	3402	375	188	412	397	481	149	375	346	466	3189	6591		
EGRET	379	390	408	452	150	385	356	148	471	3139	347	158	389	382	439	125	352	309	440	2941	6080		
HANDICAP	7	5	1	15	9	3	17	13	11		6	18	2	4	10	16	12	14	8				
PAR	4	4	4	5	3	4	4	3	5	36	4	3	4	4	5	3	4	4	5	36	72		
CARDINAL	361	350	351	380	126	355	329	132	437	2821	321	139	362	347	399	102	329	283	409	2691	5512		
HUMMINGBIRD	348	319	298	350	116	329	307	108	411	2586	295	113	335	324	359	91	305	258	375	2455	5041		

Another championship course by Willard Byrd, Calabash Golf Links is a traditional course that winds through hardwoods and coastal pines and wraps around ten sparkling lakes.
(Courtesy Himmelsbach Communications/Bill Woodward)

CALABASH GOLF LINKS

820 Thomasboro Road   P.O. Box 4610   Calabash, NC 28467
(800) 841-5971   (910) 575-5000
Architect: Willard Byrd   Year opened: 1996
Course rating/Slope rating:
Blue - 72.0/128   White - 69.2/118
Gold - 66.9/106   Red - 68.4/108

Noted as being especially friendly to lady golfers, Calabash Links also can be tough enough to challenge the low-handicap, long-hitting men and boys who have expressed appreciation of this 1997 addition to the Myrtle Beach golfing scene.

Calabash Links is a traditional course that wanders through hardwoods and coastal pines and wraps around ten sparkling lakes. Jack Lewis, one of the state's better-known professional golfers, established the course record from the blue tees, firing a 65 just after the course opened.

Willard Byrd again has done a very good job of building a championship course. The two nines are quite different: The front side was carved from hardwoods, and the back side used to be a large bean field. Byrd had to create some landscape features from a relatively small piece of ground (175 acres) that is very close to sea level. He created mounds and skillfully used existing water to form ten sparkling lakes, using much of the dirt from those lakes to do the mounding.

Only a couple of miles from the popular seafood and fishing village of Calabash, this new course is right in the middle of a hotbed of golf activity. Byrd has designed the course so that on most days you can finish your round in three-and-a-half to four hours, letting you go into Calabash for a fresh seafood lunch or enjoy the dining facility at Calabash Golf Links. Within five to six miles are Brunswick, Meadowlands, Sand-piper Bay, The Pearl, Carolina Shores, and Marsh Harbor. Likewise, the three Sea Trail courses, Panther's Run, Lion's Paw, Glen Dornoch, Heather Glen, Angels Trace, and Oyster Bay aren't more than a ten-minute drive from Calabash. It would not be stretching a point to say that golfers can easily play Calabash Golf Links in the morning and finish the day at Ocean Harbor, Cypress Bay, River Hills, or Eagle Nest. Thus, the golfer has a choice of twenty-two championship courses between the bridge over the Intracoastal Waterway in North Myrtle Beach and the Ocean Island Beach road!

Like most Byrd creations, this course is of a traditional nature and features elevated greens. The par-four holes are relatively short but still are good tests of golf, and the four par threes are very good, all stretching more than 180 yards from the blue tees and generously endowed with sand and water hazards.

Three of the par-five holes are more than 520 yards long, making them difficult birdie holes, but #18 is the one most golfers go home talking about. If you get the wind behind you, you have an excellent chance of getting home in two. How long has it been since you last eagled a hole? Are you thinking of Gene Sarazen and a double eagle? This might be your opportunity. Then again, you might card a 7, an 8, or even more. There's a big lake to navigate off the tee, and water is to the left and right as you approach the green itself—not to mention several sand bunkers. . . . If you're thinking eagle, your second shot had better be close to the pin or at least on the right level of this devilishly two-tiered, sloping green. Most players don't consider this a two-shot hole. Even a good drive can warrant a well-placed long iron into a safe landing area and a short pitch to the Bermuda green, whose firmness demands delicacy.

Several other holes at Calabash are memorable. One is #6, a par-three hole that departs from the norm by offering five sets of tees, four of which have you shaking behind a lake that runs all the way to the green. The hole plays uphill and 20 yards longer than the designation on the scorecard. In addition to the menacing lake, traps are on both sides of the green and on the back. Byrd throws in another twist by sloping the front of the green back toward the water. Don't be short on this one or you'll be wet and hitting three from the tee box!

Number 9 is a fine finish to the front side and almost a mirror image of #18. This time, of course, the lake is on the right, and the green is three-tiered, making a par four a good score.

The 10th hole is a tough start on the back, a dogleg left with plenty of sycamore trees ready to throw the errant tee shot back at you or—even worse—send it careening into

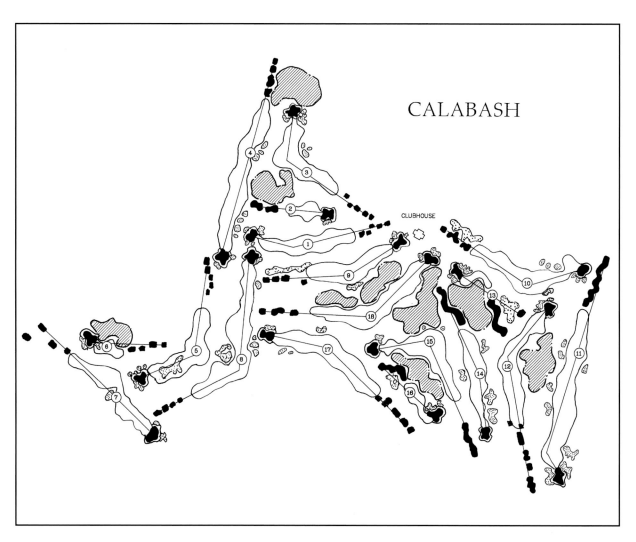

CALABASH

CLUBHOUSE

268

more trouble. When you hear the name of Willard Byrd, do you think pot bunkers? Right on. Number 10 has three of them that guard the right side of the fairway and green from 60 yards in. Sure, it's a pretty golf hole, but be very careful.

Some think of #14 as the best par four on the Calabash Golf Links. At more than 425 yards from the blue tees, it is long and is classified as the second-highest handicap hole on the back nine. The fairway is a slight dogleg to the right. Don't try a shortcut. To avoid sand traps you are much better off hitting the ball as close to center as possible.

Calabash

HOLE NUMBER	1	2	3	4	5	6	7	8	9	OUT	10	11	12	13	14	15	16	17	18	IN	TOT	HCP	NET
BLUE	357	180	374	513	371	195	380	520	374	3264	372	528	396	179	429	378	180	400	486	3348	6612		
WHITE	330	167	341	466	336	172	344	488	342	2986	347	504	364	155	370	359	160	354	451	3064	6050		
GOLD	290	130	303	435	305	155	271	443	320	2652	322	461	340	126	338	330	140	299	407	2763	5415		
HANDICAP	17	5	15	3	7	9	13	1	11		6	4	10	18	2	12	8	16	14				
PAR	4	3	4	5	4	3	4	5	4	36	4	5	4	3	4	4	3	4	5	36	72		
RED	240	102	282	410	290	115	223	406	287	2355	277	440	312	105	306	300	120	285	350	2495	4850		
LADIES HCP	17	11	9	3	5	7	13	1	15		6	2	16	10	4	18	8	12	14				

The North course at Angels Trace, cut from virgin pines, has been imaginatively and beautifully contoured by Clyde Johnston. With 807 acres at his disposal, the architect used the land to great advantage. (Courtesy Himmelbach Communications/Bill Woodward)

Angels Trace (North Course)

HOLE NUMBER	1	2	3	4	5	6	7	8	9	OUT	10	11	12	13	14	15	16	17	18	IN	TOT	HCP	NET
BLUE	547	376	161	426	382	175	409	368	497	3341	366	510	383	163	352	191	399	363	572	3299	6640		
WHITE	527	355	132	405	338	150	390	348	472	3117	346	490	364	148	320	169	380	331	551	3099	6216		
YELLOW	510	280	103	346	298	137	338	278	375	2665	278	416	306	121	287	147	320	285	491	2651	5316		
HANDICAP	1	13	17	7	9	15	5	11	3		10	6	8	16	14	18	4	12	2				
PAR	5	4	3	4	4	3	4	4	5	36	4	5	4	3	4	3	4	4	5	36	72		
RED	450	247	83	284	259	92	276	246	329	2266	241	389	260	105	265	116	253	211	418	2258	4524		
HANDICAP	1	13	17	7	5	15	9	11	3		10	8	14	18	12	16	6	4	2				

ANGELS TRACE

1215 Angels Club Drive S.W.   Sunset Beach, NC 28468
(800) 718-5733   (910) 579-2277

Architect: Clyde Johnston   Year opened: 1995

Course rating/Slope rating:

NORTH
Blue - 73.6/139   White - 70.8/130
Yellow - 67.6/125   Red - 68.2/118

SOUTH
Blue - 74.3/138   White - 71.4/132
Yellow - 68.8/122   Red - 69.1/118

When golfing historians review the final decade of the twentieth century, honing in on golfing activity on the Grand Strand, the name of Clyde Johnston may be the most important entry in these golfing journals. Why? The man knows how to design and build golf courses!

The two courses at Angels Trace, in nearby Brunswick County, are another tribute to his ability to take a virgin piece of ground and carve it into a magnificent golf course. At Angels Trace he has done it twice, and one of the most important decisions a golfer can make is which course to play.

To be sure, having enough ground for true expression is important, and Johnston, once a close friend and valued architect for Willard Byrd, likes to build big, wide-open courses. When 807 acres are available for course design, the creative bent has ample opportunity to express itself. However, the spaciousness of these courses alone isn't what has stamped Johnston as one of the world's best golf architects. Rather, he knows how to move dirt, and again at Angels Trace he has built rolling fairways and oversized, gently rolling greens while taking advantage of virgin pine forests, natural water hazards, and environmentally protected wastelands to create a memorable course.

Building one golf course is tough enough, but at Angels Trace a carefully coordinated effort enabled the course owners to open two courses simultaneously. Winding through tall Carolina pines and a mixture of hardwoods such as oaks, poplars, and dogwoods, the courses are similar but at the same time offer different tests of golf. The trees on the North course are older, never having been forested, and the course is much tighter than the South course, where the trees, forested one time, still are twenty-five to thirty years old. While the South course is longer, the slope ratings for these two courses are just about the same.

Angels Trace, with its two heavenly golf courses, was opened in the fall of 1995 to rave reviews and continues to enjoy great popularity. Angels Trace is located within a dense population of golf courses. The three Sea Trail courses are directly across Angels Club Drive; Sandpiper Bay is in plain view across the highway; and the entrance to three animalistic courses—Lion's Paw, Panther's Run, and Tiger's Eye—is less than two miles away on Highway 904, as are the two courses at The Pearl. While they are all very good courses, Angels Trace does not take a back seat to any of them.

The North Course

Number 5, the signature hole on this course, is quite a challenge, although it is a relatively short par four. The landing area for the tee shot is surrounded by sand bunkers, three on the right and one huge monster on the left. Select a club that enables you to proceed 175 to 225 yards from the tee box and still keep the ball in the narrow fairway. Then the course doglegs sharply to the left, and the golfer faces a deceptive downhill approach over water to the green, which is completely bounded on the front by the water and guarded by two bunkers just beyond the water.

One of the friendly rangers (another plus for Angels Trace) told us that #16 is almost a carbon copy of the signature hole, and they are indeed very similar. Number 16 is a little longer and its dogleg is not as sharp as #5's. Otherwise they could be twins, and both can give you as many problems as there are in math books.

Number 1 is a very good starting hole, but you might want something easier. This par five stretches 547 yards from the blue tees and can pose plenty of trouble. The second shot is critical because the landing area is narrowed by a large pond on the left side of the fairway that is not visible and which crosses the fairway directly in front of the green. Because there is no place to bail out, the thinking golfer must realize the importance of keeping his second shot in play and short of the water and then hitting a lofted iron to the pin.

Number 9 is another of the front side's holes that brings back memories—many of which are not good ones. This par five yields some birdies as well as double bogeys. Bring out the driver and swing away to a wide-open landing area. The second shot, for those who dare, must carry over water to a green surrounded by four sand bunkers.

The back nine also features many good holes. Number 12 makes you think twice about which club to use off the tee. Because of its narrow fairway, this hole requires a drive with more accuracy than distance. The approach shot is difficult because the green is fronted on the left by sand bunkers, and the steep drop-off on the right front of the green resembles a valley with a huge elevation change. "Hitting the green is very tough because it plays away from you," the ranger said. "It's just not in line with your fairway shot."

The 18th hole is the number-one handicap hole on the back side with good reason. A great finishing hole, it is more than 470 yards long from the blue tees and plays all uphill! It requires two solid shots with a long approach to a huge green surrounded by sand bunkers.

The North course is a good golf course.

The South Course

This one is good, too. Andy Snead, golf professional at Angels Trace, told us that his favorites on this big, big course are consecutive holes: #6, #7, and #8. "And," he said, "don't forget #18.

Even though water is not as prevalent on the South course as on the North, the hazards are still more than enough to plague most golfers. Number 6 is a perfect example. Sure, this par three is beautiful, but the water runs laterally along the right side of the entire hole, whose length also is downright scary. Number 6 requires a long carry to the green, which is 220 yards from the blue tees and 194 from the whites. Only the ladies get a break on this one: They tee off on the left side away from the water hazard and must hit the ball less than 100 yards. Men, if you must miss the green, do so on the left because nothing but beaches and watery graves await you on the right. The water extends from tee to green, so please don't hit a slice.

The 7th hole is long enough to be rated the third most difficult on the front side, but

The South course is "heavenly," too. The trees aren't as old as those on the North course, but these two are equally difficult and very pleasant to the eye. Neither is easy. (Courtesy Himmelsbach Communications/Bill Woodward)

it can be a two-shot par five. The tee shot favors left-to-right hitters because the fairway devilishly slopes right to left toward the water, which runs the length of the fairway. The approach shot is not the end of your troubles, either. This green is large and elevated, with a big hump in the middle of the right side of the putting surface.

Now, try the number-one handicap hole on the South course. Number 8 is a par four that measures 422 yards from the blues, 398 from the whites. You need an accurate drive because the fairway narrows at the 150-yard marker. The approach shot is to an elevated green (thanks just the same, Clyde) that is guarded by water and sand on the left and by mounds on the right.

Number 8 is tough for men, but oddly enough it is rated as the fifth most difficult hole on the front for the ladies, who again play on the right away from the water. This 287-yard hole can yield some birdies for the longer-hitting ladies.

Conversely, #18 is the number-one handicap hole on the back side for the ladies and the second most difficult hole for the men (#14 is their toughest). This par-five hole with its very sharp dogleg to the right is a very challenging finishing hole. For those who dare (and you probably shouldn't), the best angle from which to approach the green is from the left side of the fairway, but you are cautioned to be aware of the water that comes into play on the left and into the dogleg. By the same token, don't go too far right because trees will block your approach shot to a very wide, well-protected green.

The South course is good, but so is the North. While at Angels Trace, you might want to play both of these heavenly Clyde Johnston gems.

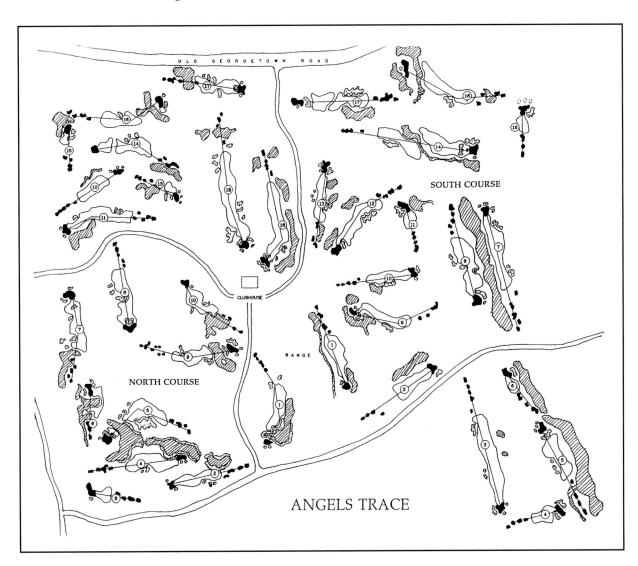

Angels Trace (South Course)

HOLE NUMBER	1	2	3	4	5	6	7	8	9	OUT	10	11	12	13	14	15	16	17	18	IN	TOT	HCP	NET
BLUE	385	383	541	175	387	220	524	422	397	3434	398	198	387	397	568	178	387	398	531	3442	6876		
WHITE	356	363	522	147	356	194	502	398	377	3215	381	187	377	366	544	168	366	373	465	3227	6442		
YELLOW	328	324	452	129	327	124	447	330	314	2775	329	134	320	344	496	110	312	337	436	2818	5593		
HANDICAP	11	15	7	17	3	13	5	1	9		12	18	6	14	2	16	8	10	4				
PAR	4	4	5	3	4	3	5	4	4	36	4	3	4	4	5	3	4	4	5	36	72		
RED	277	279	400	109	266	88	410	287	278	2394	290	118	284	261	440	88	270	288	378	2417	4811		
HANDICAP	13	11	1	17	7	15	3	9	5		14	18	12	10	4	16	6	8	2				

PANTHER'S RUN

351 Ocean Parkway   Ocean Isle Beach, NC
(800) 233-1801   (910) 287-1717

Architect: Tim N. Cate   Year opened: 1995
Course rating/Slope Rating:
Black - 72.4/142   Blue - 70.2/136
White - 68.1/119   Gold - 66.6/114
Red - 68.3/118

The second in a trilogy of superior courses, each named for a ferocious feline, Panther's Run is located in a prime development area carved from 1,300 acres of maritime forestry and shares those acres with Lion's Paw (the original course) and Tiger's Eye, another Tim N. Cate design set to open in the fall of 1999.

Most of the people who live here are golfers, and they dwell amidst three excellent courses in this planned unit development known as Ocean Ridge Plantation. It seems as if each course just keeps getting better. If anyone should tire of playing "at home" (which is almost unimaginable), many other quality courses such as Sea Trail, Sandpiper Bay, and Oyster Bay are just down the road. This is a great place to live for those who love golf!

"At some point in time we may have as many as 1,200 residences at Ocean Ridge," said developer Ed Gore, "but none of them will intrude on the golf course." While individual homes are going up around Lion's Paw and Panther's Run, Gore contemplates the addition of some multi-unit construction for the third course, Tiger's Eye. However, "the natural, unspoiled beauty of the courses continues to be our top priority," Gore emphasized.

One of the words applied to Panther's Run is "stealth," and it's not too difficult to imagine a panther lurking in the woods and lovegrass, leaping from hiding to mangle your golf shot or carry it into a location where par becomes impossible. Even the rangers and starters employed at this beautiful course and dressed in traditional safari shirts, shorts, and pith helmets are of little help against the ferocious feline.

Putting together this book, the author had the opportunity of viewing some of the great holes of Panther's Run firsthand with golf architect Tim Cate, who has developed a style all his own. "It isn't hard when you have a beautiful piece of ground like this," Cate said. "We don't move tons of dirt like some others do; we allow the natural contours of the land to dictate much of our design."

An example of Cate's thinking can be seen on the 8th hole. "We didn't build mounds here. We just dug a big hole and created intricately deep grassy bunkers which are used to define fairways. They frame the hole to perfection."

Cate grew up with the land. His dad was in the grading business, and he learned nuances of golf-course architecture while working for Willard Byrd, architect of the first course at Ocean Ridge, Lion's Paw. However, "The courses I build today are very different from the Byrd style," Cate said.

Tim N. Cate has become a highly sought-after golf-course designer and is doing some outstanding work. As this book went to press, he maintained offices at Panther's Run while developing Tiger's Eye, completing the outstanding Players Club some ten miles to the north, and beginning work on

Tim Cate is well on his way to building a reputation as one of the nation's best golf architects. This is the second in his trilogy of pleasant but difficult courses, each one named for a ferocious feline. Cate took full advantage of natural contours, moving a minimal amount of dirt to create subtle and not so subtle moundings on this very good course. (Courtesy Himmelsbach Communications/Bill Woodward)

a thirty-six-hole layout at nearby Calabash.

Let's look at some of the memorable holes at Panther's Run:

Number 4 is a par four that requires a very long and well-placed drive. The hole itself is a dogleg to the left, and to reach the green in two the golfer must clear a lake that crosses the fairway in front of the well-bunkered green. The green slopes to the front and necessitates a shot that must "carry" all the way to the putting surface.

The 6th hole is another good one on the front side. Length (215 yards) makes this par three tough, and the hole plays even longer than it looks. The green is elevated, well bunkered, and huge! To further complicate making par, this green is two-tiered, so the golfer must fire at the pin to avoid a probable three putt.

As you might expect on a course that plays to a slope rating of 140 and a course rating of 74.8, the finishing hole on the front nine also is formidable. It stretches 571 yards from the back tees and is fortified with wetlands on the right, fairway bunkers in the two landing areas, and a deep and extremely large sand trap at the green. Number 9, rated as the number-one handicap hole at Panther's Run, is as beautiful as it is difficult.

It doesn't get any better on the back nine, which—like the front side—is more than 3,500 yards long. Number 13 is memorable because even though it measures more than 550 yards from tee to green, it is a sharp dogleg that a daring long-ball hitter can reach in two. Water crossing the fairway shouldn't come into play.

Numbers 15 and 18 are the signature holes of this back nine. Fifteen is a long par four with a pretty lake going all the way down the right side of the fairway and coming across to protect most of the green, which is long and narrow. The approach to a small target area is very tough.

Number 18, the magnificent number-one handicap hole that is pictured with this chapter, is straightaway, but the second shot must go over a large lake that completely guards the green, bisecting the entire fairway. Position is everything on this 420-yard-plus hole; you must determine whether the second shot must be "laid up" or (if going for the green) how much of the lake can be "chewed off."

Ocean Ridge executives describe Panther's Run as a traditional course, carved out of woods in a parkland style, and a favorite of local and tourist golfers. Several members of The Players Tour, which visited Panther's Run in their 1996 tour, were very complimentary of this golf course, declaring it "perhaps the best course we have played."

See also Lion's Paw (p. 211).

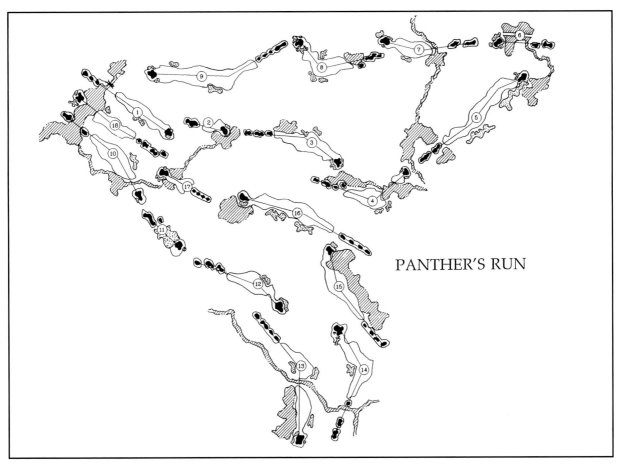

PANTHER'S RUN

Panther's Run

HOLE NUMBER	1	2	3	4	5	6	7	8	9	OUT	10	11	12	13	14	15	16	17	18	IN	TOT	HCP	NET
BLACK	404	177	427	431	525	215	396	389	571	3535	401	192	384	554	434	412	548	204	425	3554	7086		
BLUE	384	164	408	397	504	191	386	378	548	3360	375	170	369	514	419	394	513	182	410	3346	6706		
WHITE	362	150	371	378	482	171	357	353	518	3142	361	143	341	493	396	357	492	162	380	3125	6267		
GOLD	330	126	316	348	432	137	318	311	462	2780	293	137	310	458	372	310	441	130	315	2766	5546		
HANDICAP	11	13	5	3	9	7	15	17	1		16	14	18	2	6	12	4	8	10				
PAR	4	3	4	4	5	3	4	4	5	36	4	3	4	5	4	4	5	3	4	36	72		
RED	251	103	301	320	416	95	307	276	437	2506	264	115	275	425	328	295	410	118	287	2517	5023		
HANDICAP	11	13	5	3	9	7	15	17	1		16	14	18	2	6	12	4	8	10				

Sand and water are very much in evidence at Magnolia Greens, and architect Tom Jackson maintains that each individual hole has "a character all its own." (Courtesy Magnolia Greens)

MAGNOLIA GREENS

1800 Linkwood Circle (U.S. 17 North)
Leland, NC 28451
(800) 677-7534   (910) 383-0999

Architect: Tom Jackson   Year opened: 1998

Course rating/Slope rating:
Black - 75.3/138   Blue - 72.0/130
White - 68.6/119   White - 74.9/135
Red - 70.3/120

Located in Brunswick County, the home of many of the courses featured in this book, Magnolia Greens is the perfect companion piece to the three great golf courses of St. James Plantation and the Fred Couples-designed Carolina National at Winding River Plantation. The opening of this course on the county's northern edge is a big step toward making the area "wall to wall" with golf facilities—from the southern regions of Myrtle Beach all the way into Wilmington, North Carolina.

"From a golf architect's point of view, planning this course was both challenging and fun, and I believe that everyone who plays it will discover these same qualities. It ranks at the top of all the courses I've designed," said architect Tom Jackson, who has put his signature on seven other excellent layouts pictured and described in this book.

Making Magnolia Greens even better, as far as many golfers are concerned, is its price. Golf professional Patrick Crean, who worked closely with Jackson and the builders before opening the course, called it a "a reasonably priced course," with greens fees (including carts) going for $35 to $55, depending on the time of the year. The clubhouse is 5,000 square feet, and excellent practice facilities are available.

Magnolia Greens stretches out to a daunting 7,156 yards and has a slope rating of 138. It can be a monster if played from the black tees, but with multiple tees it is "a very fair course with no blind shots."

The greens are G-2 bent grass, and every hole has at least four sets of tees. The par-four 4th, generally considered the signature hole of this Tom Jackson masterpiece, can be played from any of *seven* separate tees, each elevated and built into a small mound. Reaching the fairway from the black tees requires an awesome swat of 233 yards over rough, so most golfers opt for one of the forward tees on this hole. The hole slopes left toward Sturgeon Creek, and the green itself is well protected, with bunkers to the right and one tucked to the left front. Five mounds to the left side and behind the green enhance the hole's beauty and frame the target area.

The 14th, however, is the number-one handicap hole. It's long enough to challenge any golfer—467 yards from the black tees, 431 from the blues. To complicate matters, a vast expanse of wetlands separates two fairways, and at the far edge of this hazard Jackson diabolically left two hardwoods that wait to knock down your second shot and make a double bogey very realistic. Again, the hole slopes left toward Sturgeon Creek, and the strand of hardwoods bordering this creek make it a very pretty hole. You'll want to keep your tee shot to the right of the fairway, but don't let it go too far in that direction because there are plenty of trees just off the fairway. You also want to be aware of a

Looking across the water to #18, nestled below the clubhouse at Magnolia Greens
(Courtesy Magnolia Greens)

big bunker to the right front of the green.

"I always like to finish with a five-par hole," Jackson said, "and #18 at Magnolia Greens is a real good finishing hole." The hole plays as a dogleg left, and a vast expanse of water lies to the left of the green. The view from the clubhouse across the water is pretty, but it can be a frightening one for the golfer who has navigated almost 600 yards of real estate to reach the green. Wetlands run up the left side all the way from the tee boxes to the large pond, and golfers *know* they must keep almost every shot to the right. They get an assist from the architect, who installed a set of moundings on the right side that frame the proper direction and keep the wayward shot from hardwoods that really should be out of play. This hole is a good one.

With most golfers choosing to play white tees, the three-par holes demand more accuracy than length, and those golfers with the finely tuned short irons and wedges should do well. Number 3 conveys an unusual sand-dunes effect, with a large green that slopes to the front. Pin placement can be difficult, and if you think 113 yards is just too short, then go on back to the black tees. It's 175 yards from black tee to green, and the four bunkers that front the green will probably make you sorry. If you pull your shot or come up short, you're in the kitty box.

Number 8 is a very pretty three par, stretching from 145 (white tees) to 195 yards (black tees), and the hole is encircled with oak and pine trees. This time the green slopes left toward the creek, and three putts are not infrequent. Number 13 also has a severe slope in the green, and while #16 does not have that much undulation, it is longer than the other three pars.

Overall, Magnolia Greens is a well-designed golf course, and each individual hole has a character all its own. However, getting to the course requires driving time of about one hour for the "package" golfers who are staying at facilities in the northern part of northern Myrtle Beach. Still, if your plans call for playing one of the many good courses north of the South Carolina border and you want to play thirty-six holes, this very rewarding course is easily reached via four-lane highways and is easy to find, located right on U.S. 17. Because developers of the property envision a continued expansion of golf's popularity, they are planning to construct a hotel on the property along with condominiums.

If you have the time, play this course. Magnolia Greens has the Tom Jackson stamp of approval, and that's good enough for us.

(Courtesy Magnolia Greens)

Magnolia Greens

HOLE NUMBER	1	2	3	4	5	6	7	8	9	OUT	10	11	12	13	14	15	16	17	18	IN	TOT	HCP	NET
BLACK	394	602	174	393	555	392	384	195	444	3533	421	520	425	152	467	388	190	468	592	3623	7156		
BLUE	365	563	151	355	532	359	354	165	412	3256	396	494	401	119	431	356	163	435	568	3363	6619		
WHITE	340	539	113	309	494	306	299	145	381	2926	350	424	367	104	367	334	137	407	520	3010	5936		
HANDICAP	10	2	18	8	6	14	16	12	4		13	11	3	17	1	9	15	5	7				
PAR	4	5	3	4	5	4	4	3	4	36	4	5	4	3	4	4	3	4	5	36	72		
RED	275	500	82	266	437	266	253	115	352	2546	302	375	328	61	336	300	104	360	461	2627	5173		

CAROLINA NATIONAL
GOLF CLUB AT WINDING RIVER

1643 Goley Hewett   Bolivia, NC 28422   P.O. Box 11107   Southport, NC 28461
(800) 711-5263   (888) 200-6455

Architects: Fred Couples/Gene Bates   Year opened: 1997

Course rating/Slope rating:
MEN'S
Black - 73.4/136   Gold - 70.8/130
Blue - 68.7/125   Teal - 66.3/120
White - 63.5/116
WOMEN'S
Blue - 73.9/135   Teal - 71.2/128
White - 67.5/118

Developers of Winding River Plantation have a master plan that includes much more than this exciting championship course, the third Fred Couples signature course in the United States, which opened on November 17, 1997. Couples currently is working as a designer on two other courses.

Opening as an eighteen-hole course with bent-grass greens, five sets of tees, and the length you would expect from a Couples-flavored golf course, Carolina National soon will expand to twenty-seven holes. Golfers and nature lovers who intend to make Winding River Plantation a permanent home will enjoy their own beach club directly on the Atlantic Ocean, boating and fishing on the wide and winding Lockwood Folly River, and two private marinas within the community.

Winding River is a large tract of ground, more than 1,100 acres, bounded on the east by Lockwood River and pristine marshland. As an environmentally aware group, the developers took every precaution to leave the land in as natural a state as possible. As a result, the property remains heavily wooded with magnolia, dogwood, bay, oak, and pine trees. Trees are nice, but the golfer tends to focus on the golf course itself.

Bates, who did most of the routing, worked with the Jack Nicklaus organization and is pleased with the effort, calling Carolina National unique to the area. The course is equipped with five sets of tees on each hole and is adorned with native grasses and flowers. Indeed, the architect's goal was to create a course sporting the largest inventory of native and nonturf grasses on any course in the United States.

The fairways are wide, and the landing areas are very generous, making the length of this course a little less threatening. Carolina National can be very formidable from the back tees, but the golfer who chooses to play "up front" will find the tees are forward of all hazards and wetlands.

The fairways are planted in 419 Tifway, and the bent-grass greens are a combination of the Crenshaw strain and L93, affording both speed and longevity. These "quick as lightning" greens average 7,500 square feet in size, and #18 is an oversized 9,400 square feet, making a three putt a definite possibility.

The par-five holes measure between 517 and 568 yards, but even the shortest (#9) does not lend itself to becoming a two-shot hole because of a demanding dogleg left and water placed strategically in front of the green. Six lakes are located within the playing area of the initial eighteen holes, and the completed course will be an interesting mixture of both wide-open spaces and holes that wind through residential areas to create a man-made canyon effect without infringing on the course itself.

Number 14, the signature hole of Carolina National, offers five tee boxes set in a semicircle so that the angle approaching the green is 180 degrees from one through five. The tee shot must carry both marsh and water and can be intimidating, ranging in distance from 144 to 198 yards.

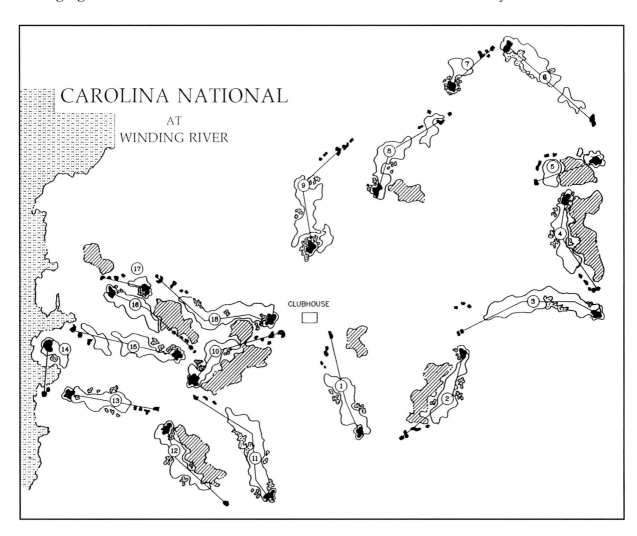

Carolina National

HOLE NUMBER	1	2	3	4	5	6	7	8	9	OUT	10	11	12	13	14	15	16	17	18	IN	TOT	HCP	NET
BLACK	388	427	577	384	184	445	219	390	486	3500	400	530	384	365	203	432	443	173	587	3517	7017		
GOLD	361	412	548	366	156	412	185	374	457	3271	378	502	325	348	191	370	401	158	549	3222	6493		
BLUE	350	357	506	340	156	369	181	316	427	3002	361	458	312	312	182	350	374	141	508	2998	6000		
TEAL	322	343	463	295	138	309	162	303	393	2728	330	420	298	303	162	271	313	112	469	2678	5406		
WHITE	276	300	421	257	131	279	139	271	347	2421	318	393	201	243	121	247	267	105	443	2338	4759		
HANDICAP	17	5	3	11	7	1	9	13	15		12	8	14	16	10	6	2	18	4				
PAR	4	4	5	4	3	4	3	4	5	36	4	5	4	4	3	4	4	3	5	36	72		

Highway 9 West

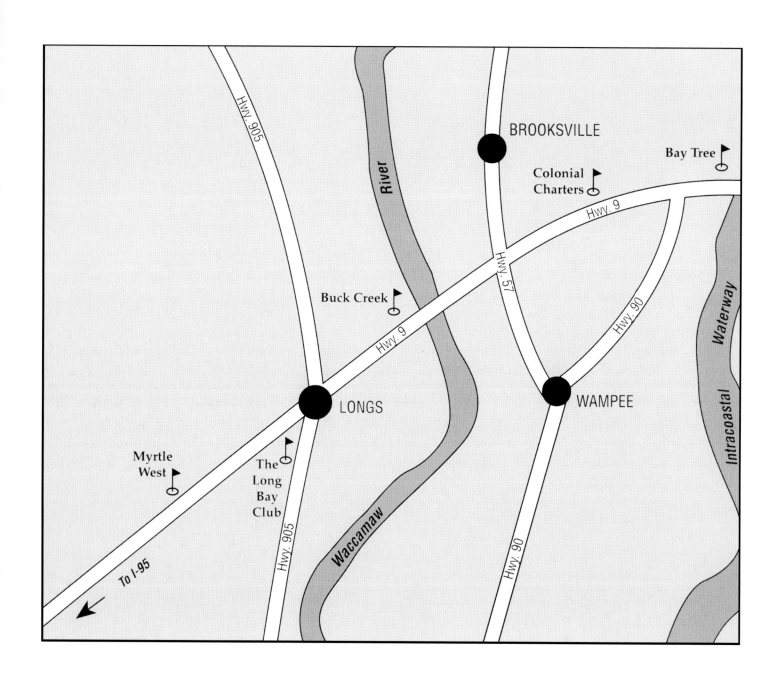

286

MYRTLE WEST

Highway 9   P.O. Box 3371   N. Myrtle Beach, SC 29582
(843) 249-1478   (800) 842-8390

Architect: Tom Jackson   Year opened: 1989

Course rating/Slope rating:
Gold - 72.7/128   Silver - 66.7/113
Blue - 69.7/118   Red - 67.6/113

Golf is growing in all directions on the Strand, and the Highway 9 corridor, reaching from North Myrtle Beach west through Loris and Dillon toward Charlotte and the Piedmont, is a promising development area.

Joining the three courses of Bay Tree, the twenty-seven holes of Buck Creek, Colonial Charters, and the Long Bay Club as an enticement to golfers is Myrtle West, an innovative Tom Jackson design which opened in October 1989. Easily accessible to Beach golfers because of a wide four-lane highway, Myrtle West is less than fifteen minutes from the bridge connecting North Myrtle Beach and Little River, NC.

According to Billy Cole, golf director when this course first opened, Myrtle West is "a tremendous golf course for the golfer who is looking for a test, but is not looking to get his brains beat in."

Jackson wanted a course that was different and partially accomplished this aim by creating a course that is "grass wall to wall." It is a superintendent's dream, easy to manicure. There are no pine needles and no rough area. "Hit the ball and go find it," laughs Jackson. "It's either in the grass or in the water."

The course is designed to give the golfer an opportunity of staying away from water if he so chooses. The water on the course is visible and it doesn't take a lot of imagination to determine which side of the fairway you should avoid. Hit it down the middle, or take a little longer route to the green by going down the side of the fairway not guarded by water.

Sometimes that's easier said than done.

Jackson has designed some excellent holes where the water does come into play. Numbers 8 and 18, two favorites, are typical.

Both are doglegs to the right, and, on both holes, the golfer needs to go over water on his approach to the green or take the long way around, needing an extra shot.

Number 8 might be termed a "little four par" because of its relatively short distance of 352 yards from the professional tees, but it is a dangerous hole with water running all the way down the right side of the fairway,

Myrtle West

HOLE NUMBER	1	2	3	4	5	6	7	8	9	OUT	10	11	12	13	14	15	16	17	18	IN	TOT	HCP	NET
GOLD	370	579	174	370	406	221	526	352	414	3412	374	360	513	175	353	410	203	454	533	3375	6787		
BLUE	341	552	135	331	375	195	506	315	375	3135	337	332	476	142	319	373	175	407	495	3056	6191		
SILVER	305	517	115	296	354	159	462	286	343	2837	300	267	443	113	283	340	134	376	462	2718	5555		
HANDICAP	12	2	18	16	6	8	10	14	4		17	3	13	11	15	5	9	1	7				
PAR	4	5	3	4	4	3	5	4	4	36	4	4	5	3	4	4	3	4	5	36	72		
RED	269	488	71	250	321	121	443	259	306	2528	272	228	374	85	233	281	105	327	426	2331	4859		
LADIES' HCP	12	2	18	16	6	8	10	14	4		17	3	13	11	15	5	9	1	7				
LADIES' PAR	4	5	3	4	4	3	5	4	4	36	4	4	5	3	4	4	3	4	5	36	72		

Number 18 at Myrtle West . . . a five par over water with the clubhouse in the background.
(Courtesy Myrtle West Golf Course)

ready to catch an errant drive from the tee. To reach this green in two, you must go over the water with the second shot.

Number 18 is similar, but much longer, and a good par five to the degree that you can birdie it, score an eagle, or play it as a traditional five par. The daring golfer, going for a birdie, needs to bite off a huge chunk of water that sweeps completely in front of the green. Most golfers will keep their first two shots well to the left, reducing the amount of water on the hole.

Myrtle West, a "fun place" to play golf, is reasonably short from the four sets of tees (6,787, 6,191, 5,555, and 4,859). Jackson built undulating, mounded greens to put a premium on good putting.

The greens are good—Tift Dwarf Bermuda—but they feature lots of contours.

The golfer reaches the clubhouse at Myrtle West by turning from Highway 9 onto a picturesque lane ambling through a covered bridge. This amenity sets Myrtle West apart, gives the course a Low-Country atmosphere, and makes the course more memorable.

Terry Mauney, a North Carolina sportswriter who once played on the PGA Tour, has fond memories of Highway 9. He holds the course record (63) at Myrtle West, set in the 1990 Sports Reporters Tournament, and also has the course record at nearby Buck Creek.

His record-setting round at Myrtle West was near perfect, nine pars and nine birdies!

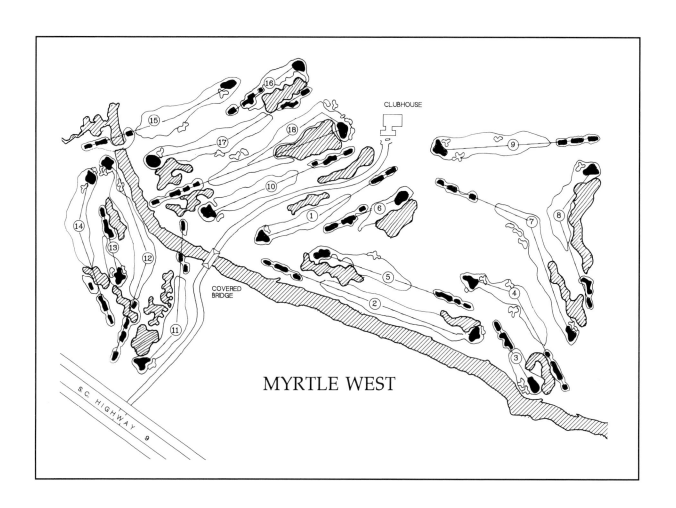

MYRTLE WEST

The two-level tee box at #8 of Cypress, one of Buck Creek's three nine-hole layouts.
(Courtesy Himmelsbach Communications/Bill Woodward)

BUCK CREEK

Highway 9   P.O. Box 3629   N. Myrtle Beach, SC 29582
(843) 249-5996   (800) 344-0982

Architect: Tom Jackson   Year opened: 1990

Course rating/Slope rating:
Stag - 71.1/126   Doe - 66.9/111
Buck - 68.7/119   Fawn - 67.5/117

Most people who played Buck Creek for the first time before the third nine was opened in October 1990 agreed that this course lived up to the glowing description printed on the back of the scorecard:

Nestled amidst the hardwoods and the flowing waters of the Waccamaw River lies a fascinating blend of beauty and adventure. Buck Creek's 27 holes, encompassing 500 acres, present a variety of fairways, greens and intricate mounding that will enhance your golfing experience and provide challenges that will test your shot-making skills. At the conclusion of your round you will realize that you have just completed 18 of the finest golf holes that you may ever play.... Nominated by *Golf Digest* as America's best new course for 1990 ....

The words come from the golf course.

However, we agree with this assessment of Buck Creek, and can tell readers that it became even better when the third nine (Tupelo) was ready for play!

This is a first-class project. Much attention is given to floral plantings at the clubhouse and around the course, and this is a truly scenic, colorful, and beautiful layout. The clubhouse itself is handsome, with wicker furniture, a striking floral-patterned carpet throughout, and a well-stocked pro shop.

Golf architect Tom Jackson and builder John McWhite did a fine job creating a course that would be pleasing, demanding, and esthetic.

If Buck Creek hosts a tournament for professionals or low-handicap players, they will probably use Tupelo as the front nine and Cypress as the back, giving a championship layout of 6,865 yards with enough water, sand, and trouble to make a par round very good indeed.

The Cypress is generally considered the most difficult of the three nines, but Tupelo is just as long and the golfer still is aware of water on every hole!

Because Cypress and Tupelo are so very tough, don't fall into the trap of thinking that Meadow is a "piece of cake." It's shorter, but Jackson designed this course to be challenging every inch of the way, and there are some very good golf holes on Meadow.

With three nines, Buck Creek can accommodate a lot of golfers. Ordinary rotation is Meadow to Cypress to Tupelo to Meadow.

Buck Creek is as pretty as it is difficult. Of the 500 acres, more than 170 were set aside for wildlife. And more than 1,000 feet of bridges have been constructed on the property.

Only seven of the holes are situated near residences, so golfers can enjoy a fairly wild course, spotting a deer, a raccoon, quail, or ducks during a round.

Buck Creek flows through the course, which adjoins the Waccamaw River and the old Loris Hunt Club, some 30,000 acres of protected, unspoiled natural beauty.

Each of the three nines has a distinctive

character, but every hole offers four sets of tees. Calling attention to the natural environment around the course, these tees are aptly named Stag (6,726 yards), Buck (6,115), Doe (5,574), and Fawn (4,684). All measurements are for a combination of Meadow and Cypress.

Terry Mauney, once a touring pro and now a sportscaster in North Carolina, holds the competitive course record from the Buck tees—a one under par 71. That score might be surprising to anyone who looks only at the relatively short distance of 6,115 yards, but can be appreciated by players who have seen firsthand the great expanse of waste land, the various unsuspected water haz-

ards, and the formidable stands of trees that abound on the course.

This is a course that challenges your game management. You can't just stand on every tee with a driver in your hand.

Not only is the course difficult, but the greens are huge, allowing some tough pin placements. Yardage books, available in the clubhouse, give you fair warning. For instance, as you play #1 on the Tupelo nine, and approach the green on this five-par hole, the golfer who consults the yardage book will read, "Club selection is vital on your approach as the green is five clubs deep!"

Every hole is a good one, but #5 on

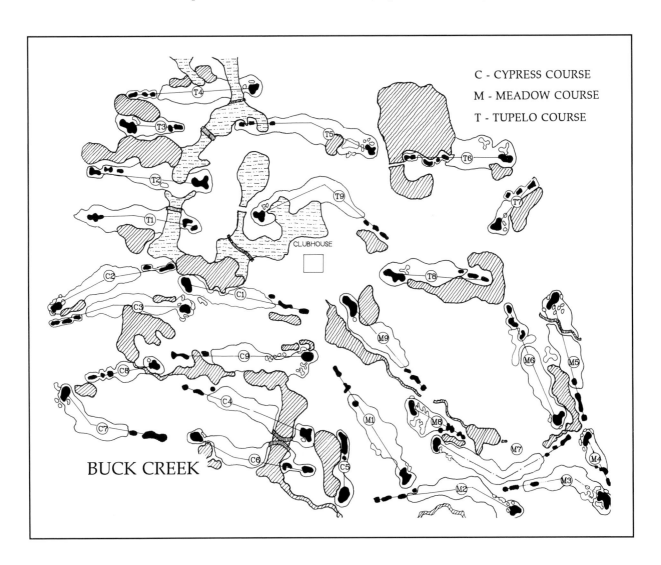

C - CYPRESS COURSE
M - MEADOW COURSE
T - TUPELO COURSE

CLUBHOUSE

BUCK CREEK

Tupelo has been hailed as the most dynamic par five in the world. That probably is an overstatement, but it is a very demanding golf hole. Length and strategy are the key thoughts here. To begin play, you need a long tee shot that must carry 190 yards of waste area—and that's only the beginning. Any golfer with an idea of reaching the green should think again. He needs a shot of more than 250 yards, must traverse water and waste sand, and must be able to stop the ball on a green that was built for a wedge shot! Play it safe and you're flirting with a tree that Jackson devilishly left standing in the fairway.

By the time most golfers get to #9 on Tupelo, they will be thankful it's almost behind them, but #9, too, is outstanding, one of the hardest, most challenging four pars you will find. The drive must be an extremely accurate tee shot over a waste area to a target area of fairway.

Then comes the hard part.

The approach shot requires a 175-yard effort of extreme accuracy that must have plenty of spin to stop the ball on the green. An errant shot, left or right, is in deep trouble, and if you're short you're out of play!

Space prohibits describing all of the excellent holes at Buck Creek, but #3 and #4 on Cypress are especially worthy of mention. As on most holes, #3 demands accuracy and good judgment. There is a lake approximately 250 yards from the tee so the golfer must hit his tee shot short of the water and down the left side of the fairway to minimize the amount of water he must carry on the second shot. Even getting over the water is no guarantee of success, and the smart golfer will aim at the greenside bunkers on the right because there's another lake on the left of the green! To some people, it's a great hole. To others it is very controversial. Some really like it, but some find it too difficult.

Without question, Buck Creek rates in the upper third of golf courses on the Grand Strand, for both challenge and enjoyment.

Meadow Course

Cypress Course

HOLE NUMBER	1	2	3	4	5	6	7	8	9	OUT	1	2	3	4	5	6	7	8	9	IN	TOT	HCP	NET
STAG	342	522	331	147	391	400	570	216	387	3306	432	426	535	421	167	411	351	158	544	3445	6726		
BUCK	306	494	300	129	358	365	546	160	352	3010	380	402	502	388	151	400	320	141	517	3201	6115		
DOE	286	472	280	101	321	343	499	128	329	2759	368	383	465	363	119	335	298	111	487	2929	5574		
FAWN	239	373	222	74	271	298	465	103	305	2350	323	345	441	331	92	319	262	85	424	2622	4684		
HANDICAP	15	5	13	17	9	11	1	3	7		6	8	2	4	18	14	12	16	10				
PAR	4	5	4	3	4	4	5	3	4	36	4	4	5	4	3	4	4	3	5	36	72		

Number 16 at Colonial Charters, one of four fine holes "down the stretch." (Courtesy Chip Smith Advertising)

Colonial Charters

HOLE NUMBER	1	2	3	4	5	6	7	8	9	OUT	10	11	12	13	14	15	16	17	18	IN	TOT	HCP	NET
GOLD	484	364	422	158	368	408	204	509	460	3377	355	180	500	365	171	390	522	450	424	3357	6734		
BLUE	472	339	378	148	351	382	192	487	409	3158	338	167	480	345	157	365	496	426	401	3175	6333		
WHITE	461	326	352	137	329	365	179	466	386	3001	321	159	473	300	148	347	470	402	385	3005	6006		
MEN'S HCP	5	15	7	17	11	3	13	1	9		14	18	4	12	16	10	2	6	8				
MEN'S PAR	5	4	4	3	4	4	3	5	4	36	4	3	5	4	3	4	5	4	4	36	72		
RED	397	275	311	101	275	278	151	409	335	2532	258	139	398	258	125	313	431	342	324	2588	5120		
LADIES' HCP	3	15	7	17	9	11	13	1	5		12	16	4	14	18	10	2	8	6				
LADIES' PAR	5	4	4	3	4	4	3	5	4	36	4	3	5	4	3	4	5	4	4	36	72		

COLONIAL CHARTERS

Highway 9   301 Charter Drive   Longs, SC 29568   (843) 249-8809
Architect: John Simpson   Year opened: 1988
Course rating/Slope rating:
Gold - 73.0/131   White - 70.1/118
Blue - 71.5/126   Red - 70.2/120

With large, excellent Bermuda greens, wide fairways, and water coming into play on most of the very good eighteen holes, Colonial Charters is a comfortable golf course. You have to hit the ball fairly straight, but high handicappers and really good players alike enjoy playing here. The course is long enough (6,734 yards from the back tees) to earn a rating of 71.8, and very few golfers have equaled that mark. Now deceased, Hamp Auld was always one of our favorites: He won every major championship in the Carolinas, and his course records at Colonial Charters still stand—65 from the middle tees and, surprisingly, 69 from the front.

The women's record—74—is held by Alice Simpson, wife of the course architect.

There are many memorable holes, but Auld said that the final holes on Colonial Charters—#17 and #18—are "the Hell Holes," and indeed, they often are featured on lists of the most devilish holes on the Grand Strand.

Both are extremely long four-par holes, and to the golfer trudging up the 18th fairway, the final green looks as if it is perched on a cliff. "There's one heck of a big hole in front of that green," said Auld, "so it's very hard to run the ball onto the green. You've got to hit it in the air all the way."

Number 18 is 424 yards from tee to green. Water to the left of a big trap protects the left front, and fairway traps are placed some 200 yards from the tee on both sides of the fairway. Number 17 is even longer, 450 yards, requiring a tee shot of 200 yards over a stream that cuts across the fairway, which has a lake running along the entire left side of it. However, these two holes are not regarded as the most difficult.

Two other holes on the back, #16 and #12, are rated as the number-two and number-four handicap holes. Many good golfers can argue that #16 isn't that tough, but it is a very pretty five-par hole, 522 yards from tee to green, with water to the left and a series of bunkers to the right of the green. Water in front of the tee should not come into play, and it is possible, but not probable, to get home in two.

Number 12, however, is tough. "It's the toughest hole on the entire course," said Auld. "You can't get home in two on this five par. You gotta hit it straight with an iron or fairway wood off the tee, and then you have to handle your second shot the same way. That's because trees have been left in the middle of the fairway. Simpson wanted to take them down, but I talked him into letting them stand."

The hole is a dogleg to the left, and although only 500 yards in length, trees to the left and those sentinels posted in the middle of the fairway make it a "target golf"-type hole.

The course architect made good use of a creek on the front side, and #3 is very memorable—a 422-yard (from the back tees) four par with the stream crossing the fairway 90 yards in front of the green, which is ringed with four sand traps. This is a hole that calls for a very accurate drive, with water all the way down the right side and a big bunker on the left.

Number 6 is a similar hole, and while there is less water on this one, it is rated as a tougher four par than # 3, with the stream coming across the fairway much closer to the putting surface. This hole features an extremely tight driving area, and it has some length. Accuracy is necessary, and to compound the difficulty, there is a pot bunker on the right that is not visible from the tee.

Golfers will remember the big waste bunker on #7, which runs alongside the fairway for most of the hole. The 14th hole is another good three par, which plays in a similar fashion. The green is elevated and calls for a right-to-left shot because of the waste bunker that guards the front and left side of the green. Beyond that expanse of

sand is a big lake, and many golf balls find their way over the sand and into the water.

Clearly visible, hanging from a branch of an oak to the right of the green, is a rope fashioned as a hangman's noose. "Once, a guy was even par until he got to this hole, and then he hit two balls into the water, made nine, and decided to hang himself," Auld said. Well, it makes a nice story, and the rope really is there!

Colonial Charters became part of "The Links Group" in 1996, and Ken Fowlkes and his staff have done extensive work on what already was a very fine course. The course is well conditioned, and the greens, often referred to as the best on the Strand, continue to be a true putting delight. This is not a surcharge course, but it is one you will enjoy playing.

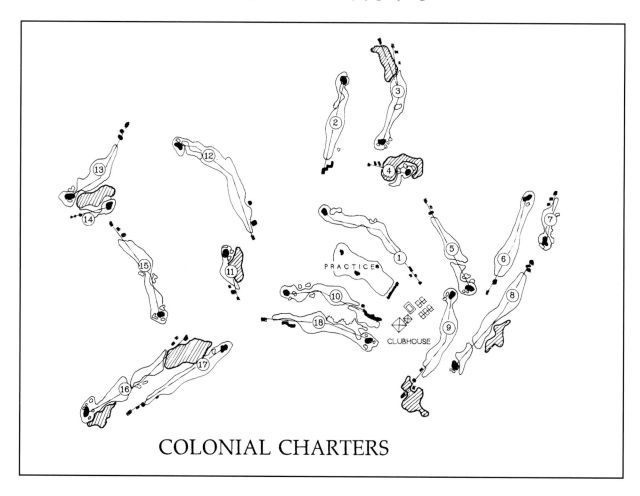

COLONIAL CHARTERS

BAY TREE

Route 2, Highway 9   N. Myrtle Beach, SC 29582
(843) 249-1487   (800) 845-6191

Architect: George Fazio and Russell Breeden   Year opened: 1972

Course rating/Slope rating:

GREEN	GOLD	SILVER
Blue - 73.5/135	73.4/135	72.7/131
White - 71.5/126	71.0/128	70.3/122
Red - 70.8/118	70.0/117	70.6/116

Bay Tree, located in North Myrtle Beach just west of the Waterway, on Highway 9, is a mature golfing facility. This fifty-four-hole golf resort with the landmark golf ball in the sky is not only popular, but also first class.

Never before in the Myrtle Beach area had any entrepreneur attempted to build and open three golf courses at one time, but that is exactly what five Beach residents with great foresight did in 1970. Enlisting George Fazio and Russell Breeden, well-known golf course architects, these five—Ed Martin, Bryan Floyd, Howard Anderson, Skeets Bellamy, and Gen. Joe Hackler—bought more than 600 acres of property from Myrtle Beach Farms and gave Fazio and Breeden the green light to build, right now, three championship courses!

On paper the Silver course was to be the most difficult, but it didn't turn out like that. Instead, the Green became the longest and most difficult, and the Gold became the most popular.

The course names reflect the theme of money in honor of the principal investor, a banker. The courses were built for $2.2 million, including the cost of the land. Bay Tree has been offered more than ten times that amount by interested buyers.

Profitability means a great deal to the investors, but that is not the factor that sells millions of golfers on these Bay Tree courses. They are as good today as they were twenty years ago, and continue to attract golfers who are serious about their game.

Most golfers will tell you that the Green is the most difficult, but that the Gold and Silver could be more fun. An LPGA Tournament was hosted at the Gold, which gave that course a lot of exposure.

Nevertheless, all three courses have more than their share of memorable holes, and all can be stretched to true championship caliber, measuring 6,871, 6,942, and 7,044 yards from the back tees. That's a lot of golf!

These are beautiful courses, with an abundance of tall pines, cypress, natural lakes, creeks, well-placed sand traps, and wildlife. North Myrtle Beach and Little River have grown up around Bay Tree, but evidence of deer can be seen around water holes, and stately herons and fierce hawks are a part of the scenery.

Bay Tree lost its alligator in 1991. A lot of people wanted to play #12 on the Silver course so they could see him, but he strayed into a new housing development beyond #12 and the Wildlife Department had to move him.

The most talked about golf hole at Bay Tree is #13 on the Green course. It has been voted to the list of the toughest eighteen holes on the Strand every time such a list has been compiled. It is a par four with a severe dogleg left and is tough. It requires a long drive into a small landing area so that the golfer can negotiate the second shot over a lake to an elevated green. You must hit your drive about 250 yards in order to have a 170-yard second shot over water onto the green. Once reaching the putting surface, the golfer finds a lot of work still to be done on the steeply banked, undulating green.

Another memorable hole on the Green course is the first one you see, which features a ten-acre lake in the center of the fairway, demanding good club selection. No one

has reached this hole in two. You can't drive over the lake, and you don't want to hit into it, so usually you're a long way out for your second shot.

The Gold course has its share of good holes. Number 5 is very long, 472 yards from the back tees with a lake to the left at the bottom of a small hill. This creates a very small landing area and leaves the golfer with an uphill second shot to the hole.

Number 8 on the Gold is a favorite, too—a three-par hole over water and the golfer can use the "Golf Ball Tower" as a directional guide. The hole that golfers see from the highway as they drive past Bay Tree is

Golf ball in the sky—a memorable symbol of Myrtle Beach and the three championship courses at Bay Tree. (Courtesy Brandon Advertising/Michael Slear)

#16, and, while not as difficult as some of the others, the big lake to the right of the fairway can cause problems.

Many long hitters are partial to the five-par 18th on the Gold. If you hit a good drive out of the chute, you can try to go for the hole in two.

Another favorite of golfers is the five par 12th on the Silver course. Leaving a natural cypress crater lake intact, golf architects created a 525-yard dogleg hole with sand traps to the right directing a good shot. It is a very narrow fairway and the pond actually is beyond the landing area of the drive. Traps really are not in play and are there for direction. However, there are a lot of tall pines and the water comes into play on the second shot.

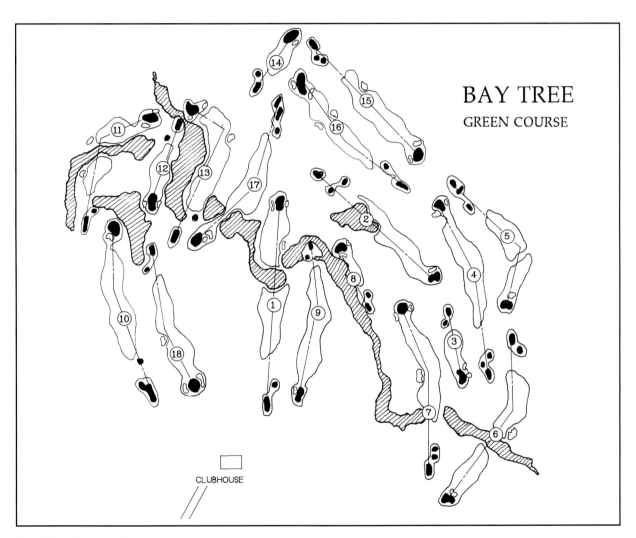

Bay Tree/Green Course

HOLE NUMBER	1	2	3	4	5	6	7	8	9	OUT	10	11	12	13	14	15	16	17	18	IN	TOT	HCP	NET
BLUE	563	454	197	385	403	510	451	198	411	3572	502	415	187	417	182	411	387	530	441	3472	7044		
WHITE	537	385	168	343	370	489	428	174	389	3283	481	383	164	395	166	366	357	489	408	3209	6492		
MEN'S HCP	8	2	12	16	10	6	4	18	14		9	5	15	1	17	11	13	3	7				
PAR	5	4	3	4	4	5	4	3	4	36	5	4	3	4	3	4	4	5	4	36	72		
RED	480	338	125	305	288	427	333	130	355	2781	374	292	135	300	158	311	286	421	304	2581	5362		
LADIES' HCP	2	12	16	14	10	8	4	18	6		7	11	15	1	17	9	13	3	5				

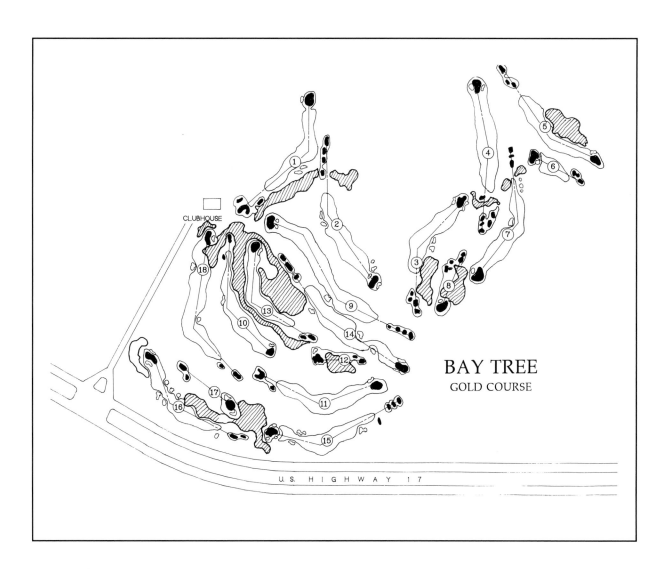

Bay Tree/Gold Course

HOLE NUMBER	1	2	3	4	5	6	7	8	9	OUT	10	11	12	13	14	15	16	17	18	IN	TOT	HCP	NET
BLUE	369	526	351	417	455	181	414	176	546	3435	413	372	191	393	540	425	445	213	515	3507	6942		
WHITE	350	452	281	387	409	148	376	147	524	3074	397	359	173	377	517	394	414	189	496	3316	6390		
MEN'S HCP	15	7	17	5	1	11	3	13	9		4	16	12	18	8	10	2	6	14				
PAR	4	5	4	4	4	3	4	3	5	36	4	4	3	4	5	4	4	3	5	36	72		
RED	261	422	246	288	374	140	270	100	445	2546	330	298	124	333	437	331	317	145	403	2718	5264		
LADIES' HCP	17	3	15	7	1	9	13	11	5		4	14	12	10	2	6	16	18	8				

Bay Tree/Silver Course

HOLE NUMBER	1	2	3	4	5	6	7	8	9	OUT	10	11	12	13	14	15	16	17	18	IN	TOT	HCP	NET
BLUE	428	211	483	366	374	193	383	388	508	3334	385	187	544	464	209	385	529	415	419	3537	6871		
WHITE	382	168	464	339	345	169	374	351	492	3084	332	158	516	418	196	359	516	387	397	3279	6363		
MEN'S HCP	2	14	12	16	8	18	4	6	10		13	11	3	1	15	17	5	9	7				
PAR	4	3	5	4	4	3	4	4	5	36	4	3	5	4	3	4	5	4	4	36	72		
RED	330	97	427	287	287	115	340	300	418	2601	311	125	464	392	156	293	418	343	314	2816	5417		
LADIES' HCP	4	18	12	10	6	16	2	8	14		9	15	3	1	13	11	17	5	7				

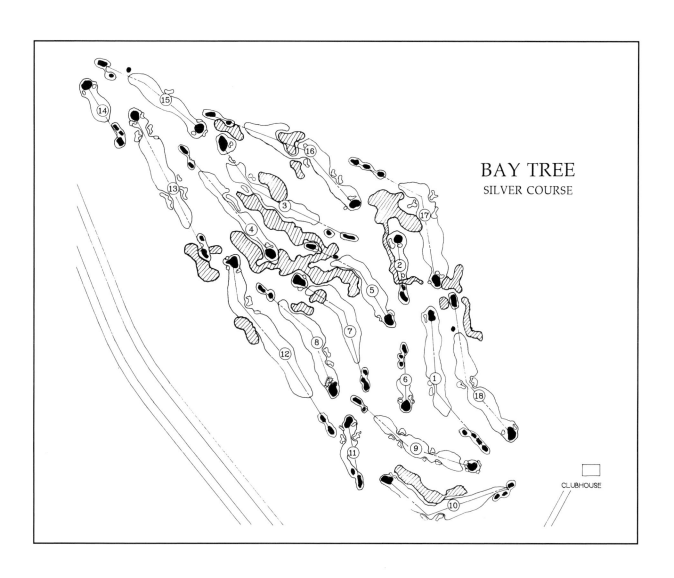

BAY TREE
SILVER COURSE

CLUBHOUSE

Number 10 at the Long Bay Club, with fairway surrounded by sand. (Courtesy the Long Bay Club)

Long Bay

HOLE NUMBER	1	2	3	4	5	6	7	8	9	OUT	10	11	12	13	14	15	16	17	18	IN	TOT	HCP	NET
CHAMPIONSHIP	408	568	401	472	182	394	543	179	370	3517	352	547	443	156	426	492	433	210	445	3504	7021		
MEMBERS	386	538	377	443	166	377	500	166	357	3301	327	513	408	140	390	463	408	194	412	3255	6565		
SENIORS	368	524	354	419	149	356	468	147	327	3112	315	480	375	123	361	449	380	176	368	3027	6139		
MEN'S HCP	11	3	5	1	13	17	7	15	9		16	10	4	18	8	14	2	12	6				
PAR	4	5	4	4	3	4	5	3	4	36	4	5	4	3	4	5	4	3	4	36	72		
LADIES	319	491	338	382	133	319	428	123	288	2821	289	464	354	86	323	429	357	146	329	2777	5598		
LADIES' HCP	9	3	7	1	13	15	5	17	11		16	4	8	18	10	6	2	14	12				

THE LONG BAY CLUB

Highway 9   P.O. Box 330   Longs, SC 29568   (843) 399-2222
six miles from the Waterway bridge toward Loris
Architect: Jack Nicklaus   Year opened: 1988

Course rating/Slope rating:
Championship - 73.0/129   Seniors - 69.5/122
Members - 71.4/129   Ladies - 71.2/110

No one, not even course record holder Randy Fuqua, will tell you that the Long Bay Club is an easy golf course.

"It's too tough for the average golfer," says George Lindsay, NBSC bank executive and a very good amateur player who is a student of the golf game on the Grand Strand. "It's not the drive that makes the course so tough—it's the second and third shots."

The author's son, Tommy, a good three-handicap player, defines Long Bay as "a typical Jack Nicklaus course. He builds courses that you have to play in the air. You must fly the ball to the green. There are no bump-and-run shots, no roll-ups that you can play on this course."

Long Bay is one of two Jack Nicklaus designs on the Strand (Pawleys Plantation at the south end of the Beach is the other) and is widely heralded as one of the area's finer golf courses. Water comes into play on eight holes and many of the greens are elevated, guarded by well-manicured bunkers and waste areas.

There is, indeed, a tremendous amount of sand on this private championship course, which measures a formidable 7,021 yards from the championship tees. Long Bay is notable for huge waste bunkers that seemingly dominate the length and breadth of the entire course. On four separate holes at Long Bay, the waste bunkers are so huge and so dominant that the golf cart paths run right through the hazard!

There are several memorable holes. The waste area encircles the fairway from tee to green on the 10th and further complicates the approach shot by running across the front of the elevated green.

Nor is there a landing area in front of the green on the par-five 2nd hole. Then, too, you will have difficulty finding a landing area with your tee shot on the awesome 16th, a dogleg right where the waste bunker not only runs along both sides of the fairway but bisects that fairway with a 40-yard-wide expanse of sand some 200 yards from the green. Can you carry that waste area with your tee shot? Maybe, but most players must choose a club to be short and then face a very long second shot to the green.

Golfers find hazards of a different color at the signature 13th hole, a devilish island green with no bailout area. It's more than 150 yards from tee box to green, and, when the wind is blowing, this hole becomes a monster. This is a true "island green" and the golfer, leaving the tee, drives his cart to the left of the green and crosses a footbridge to the putting surface.

Water, in the form of a very big lake, decorates and dominates the 9th and 18th holes, and the 18th, in particular, invites the golfer to reach the green with a perilous shot over water. Both are excellent finishing holes and can ruin an otherwise good round.

The course record is 64 but that is misleading.

No one has come close since Fuqua set the standard and most people who play here think the record will never be threatened.

The general impression a golfer playing Long Bay will take home is that of a fine, demanding golf course, featuring a vast amount of sand and water. It is beautiful, with awesome mounding, lush fairways, carefully tended greens and waste areas. It is long, tough, and fair for the low handicapper, a course that rewards good shots. If you are a high-handicap player you will have a lot more fun playing the course from the forward tees.

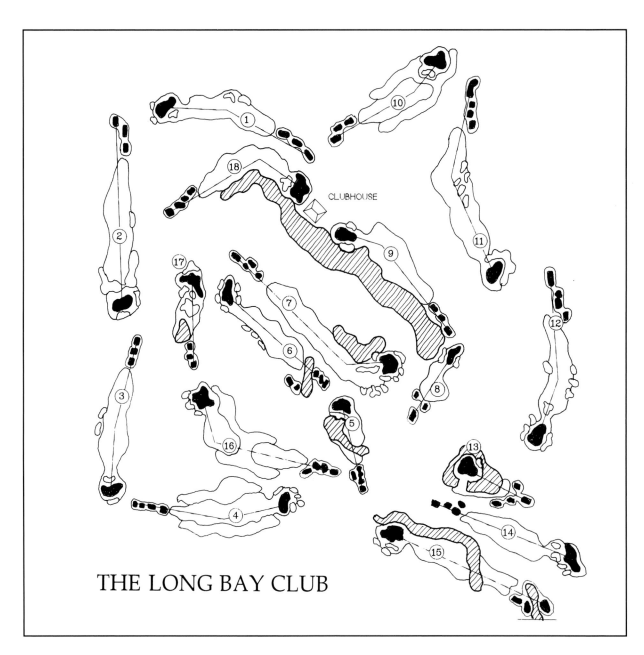

THE LONG BAY CLUB

The Little River Area

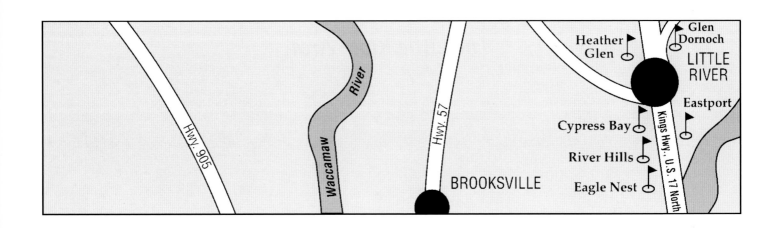

HEATHER GLEN

Highway 17   Little River, SC 29568
P.O. Box 297   N. Myrtle Beach, SC 29597
(843) 249-9000   (800) 868-4536

Architect: Willard Byrd and Clyde Johnston   Year opened: 1987
Course rating/Slope rating:
Blue - 72.0/130
White - 70.3/123
Red - 68.0/118

First impressions at Heather Glen are absolutely fantastic . . . the oak-lined driveway at the entrance to the club, the Scottish-inspired clubhouse, the kilted Scotsman who greets you, the first hole on the first nine. Everything is first class, and the best thing about the first impressions is that they become lasting impressions of a first-rate, championship golf course.

Heather Glen, chosen by *Golf Digest* magazine as America's number-one new public course when it opened in 1987, in itself is worth a trip to Myrtle Beach.

It is a golf course you will remember.

Your first view of Heather Glen from the elevated first tee of the first nine (there are three nine-hole layouts) is as frightening as it is beautiful, and this is typical of the masterpiece designed by golf architects Willard Byrd and Clyde Johnson.

That first hole, 363 yards from the championship tees, is all uphill. There are many features at the tee to divert the attention of the golfer, including a meandering burn (Scottish for creek or stream), a waste area of 130 yards covered in love grass, Scotch broom, and most definitely, two tall pines on either side of the fairway defining the narrow landing area quite dramatically. The undulating fairway guides you into a large green that slopes toward the golfer, offering a gaping sand bunker on the left and an unusual grassed bunker on the right. The green is well defined by high mounds behind and to the left.

Mounds, pot bunkers, large waste areas, hidden bunkers, and heather-laced dunes are the rule, not the exception at Heather Glen, and there are many holes just as dramatic as #1. Try #8 on the first nine for size! With the wind blowing in your face most of the time, the green is located 224 yards from the championship tee, a large pond bordered by granite stone is cut into the fairway, completely guarding the front of the green, and, just to make it interesting, severe pot bunkers have been placed in the mounds behind the green. Oh yes. There's also a pot bunker built into the curve of the green in front, right between the pond and the usual pin placement!

Each golfer will have his own favorite, and it is possible that each of the twenty-seven holes could make the list of "best." Two that stand out are #8 and #9 of the second nine.

When tournaments are played here, the second nine is used for the finish because #9 cuts back into the clubhouse. But this would be a great finishing hole anyway. After the player has completed #8, aptly named "The Spectacle," which has been described as one of the more architecturally spectacular golf holes on the East Coast, he finds there is no rest for the weary. Having navigated one large body of water on #8, the golfer is faced with a major decision on the finishing hole.

The green is guarded by the Firth of Clyde, namesake of the big lake at St. Andrews, and there is no way to get to the clubhouse without going over the Firth! There are two ways of getting there, and that's what makes it interesting. A long hitter can hit it left to right off the tee and then be brave enough and strong enough to blast the second shot over 230 yards of water and an additional 30 yards of grass and sand to reach the green in two! Most won't try it, but will prefer to hit two shots to landing areas near the water. Directly in front of the green, the water measures 63 yards.

Golf is the primary reason golfers enjoy Heather Glen, but the owners have enhanced the reputation of this fine course by skillfully creating a Scottish flavor. Not only does a Scottish theme pervade, from golf course to clubhouse, but each of the twenty-seven holes is named with a Scottish brogue.

For example, look at the first nine holes. They are, in numerical sequence, called Hidey-Ho, Roon-The-Bin, Fin Me Oot, Scotch Broom, The Narrows, Sandy Brae, Hillocks, The Lunar Hole, and The Long Hole.

The other eighteen holes bear equally imaginative names, and each hole, with its natural roll, perfectly placed bunkers, magnificent greens and tees, will forever haunt you... luring you to return.

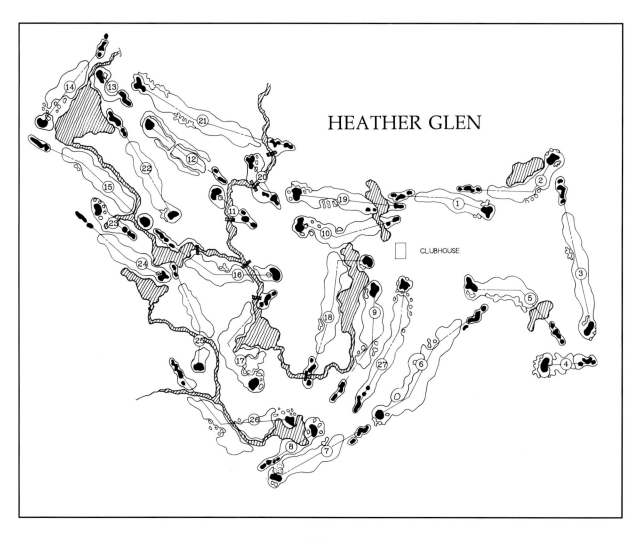

HEATHER GLEN

CLUBHOUSE

Heather Glen, a bit of Scotland at Myrtle Beach, features this three-par "Lunar" hole.
(Courtesy Himmelsbach Communications/Bill Woodward)

1st Nine

HOLE NUMBER	1	2	3	4	5	6	7	8	9		TOT
BLUE	363	366	506	180	415	484	381	224	447	3366	6771
WHITE	345	346	482	152	383	461	364	191	403	3127	6310
HCP (COURSE 1-2)	15	17	5	13	1	9	11	7	3		
HCP (COURSE 3-1)	16	18	6	14	2	10	12	8	4		
PAR	4	4	5	3	4	5	4	3	4	36	72
RED	241	294	416	127	310	413	316	110	309	2536	5053
HCP (COURSE 1-2)	17	9	3	15	5	1	13	11	7		
HCP (COURSE 3-1)	18	10	4	16	6	2	14	12	8		
PAR	4	4	5	3	4	5	4	3	4	36	72

2nd Nine

HOLE NUMBER	1	2	3	4	5	6	7	8	9		TOT
BLUE	416	153	380	165	391	527	375	409	587	3403	6769
WHITE	388	133	351	155	366	509	351	387	558	3198	6325
HCP (COURSE 1-2)	2	18	10	16	14	4	12	8	6		
HCP (COURSE 2-3)	1	17	9	15	13	3	11	7	5		
PAR	4	3	4	3	4	5	4	4	5	36	72
RED	335	105	272	115	317	402	282	320	462	2610	5146
HCP (COURSE 1-2)	4	18	14	16	12	8	10	6	2		
HCP (COURSE 2-3)	1	17	9	15	13	3	11	7	5		
PAR	4	3	4	3	4	5	4	4	5	36	72

3rd Nine

HOLE NUMBER	1	2	3	4	5	6	7	8	9		TOT
BLUE	393	171	510	404	182	400	410	525	410	3405	6808
WHITE	374	160	485	371	168	375	385	490	375	3183	6391
HCP (COURSE 3-1)	5	13	15	11	17	9	1	7	3		
HCP (COURSE 2-3)	6	14	16	12	18	10	2	8	4		
PAR	4	3	5	4	3	4	4	5	4	36	72
RED	255	120	424	276	132	296	299	420	295	2517	5127
HCP (COURSE 3-1)	5	17	11	13	15	9	1	7	3		
HCP (COURSE 2-3)	6	18	12	14	16	10	2	8	4		
PAR	4	3	5	4	3	4	4	5	4	36	72

Number 1 at beautiful River Hills, a good starting hole. (Courtesy Brandon Advertising/Michael Slear)

RIVER HILLS

P.O. Box 1049   Little River, SC 29566
(843) 399-2100   (800) 548-4148

Architect: Tom Jackson   Year opened: 1988

Course rating/Slope rating
Blue - 73.3/136   Green - 67.6/116
White - 70.6/128   Red - 67.7/120

River Hills is one of the very best of the fine championship courses on the Grand Strand that add luster to residential development. This 400-acre golf and residential complex, just off Highway 17 in Little River, South Carolina, has added tennis facilities, a health club, a swimming pool, and other amenities.

The River Hills development, conveniently located, is a rousing success, and the golf course is the linchpin. Designed by Tom Jackson, this is a fine course, stretching some 6,800 yards from the back tees through forest teeming with wildlife and a meandering Cedar Creek, which provides enough water hazards to intimidate many golfers. However, Jackson has skillfully carved landing areas through the blend of forest, water, and sand to create distinctively different golf courses from the four sets of tees. River Hills can be a roaring lion or a purring pussycat.

This does not resemble most coastal-area golf courses. There is a lot of elevation, and this is rolling land, with 50- to 60-foot variations on many of the holes. In other words,

it is hilly. This also has a very private location, and golfers can easily feel they are alone with nature. River Hills is 6,800 yards in length, and it meanders through the countryside. You don't see anything but the fairway you are playing, except for the parallel situation between holes 1 and 10.

The greens are Bermuda grass and are well maintained.

Number 7, a tough five par, is 517 yards from the gold (championship) tees and is a double dogleg. Hit your drive to the right, your second shot left, and then go back to the right on your approach to the green. Water parallels the right side on the second shot, and the overly cautious golfer, conscious of this big body of water, could easily pull his shot into another water hazard on the left side.

The 9th hole is 400 yards, requiring an accurate drive to miss the trap on the left of the fairway. From 80 yards into the green, mounds dominate the landscape, giving the golfer a blind shot to an undulating green.

Number 18 is a very good finishing hole, a

River Hills

HOLE NUMBER	1	2	3	4	5	6	7	8	9	OUT	10	11	12	13	14	15	16	17	18	IN	TOT	HCP	NET
BLUE	380	525	185	405	435	177	517	392	412	3428	398	566	182	395	418	147	374	530	435	3445	6873		
WHITE	335	502	165	380	400	152	485	370	385	3174	365	537	171	367	388	134	352	490	410	3214	6388		
GREEN	312	470	135	335	375	124	465	348	376	2940	330	515	102	327	344	110	330	444	370	2872	5812		
MEN'S HCP	14	16	18	12	2	10	6	8	4		13	3	9	11	1	17	15	7	5				
MEN'S PAR	4	5	3	4	4	3	5	4	4	36	4	5	3	4	4	3	4	5	4	36	72		
RED	260	430	105	305	340	105	420	310	330	2605	272	498	90	280	310	85	302	405	315	2557	5162		
LADIES' HCP	14	16	18	12	2	10	6	8	4		13	3	9	11	1	17	15	7	5				
LADIES' PAR	4	5	3	4	4	3	5	4	4	36	4	5	3	4	4	3	4	5	4	36	72		

dogleg right that requires a good drive and a long shot uphill to the green.

Cedar Creek dominates the back nine, very pretty and very much in play on #11, #17, and #18, running in behind the 16th green on its bubbling continuation to the Waterway.

River Hills is a challenging course. It offers a mixed array of holes—no two are alike. It is a versatile course, as the four sets of tees make it enjoyable for everyone—both the scratch golfer and the high handicapper.

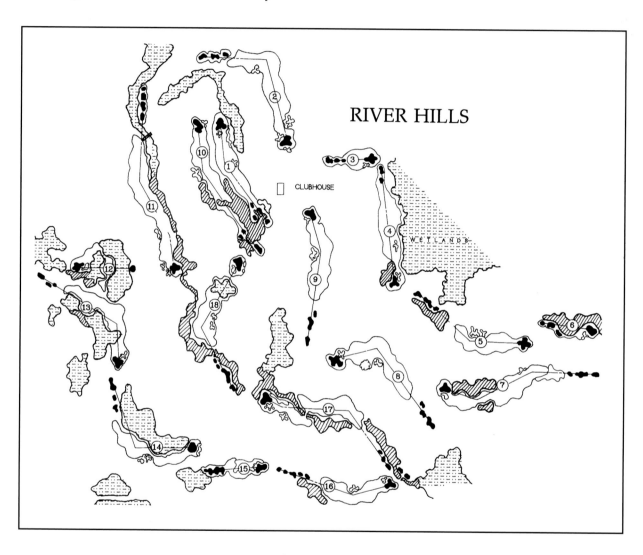

RIVER HILLS

CLUBHOUSE

WETLANDS

EAGLE NEST

Highway 17 North   Little River Section   P.O. Box 746
N. Myrtle Beach, SC 29582   (843) 249-1449   (800) 543-3113
Architect: Gene Hamm   Year opened: 1972
Course rating/Slope rating:
Blue - 72.4/120
White - 70.5/116
Red - 69.4/117

Eagle Nest is a good track, very accessible, located just off Highway 17 as you approach Little River, tucked in between two other golfing facilities, Bay Tree and River Hills.

Designed by Gene Hamm, this is a beautifully conditioned course that boasts the three toughest finishing holes on the Strand.

Some may argue with that boast, but all will admit it certainly has merit. Number 16 is a 449-yard four par from the back tees and usually plays into the wind. So does #17, which is a 616-yard five par and features a lake 100 yards wide directly in front of the green! The 18th hole is a beauty. This three-par jewel plays uphill over water and is guarded by huge bunkers, including one yawing cavern which sits between the edge of the water and the front of the green. It is 180 yards from tee to green, and because the green is at a higher elevation than the tee, plays even longer.

Those three holes are outstanding, but so are several others... #4 is a scenic three par nestled in the swamp, #8 and #9 are challenging finishing holes on the front side,

and #13 is a tease, a five par that can be reached in two, but the golfer needs to carry a large lake, then thread the needle with a long second shot to a well-bunkered green. Visitors often go home talking about #5, which is a difficult par five requiring a lay-up second shot by most golfers before they attempt to clear a water hazard that protects the green.

The greens are large and the Bermuda grass, cut short, affords a very good putting surface.

Eagle Nest certainly is not a short course, measuring 6,901 yards from the championship tees, 6,417 from the regular men's tees, and 5,105 for the ladies.

People who play the course regularly, including the golf shop personnel, are convinced this is one of the finest layouts on the Strand.

"I love it," says Bill Reese. "The course is always in good condition and it's a lot of fun, with plenty of holes that are challenging but not impossible to play."

There are some holes where you can lose

Eagle Nest

HOLE NUMBER	1	2	3	4	5	6	7	8	9	OUT	10	11	12	13	14	15	16	17	18	IN	TOT	HCP	NET
BLUE	515	348	401	186	545	429	187	422	364	3397	366	391	176	544	392	385	449	616	185	3504	6901		
WHITE	492	332	380	150	518	407	157	387	343	3166	338	359	157	507	367	367	416	576	164	3251	6417		
MEN'S HCP	14	16	8	10	4	6	18	2	12		13	15	17	5	9	11	1	3	7				
MEN'S PAR	5	4	4	3	5	4	3	4	4	36	4	4	3	5	4	4	4	5	3	36	72		
RED	418	264	297	113	400	339	121	313	259	2524	259	278	139	448	287	307	344	419	100	2581	5105		
LADIES' HCP	14	16	8	6	2	4	18	10	12		11	15	17	5	9	13	1	3	7				
LADIES' PAR	5	4	4	3	5	4	3	4	4	36	4	4	3	5	4	4	4	5	3	36	72		

your ball in the woods, but not many. For instance, #1, a five-par hole, features a wide fairway with woods on the right, rough on the left. But you can always find your ball here and continue playing.

Almost every golfer who comes to the Beach wants to have some kind of reasonable way to score. If he shoots an 80 on his home course, he doesn't want to come to the Strand and shoot 92. This certainly is not a "gimmee" golf course, but there is plenty of room to spray it. A good score is not automatic. Eagle Nest has been in existence for more than twenty years, and the course record is still 65....

Eagle Nest lays claim to the "three toughest finishing holes on the Beach." This is #18. (Courtesy Brandon Advertising/Michael Slear)

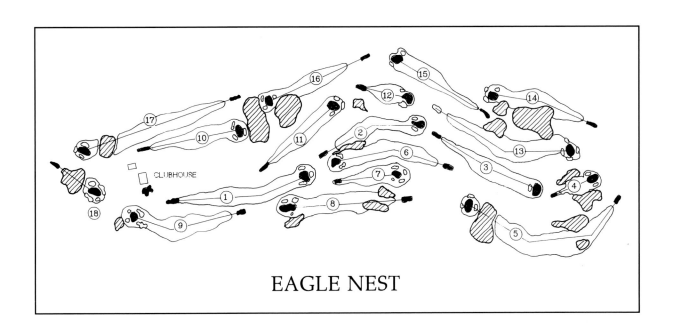

EAGLE NEST

The best-known hole at Cypress Bay...#8, nothing but tee box, water, and green.
(Courtesy Brandon Advertising/Michael Slear)

CYPRESS BAY

Highway 17   P.O. Box 680   Little River, SC 29576   (843) 249-1025
Architect: Russell Breeden   Year opened: 1972
Course rating/Slope rating:
Blue - 70.0/115
White - 69.0/110
Red - 69.0/113

Cypress Bay, conveniently located on Highway 17 in Little River, is a fun course, a delight for the skilled golfer as well as the high-handicap player. Designed by Russell Breeden and opened in 1972, this is a mature golf course featuring sharp doglegs, rolling terrain, and undulating greens guarded by plentiful sand and water hazards.

Cypress Bay can lend itself to good scores with birdie opportunities on all of the five-par holes. However, this course can penalize errant shots and the golfer who "lets it all hang out" can find he has posted a high score.

There are several very good golf holes, with 7, 8, 11, and 18 deserving special recognition. Number 8 is the hole visible from Highway 17, tucked into a corner beside the entrance to the clubhouse, lying just beyond a large body of water. As a matter of fact, the golfer will find there is nothing but water between the tee and the green and that he is hitting a long iron or four wood into a very narrow chute. It's a pretty hole—and tough!

This is the hole made famous by the challenge issued by the operators of Cypress Bay—make a hole-in-one and win $15,000! Contestants pay $5 to enter the contest. If they hit the green, they receive a sleeve of golf balls, and if they can get the ball into the cup with the tee shot they have won $15,000. Two golfers hit the Pot-of-Gold in the summer of 1990.

The four three pars, all long, rank with the best three pars of any course on the Grand Strand, and the five pars, relatively short, are fun because of the many options they bring to the player. Most can be shortened if the player can "cut" the dogleg and two of them play downwind. Long hitters have been known to reach the green with a wedge on the second shot, but usually it's a driver and three wood or long iron.

The four pars run the gamut of design and six of the ten feature sharp dogleg designs. Number 7 is esthetically pleasing, with a large pond guarding the entire front of the green. Because #7 is relatively long, many golfers will need to hit a lay-up with their

Cypress Bay

HOLE NUMBER	1	2	3	4	5	6	7	8	9	OUT	10	11	12	13	14	15	16	17	18	IN	TOT	HCP	NET
BLUE	515	389	352	194	358	471	377	191	303	3150	519	454	412	160	470	355	191	389	402	3352	6502		
WHITE	501	368	332	168	335	450	348	162	284	2948	503	434	381	154	455	322	157	367	380	3153	6101		
MEN'S HCP	15	11	7	13	17	5	1	3	9		10	6	4	16	12	18	14	8	2				
PAR	5	4	4	3	4	5	4	3	4	36	5	4	4	3	5	4	3	4	4	36	72		
RED	446	301	284	128	266	405	281	122	255	2488	416	374	285	101	342	241	123	340	294	2516	5004		
LADIES' HCP	1	9	11	15	13	7	3	5	17		6	4	8	18	12	14	16	10	2				

second shot or face the very realistic prospect of a "watery grave."

Another favorite hole is the four-par 11th, 434 yards from tee to green with a large pond on the right, but #18 is a close second, a great four-par finishing hole.

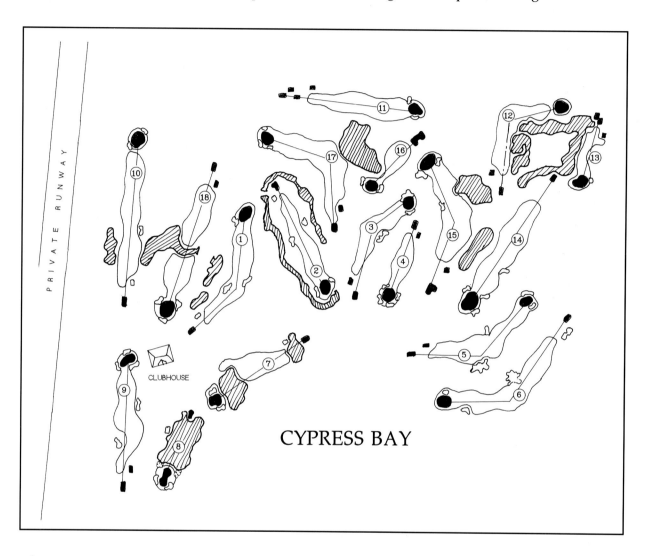

CYPRESS BAY

EASTPORT

Highway 17   P.O. Box 300   N. Myrtle Beach, SC 29597
(843) 249-3997   (800) 334-9035

Architect: Dennis Griffiths   Year opened: 1988

Course rating/Slope rating:
Blue - 69.3/117
White - 67.9
Red - 65.9/107

Eastport has a niche all its own among Grand Strand golf courses. This is a short, pretty course with a great location and it is well kept—bent-grass greens and enough water and sand to make it exciting from all three sets of tees.

The course can be stretched to 6,007 yards from the championship tees, and is a par-70 course.

Eastport didn't have a lot of land to work with, but it's beautiful. Dennis Griffiths and Associates, an Atlanta firm, laid out a nice course on ninety-five acres, making it feel much bigger than that.

This is a shotmaker's golf course particularly challenging for the women. Eastport requires careful management of your golf game. Put on your thinking cap when you

Eastport's #18, a very challenging four par. (Courtesy Himmelsbach Communications/ Bill Woodward)

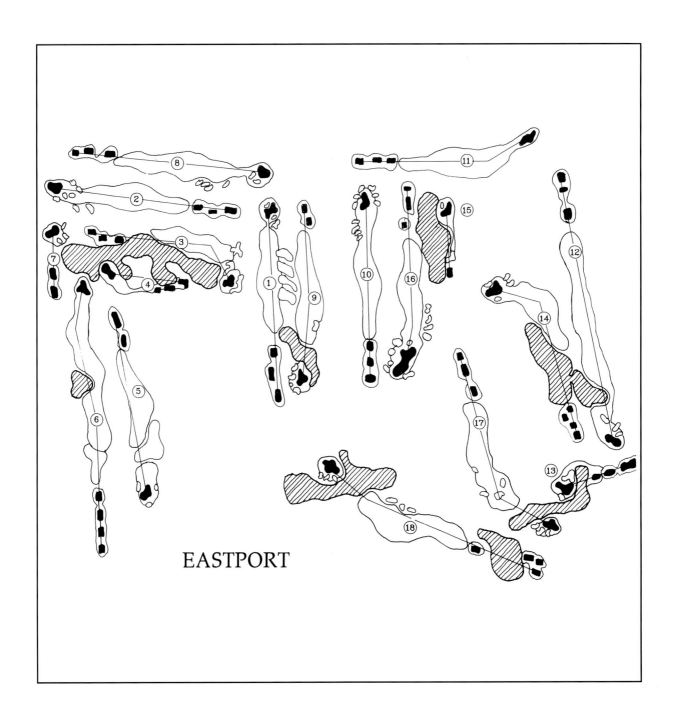

EASTPORT

Eastport

HOLE NUMBER	1	2	3	4	5	6	7	8	9	OUT	10	11	12	13	14	15	16	17	18	IN	TOT	HCP	NET
BLUE	359	366	328	150	367	508	120	371	398	2967	341	362	518	137	372	125	333	401	451	3040	6007		
WHITE	300	307	303	120	312	474	105	338	348	2607	301	332	480	115	353	110	298	367	422	2778	5385		
HANDICAP	11	9	13	15	7	1	17	3	5		12	10	2	16	8	18	14	6	4				
PAR	4	4	4	3	4	5	3	4	4	35	4	4	5	3	4	3	4	4	4	35	70		
RED	258	280	269	90	274	408	80	300	278	2237	271	263	420	85	318	92	256	308	310	2323	4560		
HANDICAP	11	9	13	17	7	1	15	3	5		12	10	2	16	8	18	14	6	4				
PAR	4	4	4	3	4	5	3	4	4	35	4	4	5	3	4	3	4	4	4	35	70		

play here. Most golf courses have 150-yard markers to the greens. At Eastport, the markers (blue stakes) are 125 yards from your destination.

Several of the holes are first class and the final two are among the best on the Strand, good enough to bring you back, wanting to challenge them again.

Number 17 goes away from the clubhouse toward the Intracoastal Waterway. It is a par-four, 401-yard toughie—a dogleg left with the second shot over water. When you have recovered from the rigors of this hole, your problems have just begun.

Number 18 starts at the Waterway near the home of Shelley Edmundson, original owner of this tract of land, and it is something else! At 451 yards from tee to green with the first shot over water and a lake guarding the green, this hole is rarely reached in two, and most hit a lay-up with the second shot.

Eastport is "short" but you will enjoy playing this course. While there is plenty of trouble, the golfer who keeps the ball in play can move around Eastport at a good rate of speed, and will find enough challenges to keep him thinking. After all, the course record is 63, only 7 under par.

The 16th hole at Glen Dornoch has everything that makes a golf hole challenging, perhaps treacherous. The slopes of the fairway threaten the driving areas. If you think this one is beautiful and difficult (a fit description of the entire course), wait until you play the holes along the Intracoastal Waterway. (Courtesy Himmelsbach Communications/Bill Woodward)

Glen Dornoch

HOLE NUMBER	1	2	3	4	5	6	7	8	9	OUT	10	11	12	13	14	15	16	17	18	IN	TOT	HCP	NET
BLACK	333	370	300	168	590	410	192	570	460	3393	535	386	350	525	183	380	431	212	455	3457	6850		
BLUE	308	342	285	155	560	394	176	540	420	3190	508	365	335	505	161	360	413	182	427	3256	6446		
WHITE	292	335	272	137	532	352	166	512	406	3004	472	351	330	487	147	342	371	164	367	3031	6035		
GOLD	263	305	255	127	515	333	150	495	387	2830	436	329	318	465	131	295	348	115	350	2787	5617		
HANDICAP	11	9	13	17	3	7	15	5	1		4	10	14	8	18	12	2	16	6				
PAR	4	4	4	3	5	4	3	5	4	36	5	4	4	5	3	4	4	3	4	36	72		
RED	246	270	225	117	497	300	130	415	314	2514	410	306	260	415	77	285	330	105	300	2488			
HANDICAP	11	9	13	17	1	7	15	3	5		6	8	14	2	18	12	4	16	10				

GLEN DORNOCH

Highway 17   Little River, SC
(800) 717-8784   (843) 249-2541

Architect: Clyde Johnston   Year opened: 1996

Course rating/Slope rating:
Black - 73.2/141   Blue - 71.5/133
White - 70.2/124   Gold - 68.6/116
Red - 69.8/129

The golfing world of the Grand Strand just keeps getting better and better. A prime example is Glen Dornoch, touted by one of its owners, Paul Himmelsbach, as "one of the best golf courses ever built. I'm not talking about Myrtle Beach or even South Carolina; I'm talking about the world!"

Early reviews of the magnificent Scottish-flavored championship course, opened in September 1996, gave credence to those glowing remarks, and most critics agree that Glen Dornoch is one of the ten best—if not the best—eighteen-hole layouts in an area that has won an international reputation for superb golfing.

Golf architect Clyde Johnston, quickly building a name for himself as one of America's foremost designers, shares Himmelsbach's appraisal of Glen Dornoch. "This is a great piece of property, one of the best I've worked with in twenty years of design. Without question it will be one of the top ten in the area. It has good elevation, several different tees, great soil," Johnston said.

Glen Dornoch boasts five sets of tees on every hole; miles of concrete cart paths; superb elevations uncharacteristic of most Myrtle Beach courses; and the Intracoastal Waterway, whose presence ensures that nothing will ever be put on the other side to mar the natural beauty. Glen Dornoch also possesses another quality that might not readily be apparent to the casual golfer, but nonetheless a quality of great importance to the developer: sandy soil, which provides the best possible drainage and reduces the number of golf rounds lost to the weatherman.

Although the course is spectacular, don't be fooled by the yardage on the scorecard. Those published yardages indicate a relatively short course, and you could be misled into thinking this course is easy. Think again. The slope rating from the championship markers is 141, and many holes are memorable because of their difficulty.

Number 16 very probably will become the signature hole of Glen Dornoch, and in a recent survey of golfing experts was named as one of the holes on "The Dream Eighteen" as published by the Myrtle Beach *Sun News*. Other beauties (or monsters) at Glen Dornoch are deserving of the same recognition.

At first this course looks benign, and the first four holes afford the golfer an opportunity of getting off to a good beginning. However, if you don't, be prepared for triple digits when you add up the numbers at the end of the round.

"This is where the golf course starts," said Head Professional Rich Bennigan. The fairway of the 5th hole is bisected by a vast expanse of environmentally protected wetlands that make this a highly unlikely two-shot par five. Once you have cleared the formidable waste area, you are confronted with a stream that not only guards the green but ambles entirely across the fairway. To give the golfer greater appreciation of the immensity of the big green, which is more than 50 yards from front to back, three wooden bridges stretch alongside the green: one in the front, another in the middle, and the third on the back. With two pot bunkers to the right of the green, pin placement can make this an awesome hole indeed.

The 6th hole, a long dogleg right with the green sitting at a 90-degree angle from the tee box, is just as frightening and has wrecked many potentially good scores. Your drive here is everything, and if you haven't "hit it a ton," it might be a good idea to bail out to the peninsula that juts into the waste area 62 yards in front of the green.

Be advised: There are a lot of "carries," a lot of "lay-ups" at Glen Dornoch, not just on #5 and #6 but all the way around this beautiful but treacherous layout.

The par-five 8th hole is another very pretty hole, stretching all the way to the Intracoastal Waterway running behind the green. Getting there in two might be possible, but the golfer must be a big, big hitter and also have great confidence in his sand play, because Johnston has dotted seven Scottish-style pot bunkers around the green.

Few who have played it will ever forget the 9th hole. The Intracoastal Waterway runs the length of the hole all the way down the right side, and the green, shared with #18, is monstrous and two-tiered. Talk about pot bunkers! Ten of those little devils surround the green, and another six are sprinkled through the fairway. Just to complicate matters, the wind often howls fiercely off the water on this very long hole. Be happy with par, and if somehow, some way, you can make birdie, be ecstatic.

Having survived the front side, the golfer now turns his attention to the back nine, where most often even higher numbers than the front are recorded! Number 10 is so deceiving that a Glen Dornoch employee stands on the tee and instructs players on the problems ahead. The main problem again is a very large environmentally pro-

tected waste area. Hit it too far off the tee and you're in deep trouble. Don't hit it far enough and face the prospect of a long carry across that area. There is hidden danger, too. A finger of wetland on the right that cannot be seen from the tee is just waiting to catch a slice or the golfer who prefers to play the right side of the fairway.

Don't overlook #11 and #12, but you might look forward to the 13th hole, a potential two-shot par five that is a dogleg left. However, water is plentiful on the right, as are formidable oaks that catch many golfers hitting away from the lake on the left. You'll want to hit a lay-up with the second shot and leave yourself a 125-yard approach.

Golf Digest architectural writer Ron Whitten calls the 14th hole a "wonderful surprise" The green is protected by another large expanse of waste area, and the green itself, of a Ridan nature, slopes severely to the back. Hit it past the pin and the shot trickles off the back.

Offering somewhat of a respite, #15 also is a memorable hole, with a large oak growing in the middle of a large waste bunker. Even here, Johnston has included subtle problems such as diabolical mounding in front of the green. Don't try a run-up shot because the mound will kick you left or right.

If the last three holes at Glen Dornoch aren't the most difficult you have played, you have been on some golf courses unknown to this writer. The green on #16 is circled by water, but that's just part of the problem. The landing area for the second shot is extremely narrow, and an attempt to lay up easily could find your golf ball rolling from left to right all the way across the fairway and down a steep embankment into wetlands and water. Yes, your second shot is scary, but you can't deny the beauty of this hole.

Although #17 is a par three, the best word to describe it is "wow." The waterway runs behind the green, and water runs along the entire left side of the hole and completely bisects the fairway. There are six bunkers and a ledge so spectacular that you almost want to hit a bad shot right so you can look down 50 feet to the Bermuda green and marvel at a pot bunker so small it is just about the size of a golfer's stance.

The 18th hole defies description. You can see the green from the championship tees, but it would take a drive of 400 yards to get there. Most people play toward a series of traps, but no matter where they hit it, the ball still needs to fly more than 200 yards to the green. Ten pot bunkers surround the deep green, which also is shared with the 9th hole.

If the management of Glen Dornoch had named each of the holes, they probably would have called #18 "Option," as you can play your tee shot into two different fairways or even three if you're foolishly tempted to try the impossible shot over all that water.

Both #9 and #18 come together at the clubhouse, which is reminiscent of Shinnecock because it borrows several architectural features from that great course. And the name Glen Dornoch also is inspired by golf history: Dornoch, Scotland, is the birthplace of Donald Ross, the architect of Pinehurst.

If Clyde Johnston keeps building golf courses like this one and Wachesaw East, Ross might have to move over and make room for the new kid on the block.

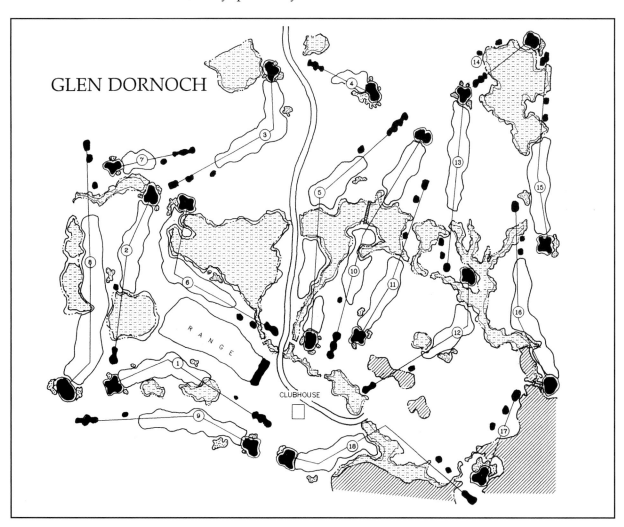

CHRONOLOGICAL
GOLF-COURSE HISTORY

Year	Course
1927	Ocean Forest Club
1944	Pine Lakes International (name changed from Ocean Forest Club)
1948	The Dunes
1960	The Surf
1962	Whispering Pines
1964	Robbers Roost
1966	Brierwood Myrtlewood (Pinehills)
1967	Seagull
1968	Beachwood Litchfield Possum Trot Quail Creek
1972	Azalea Sands Bay Tree Cypress Bay Eagle Nest Myrtlewood (Palmetto) Wedgefield Plantation
1973	Myrtle Beach National (North)
1974	Arcadian Shores Carolina Shores Deer Track (North) Myrtle Beach National (West) Waterway Hills (named changed from Skyway Golf Club in 1984)

Year	Course
1975	Myrtle Beach National (South)
1977	Raccoon Run
1978	Ocean Isle Beach
1980	Burning Ridge (West) Gator Hole Marsh Harbour
1981	Deer Track (South)
1983	Oyster Bay
1984	Indian Wells
1985	Wachesaw Plantation (private)
1986	DeBordieu Club (private) Heritage Club River Club Sea Trail Plantation (Maples course)
1987	Brick Landing Plantation Burning Ridge (East) Heather Glen River Oaks Sandpiper Bay
1988	Colonial Charters (private) Eastport Heron Point Island Green Lockwood The Long Bay Club (private) Pawleys Plantation The Pearl (East and West) River Hills Willbrook Plantation

Year	Course	Year	Course
1989	Myrtle West Ocean Harbour Prestwick (private) The Witch	1995	Belle Terre (Championship and Executive) Man O' War Panther's Run Tradition Club Wicked Stick The Wizard
1990	Buck Creek Heather Glen (nine-hole addition) Heathland at The Legends Indigo Creek Moorland at The Legends River Oaks (nine-hole addition) Sea Trail Plantation (Jones course) Sea Trail Plantation (Byrd course) Tidewater	1996	Calabash Links Glen Dornoch King's North at Myrtle Beach National The Members Club at St. James Wachesaw East
1991	Blackmoor The Gauntlet at St. James Lion's Paw Wild Wing Plantation (Wood Stork)	1997	Carolina National at Winding River Meadowlands The Players Club at St. James
1992	Brunswick Plantation Parkland at The Legends Wild Wing Plantation (Hummingbird)	1998	Dogwood nine at Brunswick Plantation Magnolia Greens Tournament Players Club True Blue
1993	Wild Wing Plantation (Avocet)	1999	Crow Creek Greg Norman's golf course The Rock The Thistle Tiger's Eye (at Ocean Ridge) World Tour Course
1994	Arrowhead Caledonia Wild Wing Plantation (Falcon)		
1995	Angels Trace (North and South) Arrowhead's third nine (Cypress)		

GOLF-COURSE ARCHITECTS

Ault, Edmund | Palmetto at Myrtlewood

Bates, Gene | Carolina National Golf Club

Brauer, Jeff | Wild Wing (Avocet)

Brazeal, Michael | Brick Landing

Breeden and Fazio | Bay Tree

Breeden, Russell | Cypress Bay
Ocean Isle Beach
Possum Trot
Robbers Roost

Byrd, Willard | Brunswick Plantation
Calabash Links
Indigo Creek
Island Green
Heather Glen
Heron Point
Lion's Paw
Litchfield
Lockwood
Meadowlands
Sea Trail Plantation (Byrd)
Wild Wing (Hummingbird)
Wild Wing (Wood Stork)

Cate, Tim N. | Panther's Run
The Players Club at St. James
The Thistle
Tiger's Eye at Ocean Ridge

Cobb, George | Bald Head Island
The Surf

Couples, Fred | Carolina National Golf Club

Daly, John | Wicked Stick

Doak, Tom	Heathland at The Legends
Duane, Francis	Myrtle Beach National (West)
Dye/Fingers/Shelley/Spann	Whispering Pines
Dye, P. B.	The Gauntlet at St. James Moorland at The Legends
Dye, Pete	DeBordieu Club
Dye, Pete and P. B.	Prestwick
Fazio, Tom	Tournament Players Club at Myrtle Beach Wachesaw Plantation
Floyd, Raymond	Arrowhead
Garl, Ron	Tradition Club
Gibson, Porter	Deer Track Wedgefield Plantation
Griffiths, Dennis	Eastport
Hamm, Gene	Azalea Sands Beachwood Burning Ridge Eagle Nest Indian Wells Quail Creek Raccoon Run River Oaks Sea Gull
Hills, Arthur	Pinehills at Myrtlewood
Hurzdan, Mike	Myrtle Beach National (Southcreek)
Irwin, Hale	The Members Club at St. James
Jackson, Tom	Arrowhead (with Raymond Floyd) Buck Creek Carolina Shores Magnolia Greens Myrtle West River Club River Hills River Oaks

Johnston, Clyde	Angels Trace (North and South)
	Glen Dornoch
	Heather Glen
	Ocean Harbour
	Wachesaw East
	Wicked Stick (with John Daly)
Jones, Rees	Arcadian Shores
	Belle Terre (Championship)
	Belle Terre (Executive)
	Gator Hole
	Sea Trail Plantation (Jones)
	Wild Wing (Falcon)
Jones, Robert Trent	The Dunes
Jones, Robert Trent and Rees	Waterway Hills
Lafoy, John	The Surf
Maples, Dan	Heritage Club
	Man O' War
	Marsh Harbour
	Oyster Bay
	The Pearl (East and West)
	Sandpiper Bay
	Sea Trail Plantation (Maples)
	Willbrook Plantation
	The Witch
	The Wizard
Nelson, Larry	Wild Wing (Avocet)
Nicklaus, Jack	The Long Bay Club
	Pawleys Plantation
Palmer, Arnold	Myrtle Beach National's three courses
	The Rock
Player, Gary	Blackmoor
Simpson, John	Colonial Charters
Strantz, Mike	Caledonia
	True Blue
Tomlinson, Ken	Tidewater

Toski, Bob	Deer Track
Wadkins, Lanny	Tournament Players Club at Myrtle Beach
Ward, Benjamin	Brierwood
White, Robert	Pine Lakes International
Young, Larry	Parkland at The Legends